Durkheim, Bernard and Epistemology

Durkheim, Bernard and Epistemology

P. Q. Hirst

Department of Politics and Sociology
Birkbeck College, University of London

Routledge & Kegan Paul
LONDON AND BOSTON

First published in 1975
by Routledge & Kegan Paul Ltd
Broadway House, 68–74 Carter Lane,
London EC4V 5EL and
9 Park Street,
Boston, Mass. 02108, USA
Set in Monotype Imprint
and printed in Great Britain by
Cox & Wyman Ltd, London, Fakenham and Reading
© Paul Q. Hirst 1975
ISBN 0 7100 8071 9

Contents

Introduction

This book consists of two studies, the first of Claude Bernard's theory of scientific knowledge, and the second of Émile Durkheim's attempt to provide an epistemological foundation for a scientific sociology in *The Rules of Sociological Method*. These two studies are complementary, certain of the themes and concepts in the analysis of Bernard illuminate the discussion of Durkheim's work, and they are linked by a common approach to the reading and analysis of theoretical and philosophical texts – an approach developed in recent years by several French philosophers – the most important of whom is Louis Althusser.

The reader would be mistaken if this rather bald description of its contents led him to suppose that the work he is about to read is a scholarly monograph in the history of ideas, or to suppose that it is an exercise in method, in which the subjects chosen are a means to display the scope and value of the method. No claim can be made that the reader will find here a full examination of the work of Bernard or Durkheim, nor can it be claimed that this work is an introduction to the concepts and methods it employs. These two studies have an 'ulterior motive', their object is not Claude Bernard or Émile Durkheim *per se*, it is to question and to challenge the dominant conceptions of epistemology in sociology. In this respect the study of *The Rules of Sociological Method* is the core of the book and the study of Bernard is a preparation for it.

Durkheim's epistemology has a central significance in relation to the question of the possibility of a scientific sociology, not because the majority of sociologists are Durkheimians, far from it, but because of the strategic place it occupies among the competing philosophical foundations for a sociology. *The Rules of Sociological Method* is significant because it attempts to provide a consistent epistemological foundation for a *scientific* sociology and one which is *not* positivist. Almost all attempts to provide an epistemological foundation for sociology have been 'subjectivist' or positivist. Subjectivist philosophical foundations of sociology have been based upon an explicit rejection of the applicability of natural scientific forms of knowledge to the realm of the social – they have sought to create a humanistic discipline based upon a conception of knowledge as 'understanding'.[1] Durkheim's epistemology, in contrast, is predicated on the unity of valid knowledge, upon the position that there is no fundamental difference between the natural sciences and sociology. Durkheim conceives the unity of knowledge in a far more radical way than modern positivism, which maintains that this unity is a unity of *method* and which refuses to make any substantive suppositions about the fundamental nature of reality. In conceiving this unity Durkheim follows Comte; knowledge has the unity of a finite *plan*, in which each of the sciences corresponds to a distinct division of natural phenomena, and in which the divisions form parts of a whole which is Nature. Durkheim's epistemology rests upon a *Naturphilosophie*.

In Durkheim's epistemology there is little immediate trace of the Kantian division of the forms of knowledge which has be-devilled the social sciences. This division is so much a part of the warp and weft of sociological discourse that its theoretical origins and its theoretical consequences are virtually unreflected – it is necessary to consider its logic in some detail before we can begin to recognise Durkheim's singularity. The neo-Kantian division of the sciences of nature and culture creates knowledges which are different in essence, the former a knowledge of a realm of objects, of non-meaningful things determined by an external and mechanical causality, the latter a knowledge of a realm constituted by subjects, of meaningful phenomena which are the products of subjective wills.[2] Each knowledge enjoys a privilege and suffers a limitation. To the sciences of nature is granted the privilege of an 'objectivity'; the relation of knower to known is a relation of non-identity, the relation of subject to object is one of externality, and the relation of object to object is not a relation of meaning, but of causality. This relation of subject and object, which grants to the former a relation of exteriority and disinterestedness to the latter, imposes a limitation on the knowledge of things – *because* the relation is an exterior one and *because* the relation of objects to one another is not a meaningful one; objects as such, things in themselves, can never be known and the subject has no guaranteed certainty as to his knowledge of things. To the sciences of culture is granted the privilege of a knowledge which is absolute, a knowledge made possible by the identity of knower and known, subject and subject, in which inter-subjective knowledge comprehends the relations of subjects and their wills which are the essence of the social realm. This knowledge which consists in the understanding of the intentions and wills of subjects by subjects is necessarily limited by the identity of knower and known; the problem of 'objectivity' arises from the nature of the phenomena of the social sciences, that they are not objects but subjects and the effects of the wills of subjects.

Durkheim's conception of the unity of the sciences denies this privileged status accorded to the subject; social relations are irreducible to inter-subjective relations and social causality is not a teleological causality in the sense that the wills of subjects are not the origin or essence of society. For Durkheim, society is as much an *object* to the human subject as physical nature is; it is prior to, irreducible to, and constraining upon the individual, and different in nature from him. Social relations are not identical to interpersonal relations, society is not 'made by man' and it does not answer to his needs any more than it is the product of his will. Durkheim's conception of society as a phenomenon like those of nature has always horrified humanists; hence the charges of 'sociologism' and of the 'reification' of society. The scandal consists in the fact that the social realm is not a cosy conspiracy between human subjects, they cannot be sure it has their interests at heart, and they cannot indulge in the hope that they can put an end to it. In a spontaneous and conscious world of immediate relations between subjects, social relations and inter-subjective relations coincide – this is the dream and illusion of radical humanism which Durkheim challenges.

Durkheim is important, then, because he offers the prospect of an anti-subjectivist and non-positivist scientific sociology. A subjectivist sociology is not and cannot be a science, even in the loosest sense of the word: it is guaranteed never to know more than it is given to know by philosophical anthropology. Such a sociology is condemned to the repetition of the philosophical postulates on which it depends in the form of pseudo-explanations and redescriptions of the given. Furthermore, a subjectivist sociology, based upon the postulate of human free-will, must ultimately degenerate into an *ethics*, into a determination of the appropriate forms of that will. Any knowledge which starts from the supposition of freedom must become an ethics: it will prescribe the laws of action and conduct appropriate to a free-being, appropriate to the nature of freedom – a subjectivist sociology cannot escape the project of Kant's *Critique of Practical Reason*, excepting, of course, that it abandons the latter's rationalist form of discourse and proof. If we consider the theoretical origins of subjectivist sociologies, if we pursue them beyond their philosophical forms to their theological foundations, we will recognise them as the continuation of Christian humanism by other means. By a paradox, it was Feuerbach, a rigorous humanist if ever there was one, who revealed the religious essence of humanism, Man is God inverted. Theology, like good whisky, is best taken straight.

A positivist sociology's fortunes depend on those of positivist epistemology – it is only possible in so far as the positivist conception of *method* is correct, in so far as it represents the mode of knowing of the sciences. Positivism as an epistemology has been subjected to vigorous criticism not simply because its particular conception of method misrepresents the mode in which the natural sciences produce knowledge but because the very conception of a scientific *method* must necessarily produce this misrepresentation. Positivism is a variant of empiricism: the conception of *method* supposes that it is a means of knowing applied to given objects, these objects are constituted as the objects of knowledges prior to the operations of these knowledges and prior to the application of the supposed method. The givenness of the objects of science necessarily entails that these objects be objects given by experience; science is the methodical study of the objects of experience. However, the objects of the sciences do not correspond to the objects of experience, they are not givens but the products of scientific knowledge itself – hence there can only be *sciences*, distinct modes of constituting and knowing non-given objects, and there can be no 'scientific method'. It is to Gaston Bachelard that we owe this critique or empiricism and this conception of the non-givenness of the objects of scientific knowledges –

Bachelardian epistemology will play a crucial role as a basis of epistemological examination and criticism throughout the two studies.[3] Bachelard is not the only scientific rationalist critic of positivism, a distinct but analogous position on the nature of science is the basis of David and Judith Willer's brilliant study of positivist and statistical empiricist sociology, *Systematic Empiricism: Critique of a Pseudo-Science* (1973).[4]

It is in this context that Durkheim's centrality with respect to the question of whether a scientific sociology is possible or not will become evident. Unlike the positivists who stand or fall by the validity of a universal method, Durkheim has a complex epistemological argument for the *specificity* of sociology's object and mode of knowing. Unlike the subjectivists he offers the prospect of a science of discoveries rather than the repetition of philosophical principles and a science which does not treat social phenomena like any other, which does not stifle itself by obedience to humanist myths. The principal question asked in this work is, is the Durkheimian theory of knowledge logically consistent and philosophically viable? In fact, as we shall see, Durkheim's difference from subjectivism and positivism, while it is a real one, in no way represents an advance on them and his epistemology suffers from the very same failings that subjectivist and positivist epistemologies do. The principal conclusion of this work is that the epistemology developed in *The Rules of Sociological Method* is an impossible one; its premises and conditions entail necessary and irresoluble contradictions – contradictions which the Durkheimian discourse suppresses as visible contradictions but which are a necessary part of its discursive and logical structure. These contradictions have their origin in the fact that, like positivism, the object of Durkheimian sociology is a given object. The attempt to provide a theoretical foundation for a science whose object is given prior to and independently of theory is an impossible one; the contradictions stem from the attempt to make the given the *necessary* object of a scientific knowledge. Positivism justifies the study of the given on the grounds of scepticism, that only the objects of experience can be known to exist.[5] The given is necessary by reason of the *limits* of knowledge. The given may be contingent but nothing else is necessary. For Durkheim the given is a necessary part of the order of things, it is their manifest form. Durkheim seeks to make the given necessary, to make this particular given, the social, the necessary object of a scientific knowledge. What makes Durkheim's epistemology *impossible*, rather than a simple variant of essentialism or idealism, is that it attempts this *within empiricism* – Durkheim is forced to assign to the knowledge of the given the task of 'discovering' what it has already been given to know. Durkheim's failure in this task is inevitable; objects already given to knowledge define its possibilities of knowing independently of knowledge; if the given is not contingent then a knowledge predicated on its necessity cannot have the form of discovery. Durkheim's empirical knowledge is impossible because it supposes a theoretical definition of the necessity of what it is given to know.

This combination of essentialism and empiricism, of the necessary given and its discovery through empirical knowledge, we will call *realism*. Durkheim's theory of knowledge is a realist theory.[6] It is in the mechanism by which the given is made necessary that the similarities between Durkheim and subjectivism become apparent. Although Durkheim displaces the human subject, he does not abolish the subject as such in his sociology. As we shall see, society is conceived as a subject, as a being of consciousness, a being which is a subject writ large. Far from abolishing the individual in an absolute sociologism, Durkheim's sociology gives the individual the status of an extra-social being, but, as a being of consciousness, with the necessary substratum and support of the society-subject. The society-subject's effectivity takes the form of its effects on the subjects who form its substratum; it is in this way that the phenomena of the given, social facts are produced. Far from having abolished the conception of social relations as inter-subjective relations, Durkheim retains a form of inter-subjectivity, although the subjects are of a distinct nature and their relations are unequal. The relation society–individual is a relation between subjects. In one respect Durkheim does transcend subjectivism: in a brilliant critique Durkheim destroys that variant of teleological explanation which reduces social relations to the needs and wills of human subjects. The Durkheimian society-subject is not a teleological being.

Durkheim's social epistemology is an impossible one, it provides no alternative to the limitations and errors of subjectivism and positivism. Durkheim's sociology reproduces many of the same limitations and errors in a variant form. A theoretical foundation for a science of the given is impossible, and what is sociology but a science of the given *par excellence*? It is well known that there is a sociology 'of' every given object, from almanacs to zoos. Subjectivism and positivism both accept the givenness of their objects; they differ in their conception of the methods necessary to study them. Sociology is an attempt to explain and to reproduce the given 'facts' of social life as necessary and rational facts – it is an attempt to explain and to reproduce the facts of experience by a mechanism which gives them a *raison d'être*.[7] It is in this sense that sociology can never be a science. And the science of an object which is not given to experience would not be a sociology. It is for this reason that the future of the 'social sciences' as *sciences* lies with those theories which do not attempt to give the phenomena of experience the form of reason but seek to explain objects not given in experience, objects constituted in knowledge, Marxism and psycho-analysis. These theories are a scandal because they contradict experience, they posit objects of study inexistent in experience, but the real scandal consists in this: that these theories are the least understood of all the theories current in philosophy, history and the social sciences. Lest it should be thought that the objects of theories which contradict experience are inconsequential, that what is not given to experience does not exist, we may note that Marxism and psycho-analysis are sciences vital to the crucial struggles of our age and to the personal struggles of individual men. The same cannot be said for sociology; for it can in no way change the given or our relation to it.

A knowledge which 'saves' the phenomena which form its object, which reproduces them as they are given, can neither provide a means of transformation of these phenomena nor can it transcend them. Its only possible value is as an ideology, and, indeed, an important element of ideology is that it is a mechanism for reproducing in a rationalised form objects, interests and answers *given* to it. It is in this that it is possible to discover the secret of empiricism. Empiricism is not merely a *limited* knowledge, a knowledge limited to given appearances but unable to attain the essence of things, a science of experience, it is a non-knowledge. The empiricist supposes that the given which he takes as the object of knowledge is truly a given, givenness being the mode of existence of objects – but the very notion of a world given to experience is an empiricist notion, it is no more true than empiricism in general is true. Empiricist knowledges do not encounter facts given in the real,

they are *given* these facts. Experience is not a simple datum, its
contents are *given* to it. Empiricist knowledges are given their facts,
objects, etc. by definite social and political ideologies. Not only is
the *content* of the given uncontrollable in empiricist knowledges,
not only are their objects constituted prior to them, but it is a content determined and constituted for them by ideologies. Correspondence with the 'facts' of 'experience' is therefore an absolute
guarantee of non-scientificity.

It is in the mechanism whereby Durkheim 'saves' the phenomena of the social world that we find the logical and rational
foundation of his conservatism. The given that is made necessary,
the facts which are made part of the nature of things, are determined in content by Durkheim's political and social ideology, but
they are secured as necessary givens by this theoretical mechanism.
It is in this sense that the Durkheimian theory, the very structure
of Durkheimian discourse, is ideological, and not merely Durkheim
the man. Clearly, the views, habits and obsessions of Durkheim
qua subject would be of no interest if he had provided a
rational foundation for a social science. Radical sociologists who
recognise only the subject, his views and opinions, criticise the
immediate ideological *content* of Durkheim's work, have no means
of determining the conditions of existence of that content, the
Durkheimian logic which necessitates the given, and no means of
avoiding that logic themselves. It is in this that we see the solution
to the apparent paradox of the identity of the basic logical and
theoretical mechanisms of 'conservative' and 'radical' sociology.

This latter point raises the question of the mode of approach to the
theories and texts analysed in this work – this mode of approach is
very different from the normal mode in which sociologists approach
sociological theories and texts of sociological theory. The approach
used here, which derives in the main from the work of Louis
Althusser,[8] makes possible an analysis of the conceptual structure
of theoretical texts and it is based upon epistemological concepts
which designate what it is that is theoretical in theoretical discourse. It is by no means a 'method' in the sense of a set of rules,
procedures and techniques which have only to be applied to
produce certain results, and it never can be, since in this approach
the analysis of theories and texts is in itself a form of theoretical
work. The dominant forms of reading of theoretical texts in

modern sociology treat discourse as a mere medium, as a mode in which the non-discursive, the mental conceptions of the thinker or the knowledge of the real, is recorded. Hence the 'life and works' literature on the major sociological theorists and the culling of 'the literature' for concepts, propositions, etc. to use in the analysis of given real phenomena. Such approaches are a necessary effect of the empiricism which is dominant in sociology; sociologists assume the meaning of theoretical discourse to be immediately given in the text as the record of the thought of its thinker or as a rational replica of the real itself. Reading is an activity as automatic and obvious as seeing. Empiricism reduces theoretical discourse to the non-theoretical and the non-discursive; it is beyond discourse that its essence, its real meaning is to be found; discourse is obliterated as a problem and as an object of study.

Once empiricism is challenged the possibility of theoretical *writing* becomes problematic: if theory is not a residue of the thought of a subject or a replica of the real, then what are its conditions of existence?

The approach used here may be called conceptual reading. Conceptual reading entails treating a theoretical text as the product of and the expositional form of *discourse*. Theoretical discourse may be defined as the form in which concepts are deployed in a particular mode of reasoning which develops answers to certain questions posed in a theory and which demonstrates the validity of those answers as answers possible under the conditions set by that theory. Theoretical discourse is at once an explanation and a proof, it concerns questions internal to theory alone, answers them theoretically and proves them theoretically – it has no domain of application exterior to theory. The conditions of existence of the questions to which answers are given and the criteria of validity of those answers, in other words the conditions which make discourse possible, are a structured set of problems and concepts, the *problematic*, of a theory. It is this structure which determines the internality of theory, which delimits a definite theoretical field with specific objects to be explained and specific forms of reasoning.

A conceptual reading is therefore one in which the text is read *in its problematic* (or problematics), as a form of discourse within a problematic, and in which the problematic of which it is a discourse is defined, and in which the form of relation of the discourse to the problematic is determined. It is on this condition alone that theoretical texts are intelligible, that the conditions of existence of discourse are determined. This type of reading is a *conceptual* reading, a reading which presupposes a concept of what it is to read and in which reading takes the form of the theoretical reconstruction of the text(s) examined, because the problematic is not given in the text; it exists only in the discourse it makes possible, in the same way that language is nowhere given as a totality but exists in the speech it makes possible.[9] The structure of a problematic is inscribed in the discourse it makes possible, but it is never present as a completed and perfect system. The structure of a problematic must therefore be constructed theoretically; such an analysis in turn entails that it be part of a problematic. The reading of theoretical discourse cannot escape the realm of theory; the validity of a reading can only be determined by conceptual argument. The text itself can in no way be the arbiter of a reading, since it is at question in the reading, and the notion that it is auto-intelligible supposes an intelligibility which is non-theoretical and non-discursive. That is why 'expositions', which suppose the givenness of meaning, suppress what is theoretical in the texts which they render; they separate manifest statements, positions, concepts, etc. from the conditions of their production, from the discourse which creates them and in terms of which they are intelligible. 'Exposition' in respect of theoretical texts must be something much more than exposition in fact, it must demonstrate that the text in question is indeed a theoretical text. A reading which lacks any concept of theory, which supposes meaning to be given, cannot do this – for the a-conceptual reading every text and no text is theoretical.

In this work we are concerned with two epistemologies, one that of Bernard which attempts to represent this openness of the mode of producing knowledge in the sciences, the other that of *The Rules of Sociological Method* which attempts to provide an epistemological foundation for a science of a given object, which generates a closed space of the repetition of the given as the necessary.

It must be emphasised that in studying *The Rules of Sociological Method* we are concerned to read it philosophically, to read it as a philosophical text concerned with the logical foundations of a science, sociology. It is solely as an epistemological argument that

we will regard this text; we shall be concerned with its logical
structure and coherence, with its demonstrative capacity as an
argument. We will in no way concern ourselves with its 'value as a
guide to social research' or its 'insights about the nature of social
reality', for such considerations presuppose that what is at question
is already settled, that this epistemology is the valid point of
departure of a social science. The analysis of the text will operate at
two levels: first, to determine the general epistemological problematic in which the text is situated, its position within classical
philosophy's spectrum; and, second, to analyse the object of this
epistemological discourse in its relation to sociology. It will be
argued that Durkheim's epistemology is in essence realist; that is,
that the object of knowledge is conceived as a given reality which
has a rational structure present in the real and that the knowledge
consists in perceiving the logic of the real itself. It will be argued
that Durkheim's discourse is structured by a series of contradictions and displacements between levels which stem from the
attempt to provide the foundations for a realist knowledge by
epistemological argument, and that this contradiction and the
series of displacements it engenders is the basis on which the discourse is a unity, that it is a unity only through a mode in which
these contradictions are produced and handled.

To our knowledge no detailed examination of the epistemological
discourse of *The Rules of Sociological Method* has hitherto been
undertaken. This new reading is not simply a possible 'interpretation' or a partisan exposition. Its analysis of this text is not a
critique which measures its 'lack' with respect to other theories;
it does not reject Durkheim because he is not something other than
a Durkheimian. The contradictions identified in Durkheim's
discourse are contradictions internal to it, they are not contradictions with the real, failures to take certain phenomena (the
class struggle, the economy, etc.) 'into account'. Paradoxically, we
dare to claim for our reading the status of being a 'Durkheimian'
reading of this text of Durkheim, not, that is, a partisan pro-
Durkheimian reading, least of all Durkheim's own reading, but a
reading which determines the contradictory unity, with all its
repressions and displacements, which *is* the particular form in
which this discourse is a coherent whole. The reading determines
the logic of this discourse – a logic, contradictory as it is, which all
who take the realist position must follow in a more or less rigorous

fashion. The Durkheimian position cannot be taken without the accompanying logic of its discursive structure and its epistemological consequences. Sociologists tend to treat theoretical texts as bundles of 'insights' from which one may borrow or select at will; if this work is of any value to them it is in challenging that kind of innocence. Durkheim's epistemology is an impossible one, but it is to his credit that he attempted to argue it rigorously – without that rigour the present work could not have been written.

Finally, it may appear curious that the analysis of Durkheim's epistemology is prefaced by a discussion of Claude Bernard. The relevance of these philosophical reflections of a nineteenth-century experimental physiologist to the epistemological problems of sociology may appear to be, at best, an obscure one. However, the choice of Bernard as a preparation for the study of Durkheim is not an arbitrary one; its pertinence will now be explained.

The analysis of Bernard's epistemology challenges the hitherto dominant interpretation of it as positivist or empiricist; it argues that it cannot be reduced to the status of a variant or repetition of any of the classical epistemological positions. This epistemology attempts to conceptualise science as a process of production of knowledge and not as a form of experience or perception, and to argue that the objects which the sciences study are intra-scientific objects, objects constructed by scientific investigation and not given objects. By reconstructing Bernard's epistemology, by showing its *difference* from positivism and empiricism, it is possible to present and to emphasise the epistemological concepts that will be employed in the critique of Durkheim.

The epistemological positions of Bernard are quite different from and opposed to those of Durkheim's system, despite certain manifest similarities in particular themes and in certain modes of presentation. Bernard's critique of realist and positivist epistemologies provides a basis for the identification and critique of Durkheim's epistemology. However, Bernard's relevance is not limited to being, as it were, a nineteenth-century representative or precursor of 'Bachelardian' epistemology – clearly, if this were the case there would be no reason to use Bernard in particular because there are more developed and better conceptualised forms of this anti-empiricist conception of science.

There are three reasons why Bernard's work is especially pertinent and why the relation Bernard–Durkheim is an especially illuminating one. Let us be clear before we proceed what a relation is *not*; it is certainly not a relation of 'influences' and manifest historical links between the two thinkers. Durkheim, to our knowledge, does not mention Bernard nor does he refer to any of his works. The coherence of this text, the appropriateness of the relation Bernard–Durkheim, does not stem from the 'coherence' of a given, the fact that the 'action' takes place in France in the time of the nineteenth century. The relations developed between Durkheim and Bernard, relations of difference rather than analogy, are relations relevant to a particular theoretical project, to the project of this work. The relation Bernard–Durkheim is in no sense a relation of the type established in the history of ideas.

The first reason for Bernard's pertinence is that his work enables us to contrast two very different relations between the sciences and philosophical epistemology. In the case of Bernard, this is the attempt to develop philosophical concepts which represent the mode of producing knowledge in experimental physiology and in doing so to develop general concepts of experimental reasoning and its conditions. Bernard is forced to break with and to transform the existing philosophical conceptions of knowledge in order to represent a form of knowledge inconceivable by them and produced independently of them. In the case of Durkheim, this is the attempt to use an existing philosophical epistemology to provide the foundation for and to legislate the conditions of knowledge in a new, and as yet unborn, science. Durkheim's philosophical point of departure determines the object and the methods of this new 'science' – it is a science constituted through this philosophic practice.

The second reason is that Bernard and Durkheim occupy certain points, and certain points only, of the same epistemological space – there is a definite analogy between the social and the biological sciences in that Durkheim and Bernard face ideological problematics with important aspects in common in their respective domains. Durkheim and Bernard both attempt to break with and to overcome the dominance of essentialist and reductionist ideologies in their respective domains. Bernard breaks with the dominance of the vitalism/materialism ideological couple in physiology and he provides in his philosophical reflections a concept of the vitalism/materialism couple and its effects. Durkheim does not break with the analogous ideologies in the social sciences, essentialism and reductionism; his work problematises certain given forms of these ideologies but, rather than breaking with them in their more general forms, his 'social science' is nothing more than a mutation or reorganisation of them.

Durkheim opposes conceptions of the social order analogous to vitalist conceptions of the organism in the biological sciences. Conceptions of society as a spiritual whole, as an entity, are similar to vitalist conceptions of the organism as animated by a unique force, 'life'. These conceptions were associated with the reactionary ideologies particularly current among Catholic social thinkers in the period immediately following the Restoration, and were incompatible with Durkheim's rationalistic and materialist position. In the Preface to the second edition of *The Rules of Sociological Method* Durkheim forcefully rejected interpretations of his work which regarded his conception of society as an essential or organic whole:

> Our principle, then, implies no metaphysical conception,
> no speculation about the fundamental nature of beings.
> What it demands is that the sociologist put himself in the
> same state of mind as the physicist, chemist or physiologist
> when he probes into a still unexplored region of the scientific
> domain. When he penetrates the social world he must be
> aware that he is penetrating the unknown: he must feel
> himself in the presence of facts whose laws are as unsuspected
> as were those of life before the era of biology (Durkheim,
> 1966, p. xlv).

No de Maistre or de Bonald could have contemplated penetrating the social world as a physiologist would the organic, to dissect, to separate, to vary, to experiment. Durkheim did; his attitude was at one with an era of heroic scientism. He hoped for a sociology which was like a natural science, an objective knowledge of an objective given, a knowledge in which the scientist was in no way privileged with respect to his object, and in which this object was no less of a real, determinate and invariable phenomenon than the phenomena of physical nature. However, we shall see that, despite these hopes, the logic of the Durkheimian theory leads it into a position as essentialist and idealist as that of vitalism.

Durkheim rejected mechanistic and reductionist conceptions of society as a combination of individuals; conceptions rooted in psychologism, biologism and voluntaristic individualism. For Durkheim the object of sociology is a distinct object, its manifestations, social facts, are facts *sui generis*. A consequence of this is that psychologistic, voluntaristic and biologistic explanations of the social stand in the same logical relation to sociology as biological reductionist explanations of the organism do to physiology. The attempt to reduce the social to individuals is analogous to the attempt to reduce life to nothing more than chemical reactions or to physical laws alone.

Thus there are analogous structures of ideology in the biological and the social sciences – in both the essentialisation of the totality or its reduction to its elements form a couple.

The third reason for Bernard's pertinence goes beyond this similarity of the ideologies confronting Bernard and Durkheim in their attempts to constitute a scientific physiology or a scientific sociology; it is that in breaking with these ideologies in the process of constructing a scientific physiology and in representing that break in philosophical concepts Bernard provides the means of identifying and criticising the effects of Durkheim's *failure* to break with ideology, the essentialism and vitalism of his conception of the social totality. Bernard's philosophical concepts, in particular the concept of the vitalism/materialism couple, provide the basis for identifying the ideological forms and their epistemological effects. Bernard's physiological concepts indicate how Bernard overcame the ideological opposition of vitalism/materialism – how he provided a scientific solution to the problem of conceiving the organism in physiology. Thus in addition to the chapter on Bernard's epistemology there is a short chapter on Bernard's main physiological concepts; the materials in this chapter will be used later to show the contrast between the effects of Bernard's scientific work and Durkheim's mutation in ideology. Bernard is not, therefore, a mere stalking horse for Bachelardian epistemology; his specific philosophical and physiological concepts are necessary and irreplaceable in the examination of Durkheim's epistemology and its consequences for his sociology.

Part One

Claude Bernard

Claude Bernard's Epistemology

Introduction

Claude Bernard was one of the leading physiologists of the nineteenth century. He is famous in the history of the sciences for, among other things, his discovery of the glycogenic function of the liver and for his concept of the *milieu intérieur*, the idea that the tissue elements of a complex organism live in an internal environment formed by the bodily fluids, which is controlled in all vital conditions, temperature, pressure, humidity, etc.[1]

Bernard was also a philosopher; his most famous text being *An Introduction to the Study of Experimental Medicine* (1865). His position in the history of philosophy is a more obscure one; he figures, if at all, in most histories of philosophy as a minor light of nineteenth-century French positivism. The character of his philosophical position is also a disputed one. Writers such as Black (1949), Charlton (1959) and Kolakowski (1972) see Bernard as a straightforward positivist or fallibilist, while Vertanen (1960) recognises in Bernard a strong affinity with Descartes and Pascal, and Bergson saw in Bernard's work a prefiguration of his own vitalist position.[2] This controversy is an index of the injustice of Bernard's obscurity. These very discrepant interpretations of Bernard's philosophy obscure concepts and positions of the first importance. Each of these readings of Bernard's texts, the positivist, the idealist, the vitalist, etc., recognises in them an element which corresponds to the reading, an element which makes it possible as a reading. But these readings do not see and cannot see the 'residue' which remains even if they are all applied in combination. It is this 'residue' which is the substance of Bernard's originality as a philosopher. It is the object of this chapter to make

Bernard's epistemology, his theory of scientific knowledge, intelligible and coherent by means of a reading which represents it in appropriate concepts. These concepts are largely drawn from the work of the French philosopher Gaston Bachelard.[3]

The point of departure of Bernard's epistemology is not to be found within the problematics of classical[4] philosophy. It is not a new theory of *human* knowledge Bernard offers us but elements of an understanding of the mode of producing knowledge in the sciences. Bernard did not enter the realm of philosophy as a pastime or in order to gain entry to the Academy. The point of departure of his philosophical work is the science of physiology and its problems. The philosophical questions Bernard tackles stem from the problems engendered by the struggle between scientific and ideological theories in physiology. Bernard's major theoretical achievements in philosophy, the separation of philosophy and science as distinct practices within knowledge, his non-empiricist conception of experiment, his conception of scientific determinism, his settling of the Vitalist/Materialist opposition, concern the major points of theoretical fragility in the physiology of the period. These points of fragility are the points of entry for ideological discourses into the problematic of scientific physiology; the discourses of vitalism and reductionist materialism, discourses whose effect is to silence and to replace scientific discourse. It is the danger of these prevalent and powerful ideologies, ideologies which contain systematic misconceptions of physiology's object, concepts and methods, which prompts the scientist Bernard to turn philosopher. Bernard's philosophical work is a representation of the epistemology immanent in the scientific practice of physiology.

Bernard's epistemological position is defined by a certain conjuncture in the history of the sciences, by a certain level of development of physiology and the other sciences, and by a certain relationship between scientific and ideological knowledges in physiology. This epistemology is resistant to the categories of classical philosophy and does not correspond to any of the variants of its theory of knowledge. But Bernard did not by any means escape from classical philosophy in the shape of the conventional philosophical doctrines of his day. It is in the categories of that philosophy that he was forced to think and to represent the conditions of a knowledge absolutely alien to them. Hence both the possibility of conventional philosophical readings and the limitations, errors and contradictions of Bernard's discourse.

However, this epistemological position is not confined to the period in which it was written nor to the philosophical struggles in the physiology of the period. As the result of the demands of a particular conjuncture concepts are produced which are of lasting value and which are relevant to all the sciences, not simply to the sciences of life.

His concept of scientific determinism is especially relevant at the present time, particularly in the social sciences. This concept destroys the whole conception of the possibility or impossibility of determinate and certain knowledge being governed by the nature of the real itself and the level of rigour and certainty of the various sciences being determined by the differences in the nature of the real objects they study. Thus, the story goes, physics is the most certain of the sciences because its phenomena are the most abstract and regular. A similar and equally familiar argument is that the social sciences are inexact and unrigorous because social phenomena are indeterminate, uncertain and especially complex. This is frequently ascribed to the freedom and diversity of human subjects. This 'argument', in essence a form of special pleading for the retention of the age-old notion of Man's free-will, mirrors exactly the vitalists' contention that 'life' is in no way determinable like the abstract and inorganic phenomena of the physical world. Bernard shatters this argument by showing that determinateness pertains to knowledge, that it is only through scientific knowledge that the nature of phenomena is known and that the argument against 'determinism' is a form of defence for a knowledge which is uncertain and indefinite because it is ideological and erroneous.

Similarly, Bernard's conception of experiment, which in many ways pre-dates Bachelard's conception of scientific experiments as forms of materialisation of scientific theory, is particularly valuable in counteracting the dominant empiricist and fallibilist conceptions of experimentation. It illustrates very clearly the quite different relation of scientific practice to experimentation as against certain types of philosophy of science. In science experimentation is a continuous process of the production of knowledge; experiments never 'fail'; they do not verify or falsify theories but represent applications of them.

Thus Bernard's philosophical work continues to be of the first importance today, but it should not be thought that the reason for this is that scientific practice is a sure defence against the errors of philosophy. There is no spontaneous 'scientist's philosophy' guaranteed against the errors of classical philosophy. To be a 'scientist' confers no privilege in questions of epistemology. A measure of Bernard's originality is the practice of certain other scientists who ventured into the terrain of philosophy in the nineteenth century. The history of those interventions in the nineteenth century is a history of the production of error and ideology by men of considerable ability. It is a history which reveals the persistent failure to recognise the difference of philosophical questions and scientific questions, to respect the limits of scientific knowledge, and the adoption of epistemologies inimical to scientific thinking and scientific experimentation. It is only possible here to briefly indicate four prevalent tendencies in the relation of the sciences and philosophy in the nineteenth century:

(i) The production of universal pseudo-sciences[5] which inextricably confuse science and philosophy, which seek to reduce 'matter' and 'nature' to a single principle, and which unite all phenomena in a single explanatory 'system'. The examples of Haeckel's system of monist materialism and Mach's universal science of 'energetics' indicate how an intelligent biologist and a brilliant physicist, both with positive achievements in their respective sciences to their credit, could be led so far into the realm of speculation and absurdity.[6] It was no necessity in biology or mechanics which produced these 'monsters' but the intervention of 'philosophical questions'.[7]

(ii) The prevalence of an ideology of materialism among philosophers and scientists which considered the disputes of philosophy to be 'settled' by the 'positive discoveries' of the sciences. Science was to intervene in the disputes of religion and philosophy as a war-engine, as the ultimate weapon of the materialist position, as an instrument of proof of the categories of philosophical materialism and a refutation of idealism. The 'discoveries' of the sciences were taken as empirical givens to be thrown in the face of pious ministers of religion. This tendency had certain very serious effects on the practice of the sciences. Darwin in particular was forced to distance himself from the struggle which followed the publication of *The Origin of Species*. His status as 'the murderer of Adam' almost absorbed the questions of evolutionary biology, in his first formulations so precarious and fragile, into questions of culture and ideology. The truths of faith in the last instance were in no way shattered by these 'discoveries', any more than they were shattered by the 'discoveries' of Galileo and Newton. Science could no more refute God's reality and existence than it could prove that the universe was ultimately composed of a colourless, odourless and invisible substance.

(iii) The collapse of many eminent physicists, at the end of the nineteenth century and in the early twentieth century, into idealism as a result of the discoveries in respect of the nature of energy, of the atom and the properties of electricity. Mach, Poincaré, Rey and Duhem all reflected on the desubstantialisation of matter into energy and the dispute about the precise nature of energy, and concluded that 'matter has disappeared'. Philosophical materialism and scientific materialism were inextricably confused in this 'crisis' in physics.

It was not in fact a crisis *in* physics but a crisis of physicists' inability to reflect in appropriate epistemological categories the logic of their own science. Matter was confused with the substance termed 'matter' in mechanical, philosophical materialism. The reality of the phenomena produced by physics was, as a function of this confusion, opened to doubt. The physicists had confused the reality they had produced with a void because they confused matter as a general (and empty) philosophical category with a particular organisation of matter (matter in classical physics and the matter of mechanical materialism). As a result they fell into scepticism. Bernard, long before confronted with the problem that the organised effectivity of living beings could not be simply reduced to the substance of mechanical materialism, had recognised that the phenomena of life were no less real and material than the phenomena of inorganic nature. It was in response to this problem that he formulated his principle of determinism as the foundation of a *scientific* materialism. Had the physicists followed this principle they would have recognised that whatever the difference between the form of organisation of phenomena in their science and that in other sciences, or in philosophy, the phenomena they produced were none the less real.[8]

(iv) The development of 'philosophies of science', that is, attempts to legislate the conditions and valid forms of knowledge of the *sciences* rather than of human knowledge in general, as was the case in earlier philosophical systems. The first major exponents of this new type of philosophical epistemology were Comte and Mill.[9] Bernard criticised these new philosophies of science most effectively for their attempt to impose external limits on the work of the sciences.

Bernard suffered from none of these tendencies which marked the relation of philosophy and the sciences in the nineteenth century. He was perhaps the only philosophically active scientist who was free from them. An important reason for this was his clear recognition of the necessary difference of philosophical and scientific questions. We will outline how Bernard effected this separation in the following section.

The Separation of Philosophy and Science

Experimental medicine (like all experimental sciences) does not need to be attached to any philosophic system. A physiologist's role, like every scientific man's, is to seek truth for its own sake, without wishing to use it to control one system of philosophy or another. When a man of science takes a philosophical system as his base in pursuing a scientific investigation, he goes astray in regions that are too far from reality (Bernard, 1865, p. 221).

Bernard conceives science as an autonomous form of the discovery of 'truth', independent of and different from philosophy.[10] Philosophy does not provide the basis of science; the production of scientific knowledge and the forms of scientific proof are internal to science. Science 'does not need to be attached to any philosophic system' because it is not an objectless 'method' or a phenomenology[11] in search of theories to prove or upon which to found the blind empiricity of its practice. Science is not the mere 'war-engine' of any philosophical system, a means of empirical proof of the postulates of a philosophy.[12] The acceptance of an object externally given to scientific investigation leads it into 'regions that are too far from reality'. Bernard here conceives the separation of philosophy and science in an empiricist form, that philosophy leads science away from the 'real' into, we must suppose, a realm of the speculative and the 'ideal'. But despite its empiricist formulations the principle of the separation remains: if scientists were to accept the pre-given objects of philosophical systems then science would become subordinate to, a secondary method of, philosophic discourse.

Philosophy is not the source of scientific methods; it cannot legislate externally the methods of investigation and forms of proof of the sciences. Bernard argues, contrary to the myth as popular in his time as in ours, that Bacon's *Novum Organum* is not the origin, the point of conception, of the modern scientific method, it is not even an adequate representation of that method.[13] Only a study of scientific practice can give an accurate representation of scientific epistemology. But philosophy, even if it were to confine itself to the reflection of the logic of the sciences, can never be equivalent to science. Bacon's object in the *Novum Organum* could not be equivalent to that of Galileo. For, at best, philosophy can only represent the method of the sciences, it cannot practise it. Philosophy does not have the same object as the sciences even when it concerns itself with scientific knowledge. Philosophy does not produce knowledge of nature nor can it subsume the sciences within its own conceptions.

Bacon neither *invented* the experimental method of the new physical sciences nor could he *use* it as the scientists did:

> Consequently, even in speaking of Bacon, it does not seem to
> me permissible to say he invented the experimental method,
> which Galileo and Torricelli so admirably practised and
> which Bacon could never use (Bernard, 1865, p. 51).

Bacon did not *invent* the experimental method because it was already existent in the practice of the new physical sciences. The new method which Galileo practised was produced in the practice of the natural sciences. Bacon misrecognised that method in conceiving it as a universal mode of cognition, a technique of obtaining knowledge, applicable to any object whatsoever. Bacon conceived the experimental method as a given external to what it is to know and explain, but in fact it was an effect of the scientific revolution in which Galileo transformed the concepts, the object and the method of physics. Bacon could not *use* the experimental method because he separated it from the problems and particular forms of explanation internal to physics in which it was, indeed, a method. Bacon conceived experimentation as a development, an extension, of the faculties of human cognition and not as a particular form of 'cognition' internal to the practice of physics:

> I think that men of science achieve their discoveries, their
> theories and their science apart from philosophers . . . those
> who make the most discoveries in science know Bacon least,
> while those who read and ponder him, like Bacon himself,
> have poor success. For scientific methods and processes are
> learned, in fact, only in laboratories, where experimenters
> grapple with the problems of nature (ibid., p. 225).

Why should Bacon misrepresent and misrecognise this element of
the epistemology of the new physical sciences? The answer is to be
found in what Bernard terms the 'systematic and scholastic' tendencies which are internal to the nature of philosophical thinking:
'Positivism, like the philosophic systems which it rejects in the
name of science, has the fault of being a system' (ibid., p. 221).
Comte, the principal representative of those 'other more modern
philosophers' to whom Bernard obliquely refers,[14] had created the
most advanced 'grand systematisation' of scientific knowledge in
Bernard's own time, positivism. Comte was an earnest and able
student of the sciences and a vigorous defender of their theoretical
autonomy. Surely then Comte's positive philosophy should have
provided an adequate basis for Bernard's own philosophical
reflections? It did not. Bernard rejects positivism because it is a
system.

Bernard's opposition to philosophical systems is not an opposition to their systematicity as such; he does not oppose philosophy's
systematic tendencies because of his commitment to an empiricist
or inductivist *philosophical* position. He opposes the systematic
tendencies of philosophy in respect of their effect upon science, of
the potential dangers of these systems for scientific practice.
'General systematisations' of scientific knowledge in philosophy,
even good ones, in spite of themselves, can only reflect a given state
of development of scientific knowledge.[15] As systems these representations of scientific reasoning formalise scientific knowledge as
it is into a 'model' of scientificity, into universal and legislative conceptions of how the sciences must operate in order to know.
Philosophical systems attempt to lay down the conditions of scientific knowledge independently of and externally to the practice of
the sciences. They create philosophical limits to scientific knowledge: 'I can no more accept a philosophy, then, which tries to
assign boundaries to science, than a science which claims to sup-

press philosophic truths that are present outside its own domain' (ibid., p. 223).

These limits are not the limits of the sciences. Philosophical systems as hypostatised representations of a given state of scientific development in practice close the problematics of the sciences. Philosophical theories of knowledge displace the conditions of proof of the validity of scientific operations from science to philosophy. Bernard rejects this displacement, this inversion of the real relations; he insists that each science establishes the limits and forms of its own knowledge: 'Processes of reasoning should endlessly vary for experimenters, according to the different sciences and to the more or less difficult questions to which they apply them' (ibid., p. 225). Bernard recognises there is no universal method common to all the sciences and external to each of them which is the model of scientificity. The validity of method, of problems and of forms of proof is determined within each science:

> But if philosophy, instead of contenting itself with this fraternal union, tried to enter the household of science and dogmatically lord its productions and methods of manifestation then their understanding would cease. Claiming to absorb the special discoveries of a science into any philosophical system would, in fact, be a delusion. For making scientific observations, experiments and discoveries, philosophic method and procedure are vague and powerless; the only means available for that are scientific methods and procedures that can be known only by experimenters, men of science or philosophers, practising some definite science (ibid., p. 224).

Science is not a simple collection of perceptions of given observables, a collection which receives increment as new discoveries are added:

> Science proceeds by revolution and not by addition pure and simple. This holds for theories, which are always successive. Chemistry is a striking example. Phlogiston explained very well . . . . Principles are needed. Propose in fact that one has never made a discovery by looking for it directly (Bernard, 1967, p. 87).

Scientific knowledge develops as a succession of distinct systems of problems, objects and methods. Sciences are not reproductions of the real, they are products of their own practice. A science is therefore intelligible only if its own terms are respected, and no universal 'method' can be abstractly legislated for the sciences.

'Science proceeds by revolution': 'A science that halted in a system would remain stationary and would be isolated, because systematisation is really a scientific encysting, and every encysted part of an organism ceases to take part in the organism's general life' (Bernard, 1865, p. 223). Bernard recognises, although in a practical form and not in adequate concepts, the necessary openness and the potentially infinite development and reorganisation that characterises scientific problematics and scientific knowledges. The effect of the domination of a science by a philosophical system is encystment, the hardening of its concepts into a dead formalist time, the stasis of its experimental practice in the form of a technical repetition.

We now see clearly Bernard's reason for opposing philosophical systems. It is not the positivist reason that philosophy is a realm of illusion pure and simple, a speculative contemplation of the 'ideal' which cannot recognise the real world. Although Bernard appears to separate philosophy and science on a positivist basis, in terms of the real versus the ideal, the concept of science he is defending is quite different from the positivist conception of an essentially realist knowledge. Bernard opposes philosophical systems because of their effect on science, or rather their scientific ineffectivity. Scientific knowledge can only be produced within scientific practice. Only the practitioners of 'some definite science' can produce scientific knowledge because it is only through induction into that problematic that it is possible to know what its 'scientific methods and procedures' are. If philosophy enters 'the household of science' and legislates the conditions of scientificity then the conditions of scientific knowledge are destroyed.

But it should not be thought that, having separated philosophy and science, having differentiated their objects, having insisted on the autonomy of science, Bernard rejects philosophy absolutely and advises the sciences and the scientist to have nothing to do with philosophy.[16] He does not counterpose science as a realm of truth, anchored in the 'real', to philosophy as a realm of illusion, lost in the speculative contemplation of the 'ideal'. He defends philosophy but in a non-philosophical spirit:

As an experimenter, then, I avoid philosophic systems; but I cannot for that reason reject the philosophic spirit which, without being anywhere, is everywhere and, without belonging to any system, ought to reign, not only over all science but over all human knowledge. . . . Indeed, from a scientific point of view, philosophy embodies the eternal aspiration of human reason toward knowledge of the unknown. Therefore, philosophers always live in controversial questions and lofty regions, the upper boundaries of science. Hence they impart to scientific thought an enlivening and ennobling notion . . . thus they nourish a kind of thirst for the unknown; the sacred fire of research must therefore never be extinguished in men of science (ibid., p. 221).

Bernard separates the 'spirit' of philosophy from philosophy's systematic and scholastic tendencies. The philosophic spirit is not present in any particular philosophic system; it is not the spirit of systematic and technical philosophy proper. Why should this 'spirit' 'reign not only over the sciences but over *all human knowledge*'? Bernard, we might say, is enough of a Cartesian to believe in the virtue of doubt. He certainly conceives systematisation as a tendency not only of philosophy proper but of the *human mind*: 'The feeble yet dominating tendency of our minds lends us to absorb other kinds of knowledge into our personal systems' (ibid., p. 223). The philosophic spirit of doubt should therefore 'reign . . . over all human knowledge' as a healthy corrective to dogmatism.

But the value of the philosophic 'spirit' is not confined to this healthy human doubt. Bernard uses the word 'philosophy' in three different senses which correspond to three quite different questions in his text:

(i) The systematic philosophies and their effect on the sciences which we have discussed above;

(ii) the philosophical 'attitude' of mind which prevents human subjects from being dogmatic and closed of mind;

(iii) philosophy is used as a substitute term for scientific, theoretical thinking. Bernard does not and cannot separate these different senses by a rigorous conceptual terminology. These different senses must be separated by any reading which attempts to expose the conceptual structure of Bernard's epistemology. We shall see later (pp. 51–7) the source of this confusion in the absence of a crucial concept. The effect of this absence in this case, unless due account is taken of it in the reading, is to confuse senses (i) and (ii), to make scientific theory subordinate to philosophy, and to confuse the theoretical problematics of philosophy and the sciences with attributes of the human mind. These effects, these confusions, are in clear contradiction with the other effects, distinctions and analyses of Bernard's epistemology.

When Bernard uses philosophy in its third sense he is warning his fellow scientists against the danger of empiricism and technicism so strongly fostered by the philosophical system of positivism.[17] He is warning against the empiricist rejection of theory for 'pure' experimentation. He argues that 'philosophy', in the sense of scientific theoretical thinking, is the means by which the unevennesses of the problematics of the sciences, their unposed and unresolved questions, are recognised and thereby made the object of scientific practice. 'Philosophy', by recognising the unknown and uncertain, makes possible that creative experimental materialisation that transforms it into the known and the determinate:

> By ceaselessly stirring the inexhaustible mass of unsolved questions, philosophy stimulates and maintains this healthful movement in science. For only the indeterminate belongs to philosophy, *in the restricted sense in which I am here considering it*, while the determinate necessarily falls into the realm of science (ibid., p. 223; our emphasis).

'Philosophy', or scientific theory, is the source of theoretical developments in the sciences. It is theoretical thinking which prevents scientific practice from becoming an empiricist system, and from suffering a technicist closure of its problematic:

> Without constant stimulation by the spur of the unknown . . . it might be feared that men of science would become system ridden in their acquirements and their knowledge. Then science would halt through intellectual inertness, just as minerals, in saturated solution, become chemically inert and crystallise (ibid., pp. 222–3).

Clearly, this cannot mean that 'philosophy' provides the basis of scientific investigation; for if that were the case science would again become a mere method, theory would be external to scientific practice, and philosophy would legislate the objects and problems of scientific investigation. However, the positive side of philosophy is not entirely included within the sense of philosophy as scientific theory:

> Philosophy and science, then, must never be systematic: without trying to dominate one another, they must unite. Their separation could only be harmful to the progress of human knowledge (ibid., p. 224).

Philosophy is not only an attitude of mind, a systematic and scholastic form of pseudo-knowledge, or a misnomer for scientific theory. Bernard's text leaves a space for a philosophy which is none of these things.[18] This 'philosophy' is the philosophy of which the *Introduction* is itself an example: a philosophy which does not try to assign boundaries to science; a philosophy which is of use to experienced scientists because it is written by 'men of science or philosophers, practising some definite science'. It is philosophical because it reflects and represents the logic immanent in scientific practice, which can be known only by knowing that practice, but is not an instance or example of that practice. Like the *Novum Organum* the *Introduction* is not a text *of* science, but a text *on* science. Unlike Bacon's texts, Bernard's text does not misrepresent but rather represents the necessary conditions of knowledge in the sciences. Its function is to defend scientific practice, to make its conditions clear in a reflected form to its practitioners, to distinguish scientific knowledge from conceptions which are dangerous for scientific practice. It is not only 'philosophy' in the third sense which protects science from a technical closure, or for that matter from idealist errors, but philosophy in the fourth and silent sense, the sense in which the *Introduction* itself is written.

Bernard therefore rejects speculative and systematic philosophy, and he rejects pragmatist science. He defends the theoretical autonomy of the sciences. He also practises, and shows in practice, the necessity of a 'non-philosophical' philosophy which defends that independence because it does not assign limits to science. The *Introduction* is not a 'general systematisation', it does not reflect scientific epistemology in the mode of closure but in the very mode of openness. Despite Canguilhem's criticisms[19] the *Introduction* does not exclude the possibility of a non-Bernardian epistemology. It is true that Bernard did not conceptualise as Bachelard did the non-philosophical philosophy necessary for the sciences, but he did write a text in that philosophy, which reflects the spirit if not the concepts of that philosophy. His epistemology is not without positivist and idealist admixtures and errors; it is limited by the conditions of the conjuncture in which it was written, but this short text is an epistemological document of lasting value for scientists and philosophers.

Determinism

Bernard's separation of philosophy and science takes the form of a rejection of the dominance of philosophical criteria of knowledge over scientific knowledge. This makes possible a new conception of knowledge in philosophy; a conception which is the product of a reflection on how it is that the sciences do produce knowledge, and which does not attempt to legislate the conditions of scientific knowledge independently of scientific practice. Far from being a manifestation of the anti-philosophical tendencies of positivism, Bernard's position represents a liberation of philosophical practice in respect of the sciences. One of the first effects of this liberation is a new concept of determinism which rigorously differentiates the determinism of the sciences from the determinism of classical philosophy. It is from the practice of physiology that the new philosophical concept of determinism is derived. This new concept both represents an effect produced by scientific practice and as a philosophical concept defends the conditions of certain knowledge in the sciences against anti-scientific empiricist and idealist epistemologies.

Scientific Materialism and Philosophical Materialism

The new concept of determinism is a key element in the demarcation between scientific materialism and philosophical materialism. The new concept defends the certainty and reality of the science's knowledges. It is in this sense that it is materialist, and not in the sense of philosophical materialism which holds that all the phenomena of the world are reducible to some universal 'matter' or 'Stoff'. This new theory of scientific knowledge does not concern itself with the same problems as the classical philosophical theories of knowledge. The central and constitutive element of the problematic of classical epistemology, the opposition of the materialist and idealist theories about the nature of the world and, therefore, of the means of knowing it, is decisively disputed: 'for physiological experimenters neither spiritualism not materialism can exist (ibid., p. 66). Materialism and spiritualism (idealism) are not rejected on the basis of an agnostic philosophical position, but because it is recognised that the question of the priority of materialism or spiritualism is a non-question as far as the sciences are concerned.

The question of the predominance of a universal 'Matter' or 'Spirit' is only possible within a conception in which a purely philosophical knowledge of nature, a philosophical explanation of the essence of things, is possible. Both metaphysical materialism and idealism conceive nature as knowable *in essence*. Materialism, as much as idealism, conceives nature as a rational order. For nature to be knowable *in essence* nature must embody a knowledge of itself in itself. It is only in this way, as reason manifest, that any knowledge of nature can escape being relative to its own operations as knowledge. Knowledge in classical metaphysics is the uncovering, discovery or recognition of a knowledge that has always existed in the real.

Bernard, on the contrary, insists that nature is an unconscious order which does not contain in itself a knowledge of that order. Experimental truths are relative truths about an essentially unconscious and blind reality; they tell us nothing beyond the knowledge they contain of the specific relations of phenomena:

> Experimental truths, on the contrary, are unconscious and
> relative, because the real conditions on which they exist are
> unconscious and can be known by us only in relation to the
> present state of our science (ibid., p. 53).

Knowledge is interiorised within the forms of knowledge; it is not given in the world. There can be no knowledge which can function as the judge or goal of the knowledge produced within these forms. Knowledge of 'matter' or 'things' must therefore always be relative and internal to the operations of the sciences themselves. What is known of 'matter' and therefore what 'matter' *is* for scientific reason can only be that matter which corresponds to the knowledge of a definite state of development of the sciences.

All questions concerning the nature of phenomena which are not

amenable to answers in terms of immediate material causes are not
questions that can be put in scientific reasoning; they are questions
of metaphysical reasoning. Bernard's opposition to classical pre-
critical metaphysics does not, however, reproduce the scepticism
and phenomenalism of the critique of classical metaphysics in
philosophy. Scientific knowledge is relative, limited and not
absolute, but it is certain and exact. It is not subject to dispute *as
knowledge* nor is it confined to single descriptive statements concerning given observables. What 'matter' *is*, is indeed internal to
the operations of the sciences but within these operations it is
nevertheless real and its conditions of existence are rigorously
known:

> The result is that a fact gains scientific value only through
> knowledge of its causation. . . . Indeed, if an experimenter
> must submit his ideas to the criterion of facts, I do not
> acknowledge that he must submit his reason (ibid., p. 178).

Scepticism, phenomenalism and conventionalism deny this
certainty of scientific knowledge and these doctrines deny that the
sciences' operations are an appropriation of real phenomena of
nature. These doctrines place scientific knowledge within question
marks; Bernard does not. For Bernard the experimental sciences
produce through their operations an appropriation and materialisation of real phenomena of nature in a form which is governed by
valid laws and is theoretically known. Any doubt that this appropriation is an appropriation of the real, that it is not merely an
illusion of scientists or a pragmatic technique, engenders a belief
in irrational facts, in a nature without causation or order, or with a
plurality of possible causes. These scepticist conclusions are
impossible for Bernard because they contradict the principle of
determinism.

Bernard's principle of scientific determinism states that if a
phenomenon is produced under specified conditions then it must
always necessarily appear in those conditions and in the same
aspect, unless some immediate material cause intervenes to change
those conditions:

> Negation of this proposition would be nothing less than
> negation of science itself. Indeed, as science is simply the
> determinate and the determinable, we must perforce accept as

an axiom that, in identical conditions, all phenomena are
identical and that, as soon as conditions are no longer the
same, the phenomena cease to be identical (ibid., p. 68).

The appearance of the phenomenon is subject to no doubt; it is not
merely probable but certain. The certainty and stability of its
appearance is directly related to the degree to which its conditions
are specified and known in the particular science concerned. The
instability and variability of a phenomenon is a function of the
rudimentary nature of scientific practice and has nothing whatsoever to do with an essential variability or lack of causation of the
phenomena itself. *Indeterminism characterises the nature of the
means of knowledge and not the phenomena to which it is applied.*
Scientific knowledge consists in determining the conditions of
existence, or in other words the *cause*, of phenomena.

For Bernard the cause of a phenomenon is nothing other than
the determinable conditions under which it appears or in which it
exists. Bernard therefore rejects all notions of an essential cause
separate from the phenomena themselves. The question, 'Why do
phenomena exist?', is a question which is unanswerable in science
unless it means merely the further specification of their immediate
conditions of existence.

Bernard's opposition to essentialist conceptions of causality and
to pretensions to absolute knowledge does not lead him into scepticism and phenomenalism. Unlike, for example, Hume he does not
take this anti-essentialist position as the point of departure of a
scepticism which in effect abolishes causality altogether and
reduces all true and unquestionable statements about the world to
descriptions of single observable phenomena. Unlike Hume he
does not consider causation to be an uncertain imputation on the
part of fallible human experience. Causality *in science* has nothing
whatever to do with making generalisations about relations between
observables of the type, 'A has preceded B on all known occasions,
therefore we suppose A to be the cause of B'. For Bernard a causal
relation in science is not merely *probable* and subject to discon-
firmation but certain and unchallengeable. Bernard's conception of
proof, of the criteria of valid knowledge, is a scientific and not a
philosophical one.

Unlike the philosophers, Bernard accepts as valid and requiring
no philosophical underpinning or foundation the proofs the

sciences use in practice. These proofs are not philosophical but concern the degree to which the conceptual and experimental operations of particular sciences have been properly carried out. Bernard does not seek to legislate the conditions of knowledge in abstraction from the forms of production of knowledge; he does not seek to produce a universal and invariant standard of knowledge but to represent the epistemological conditions of scientific knowledge.

Bernard's conception of determinism represents the conditions of the certainty and materiality of the science's investigation of nature. It is the first principle of *scientific* as against *philosophical* materialism. It is a necessary epistemological defence of scientific practice which closes the door to essentialism and scepticism alike; doctrines whose representations of the nature of knowledge destroy the possibility of that particular form of knowledge which is science.

Determinism and Indeterminism in the Sciences of 'Life'

This principle [determinism] is absolute in the phenomena of inorganic bodies as well as in those of living beings, and the influence of life, whatever view of it, we take, can nowise alter it. As we have said, what we call vital force is a first cause analogous to all other first causes, in this sense, that it is utterly unknown. It matters little whether or not we admit that this force differs essentially from the forces presiding over manifestations of the phenomena of inorganic bodies, the vital phenomena which it governs must still be determinable; for the force would otherwise be blind and lawless, and that is impossible (ibid., p. 68).

Bernard insists that the phenomena of 'life' are no different in respect of this principle of determinism than the phenomena of the physico-chemical sciences. The conception of 'life' as a form of being with properties different in essence from the mode of being which is inorganic 'matter', and which is not subordinate to the determinism which reigns in the realm of the organic, gives rise to a subordination of the biological sciences to the ideologies of essentialist metaphysics:

Aujourd'hui la physiologie devient une science exacte; elle doit se dégager des idées philosophiques et théologiques qui

pendant longtemps s'y sont trouvées mêlées. On n'a pas plus à
demander à un physiologiste s'il est spiritualiste ou
matérialiste qu'à un mathématicien, à un physicien ou à un
chimiste. Nous ne voulons pas, nous le répétons, nier pour
cela l'importance de ces grands problèmes qui tourmentent
l'esprit humain, mais nous voulons les séparer de la
physiologie, les distinguer, parce que leur étude relève de
méthodes absolument différentes. La tendance, qui semble se
raviver de nos jours, à vouloir immiscer dans la physiologie
les questions théologiques et philosophiques, à poursuivre
leur prétendue conciliation, est à mon sens une tendance
stérile et funeste, parce qu'elle mêle le sentiment et le
raisonnement, confond ce que l'on reconnaît et accepte sans
démonstration physique avec ce que l'on ne doit admettre
qu'expérimentalement et après démonstration complète. En
réalité, on ne peut être spiritualiste ou matérialiste que par
sentiment; on est physiologiste par démonstration scientifique
(Bernard, 1878–9, pp. 45–6).

The opposition of physics and chemistry as sciences of an organic
'matter' to physiology as the science of 'life', an organic and living
phenomenon of 'spirit', is the effect of the intrusion of a philosophical problematic into physiology. 'In reality it is only possible
to be a spiritualist or materialist through sentiment' because
materialism and spiritualism are epistemologically equivalent
positions within a single problematic. They are not essentially
different doctrines as their opposition would lead us to suppose.
Materialism and spiritualism merely dispute the priority of determination of the essence of the world; they counterpose the priority
of 'matter' and the priority of 'spirit'. There can be no rational
choice between these doctrines, only a choice of conviction or
preference. Materialism and spiritualism are essentialist doctrines
which cannot be subject to scientific proof nor to proofs by dispu-
tation alone.

There can be no agnosticism in respect of these doctrines in
physiology or any of the other sciences; both must be rejected
absolutely:

Ici nous serons seulement physiologiste et à ce titre, nous ne
pouvons nous placer ni dans le camp des vitalistes, ni dans
celui des matérialistes (ibid., p. 46).

The effect of the specific form of spiritualism in physiology, vitalism, is to install behind the real phenomena of living nature an immaterial essence which creates these phenomena, an essence itself without cause, and the effectivity of which is not material but spiritual:

> Il y a au fond des *doctrines vitalistes* une erreur irrémédiable, qui consiste à considérer comme force une personnification trompeuse de l'arrangement des choses, à donner une existence réelle et une activité matérielle, efficace à quelque chose d'immatériel qui n'est en réalité qu'une notion de l'esprit, une direction nécessairement inactive (ibid., p. 47).

Vitalism's explanatory principle 'life' is an inaccessible essence behind the phenomena of living nature; it reproduces the given phenomena of living nature absolutely and does not change the modality of that givenness. It explains everything and therefore nothing; it does so without effort and without problems: 'When a physiologist calls in vital force or life, he does not see it; he merely pronounces a word (Bernard, 1865, p. 67). Vitalism renders experimental science unnecessary; everything is explained, however contradictory the appearances, by a principle. Vitalism abhors determinism; it insists on the indeterminate nature of its phenomena, because determinism limits the sphere of action of the vital force:

> Les vitalistes nient le déterminisme, parce que, selon eux, les manifestations vitales auraient pour cause l'action spontanée efficace et comme volontaire et libre d'un principe immatériel. Les conséquences de cette erreur sont considérables: le rôle de l'homme en présence des faits vitaux devrait être celui d'un simple spectateur, non d'un acteur; les sciences physiologiques ne seraient que conjecturales et non certaines (Bernard, 1878–9, pp. 56–7).

Vitalism is not the only source of error in physiology. Materialism, although it is the enemy of vitalism, is no friend of scientific physiology. The effect of materialist doctrines in physiology is to reduce the phenomena of life to inorganic matter without any extension of its properties. 'Life' is abolished, and the very question of the nature of the effectivity of organic organisations and its conditions is denegated:

Nous nous séparons également des matérialistes; car, bien que
les manifestations vitales restent placées directement sous
l'influence de conditions physico-chimiques, ces conditions ne
sauraient grouper, harmoniser les phénomenes dans l'ordre et
la succession qu'ils affectent specialement dans les êtres
vivants (ibid., p. 46).

Just as 'matter' and 'spirit' are coupled as equivalent and opposed
terms in philosophy so vitalism and materialism form a couple in
their effects in physiology. Vitalism and materialism alike reduce
the problems of physiology to the philosophical answers about the
essence of nature which their philosophical progenitors spiritualism and materialism demand they must give. 'Life' is nothing
but matter. 'Life' is an essential and creative vital force. The
specific questions of physiology, the effect of organisation, and the
physico-chemical conditions of organisation, cannot exist if these
doctrines are to produce questions which conform to the answers
their explanatory principles are able to give. Vitalism and materialism form a couple in that they effect the repetition of philosophical discourse in physiological discourse. Bernard, in separating
science and philosophy, is making no idle distinction but a distinction vital to the life of science. The differentiation of science and
philosophy, and the principle of determinism, enable him to discover and to criticise from the standpoint of science the source and
the function of vitalism and materialism. This is another crucial
epistemological effect of the new philosophical concepts he
produces.

Philosophical and Scientific Determinism

Le principe du *déterminisme* domine donc l'étude des
phénomènes de la vie comme celle de tous les autres
phénomènes de la nature (ibid., p. 55).

In the *Leçons*, Bernard recognises that the resistance to the
principle of scientific determinism among physiologists and
philosophers stems from a misrecognition which confuses it with
philosophical determinism:

Depuis longtemps j'ai émis cette opinion, mais lorsque
j'employai pour la première fois le mot de *déterminisme* pour

introduire ce principe fondamental dans la science
physiologique, je ne pensais pas qu'il put être confondu avec
le déterminisme philosophique de Leibniz (ibid., p. 55).

Bernard in these passages in which he demarcates his position
from that of Leibniz gave what is perhaps the most advanced
specification of the difference of philosophical and scientific problematics (and of the difference of their objects) that could be
produced until Bachelard's formulation of the problem:

> Toutefois si le mot *déterminisme*, que j'ai employé, n'est pas
> nouveau, l'acception que je lui ai donnée en physiologie
> expérimentale est nouvelle; et cela devait être, puisque
> Leibniz l'avait appliqué seulement à des objets purement
> métaphysiques, tandis que je l'appliquais au contraire à des
> objets physiques, pour caractériser la méthode de la science
> physiologique (ibid., p. 55).

Bernard recognises that the word 'determinism' represents a quite
different concept with a different function in his problematic as
against that of Leibniz. Leibniz's use of the word is to be understood within the classical metaphysical problematic of free-will and
determinism. Leibniz's notion of determinism functions as a concept within the set of philosophical questions which seek to found
the apparently random and contingent appearances and events of
the world in a necessity:

> Lorsque Leibniz disait: 'L'âme humaine est un automate
> spirituel', il formulait le *déterminisme philosophique*. Cette
> doctrine soutient que les phénomènes de l'âme, comme
> tous les phénomènes de l'univers, sont rigoureusement
> déterminés par la série des phénomènes antécédents,
> inclinations, jugements, pensées, désirs, prévalence du plus
> fort motif, par lesquels l'âme est entraînée. C'est la négation
> de la liberté humaine, l'affirmation du *fatalisme*
> (ibid., pp. 55–6).

Leibniz is seeking a universal principle which will characterise the
essence of the world and ground its given appearances as emana-
tions of a necessary cause. Leibniz seeks to abolish all scholastic
essences *behind* the phenomena of the world; the essence must be
necessarily present in its phenomena; it cannot exist distinctly but

only in so far as it is contained in or expressed in the phenomena themselves.[20] Universal determinism is a necessity for Leibniz in order that nothing be contingent, that nothing should exist in a mode which can leave room for doubt as to the necessity of its existence, and therefore that all being is the uniform resultant of a single and unchallengeable order of nature. Leibniz's foundation of all apparently contingent events in a series of antecedents by the action of the principle of 'sufficient reason' is merely the opposed and speculative variant within classical metaphysics of scepticism and phenomenalism.[21]

The concept of scientific determinism is the product of a very different problematic. It is a product of a philosophical practice which reflects on the operations of the experimental sciences. It represents nothing more than a reflection of the epistemology of the conditions those operations require and the character of knowledge which they presuppose:

> Tout autre est le déterminisme physiologique. Il est l'expression d'un fait physique. Il consiste dans ce principe que chaque phénomène vital, comme chaque phénomène physique, est invariablement déterminé par des conditions physico-chimiques qui, lui permettant ou l'empêchant d'apparaître en deviennent les *conditions* ou les *causes matérielles immédiates ou prochaines*. L'ensemble des conditions déterminantes d'un phénomène entraîne nécessairement ce phénomène. Voilà ce qu'il faut substituer a l'ancienne et obscure notion spiritualiste ou materialiste de *cause* (ibid., p. 56).

In the physical sciences this principle is accepted with the unthinking certainty of the experimental operations the conditions of which it represents. In the sciences of life it is disputed in the same measure as these sciences' operations are less certain and in so far as these sciences are still struggling with admixtures of theological and philosophical ideology:

> Ce principe est fondamental dans toutes les sciences physiques. Là il est hors de conteste; il n'a pas même besoin d'être affirmé. Il en est autrement dans les sciences de la vie. Lorsque, en effet, il faut étendre le principe du déterminisme aux faits de la nature vivante, les médecins

animistes et vitalistes et les philosophes se mettent à la
traverse (ibid., p. 56).

Determinism is rejected by philosophers and by scientists in
respect of the sciences of 'life' and of 'morals' because it reduces
living beings and human moral agents to automata. Scientific
determinism, however, is not a universal determinism. It has
nothing to say about the question of 'free-will' for it is restricted to
phenomena whose conditions of existence can be vigorously
determined in science. Scientific determinism in so far as it is not
universal is not, however, a form of conciliation with voluntarism.
It does not admit of indeterminacy in respect of those things which
lie within its limits. Scientific determinism rejects the doctrine of
the freedom of the 'mind' or 'spirit' from material constraint, not
from the standpoint of a fatalism but because it does not admit of
the existence of real phenomena with an effectivity which are
without conditions of existence, and which therefore have no
cause.[22] It is not philosophical materialism but a scientific materialism. It rejects the essences of spiritualist metaphysics and
materialist metaphysics alike:

> Le malentendu entre les philosophes et les physiologistes
> vient sans doute de ce que le mot déterminisme est pris par
> eux dans le sens de *fatalisme*, c'est-à-dire dans le sens du
> déterminisme philosophique de Leibniz (ibid., p. 60).

Bernard's philosophical concepts which are derived from his
reflection on the sciences cannot be accommodated within the
doctrines of classical philosophy; they tear at the very fabric of
problems of classical philosophy. Bernard's philosophy cannot be
inserted into the space which unifies Leibniz and his critics for it
disrupts the homogeneity of that space by introducing the problems of another domain, that of the sciences. Determinism in its
new sense is the first conceptual effect of an intervention of the
logic of the sciences in philosophy. This intervention is unlike
those 'interventions' of Haeckel or Mach for it does not seek to
unite to reconcile the problematics of philosophy and science; its
theory of their separation is the condition of its intervention, for it
knows from what and into what it is to intervene.

Experimental Reasoning

Throughout the *Introduction* Bernard stresses that physiology is
and must be an experimental science. This insistence on the
necessity of experimental practice has led to misreadings of
Bernard's conception as an empiricist one. But for Bernard an
experimental science is characterised by experimental *reasoning*.
The greatest threats to scientific method in physiology are the construction of *a priori* 'systems' and blind empiricism. Scientific
determinism and experimental reasoning are coupled by Bernard;
without the experimental method scientific determinism is
impossible. What then is experimental reasoning?

Bernard defines the nature of scientific experimentation in
general at the beginning of the *Introduction*. Bernard's definition of
experiment produces a rupture with classical philosophical conceptions of the nature of knowledge. The definitions of experiment
and determinism contain a new conception of epistemology which
has its source in the process of production of knowledge in the
natural sciences.

> Where then, you will ask, is the difference between
> observers and experimenters? It is here: we give the name
> observer to the man who applies methods of investigation,
> whether simple or complex, to the study of phenomena which
> he does not vary and which he therefore gathers as nature
> offers them. We give the name experimenter to the man who
> applies methods of investigation, whether simple or complex,
> so as to make natural phenomena vary, or so as to alter them
> with some purpose or other, and to make them present
> themselves in circumstances or conditions in which nature
> does not show them (Bernard, 1865, p. 15).

By means of this distinction between observation and experiment Bernard demonstrates the necessity and function of reason
(theory)[23] in experimentation. Experimentation is here defined in
an essentially anti-empiricist form, and in a form which distinguishes between scientific knowledge and the 'knowledge' of the
human subject. Experimentation is an activity exclusively of the
sciences. The objects of experimental investigation in the sciences
are not domains of given facts, of phenomena 'as nature offers

them'. An object which is a 'given' can only be an object which is given to the perception of the human subject.[24] The conception of knowledge as a perception of given objects by human subjects is necessarily contained within a sensationalist problematic.[25] The 'knowledge' of the human subject and scientific knowledge are conflated in the sensationalist problematic. All sensationalist knowledge is modelled on perception or cognition; knowledge knows what an object shows. Bernard, in defining experiment as he does, produces a conception of knowledge which is based neither upon perception/cognition nor on the human subject's experience. The object of a scientific knowledge becomes an object which is potentially infinite because it is in no sense limited by the mode of givenness. If the objects of the sciences are not givens how is it that the sciences have objects? How is the object of scientific knowledge constituted if it does not exist in the mode of givenness?

In order 'to make natural phenomena vary . . . with some purpose or other', 'to make them present themselves in circumstances or conditions in which nature does not *show* them' it is necessary to have a *prior* 'purpose' and a *prior* object. This prior purpose and this prior object cannot be already given by nature; they cannot be 'natural'. It is reasoning which is the source of this prior purpose and this prior object; a purpose of reason and an object of reason. Reason (theory) is necessary for experimentation in order that those 'circumstances or conditions' be thought, that the relations and forms of phenomena be *constructed* in order that what is not given can be realised. Experimentation itself is a form of reasoning. It is an applied rationalism in which questions are put to nature but in which the answers that must be produced in the real are also formulated. 'Nature', the object of all the sciences, is interiorised within these sciences. This is the inescapable conclusion of a theory of knowledge which recognises that the objects of scientific knowledges do not exist as a given, that they are 'inexistent' as a given for human perception. The object of the sciences is interiorised within reason, and matter which the sciences construct is interiorised within experimentation.

Experimental reasoning is a form of knowledge different in essence from the 'knowledge' conceived by sensationalism. Cognition is replaced by construction. What it is that is to be produced can only be known as what it is through the specifications that reason has established. Experimental reasoning is a form of knowledge of which the conditions of proof are different in essence from any fallibilism. The 'facts' are no longer the measure of the 'hypothesis', the experimental 'hypothesis' is the measure of the 'facts' it will generate. It is experimental reason which evaluates its own products.

> In sciences of experimentation, man observes, but in addition he acts on matter, analyses its properties and to his own advantage brings about the appearance of phenomena which doubtless always occur according to natural laws, but in conditions which nature often has not yet achieved (ibid., p. 18).

An anti-sensationalist knowledge is not an idealism which thinks its phenomena into being.[26] Experimental reasoning presupposes experimental technique. Experimental reasoning is not a pure rationalism but a rationalism of application. Bernard does not believe that real phenomena are created or changed purely in the realm of thought. Matter is only acted upon by matter. The forms and relations of phenomena constructed in reason (theory) require materialisation in experiment, and they can be materialised only in so far as the material conditions of experimental production are thought out and constructed. Experiments are rational constructs, but not all experiments that are thinkable are realisable.[27] Experimental reasoning induces the rationalisation of technique, the connection of theory and experimental instruments, the rational development of instruments for acting on matter appropriate to theory. Thus it was no accident that Bernard constantly stressed the need for improved physiological laboratories, that in his monographs and textbooks he emphasised the necessity of the theoretical construction of experiments.[28]

Bernard's conception of the relation of scientific rationalism and experimental technique is contained in essence in the above quotations; its other aspects will be outlined in summary form below.

(i)
> The whole experimental enterprise comes from the idea, for it is this which induces experiment (ibid., p. 32).

Bernard here asserts both the primacy of theory in scientific work and the essence of scientific theory as a rationalism which *induces* experimentation as a logical and necessary consequence of its very mode of conceptualisation.

> As the fact which the experimenter must verify does not present itself to him naturally, he must make it appear, that is, *induce it, for a special reason and with a definite object* (ibid., p. 19, our emphasis).

Bernard's position explodes the terms of the ideological notion of inductive reasoning and installs a new conception of scientific knowledge as a process of production. Because its objects are not givens external to it, science cannot work on the basis of generalising from the collection of data, of following patiently the order of phenomena to constitute the order of its theory. The term *induce* changes its meaning. The experimenter must *induce* the phenomena he seeks for a 'special reason and with a definite object'. Phenomena are produced as material terms in an experimental argument. The place of phenomena in experimentation is no longer a given place but a rational place within the terms of experimental reasoning.

Just as the notion of induction is exploded, so is the opposed and corresponding notion of *deduction*. Experimental reasoning is not confined to the dialectic of concepts. Scientific knowledge is not developed purely deductively from the interior of the concept by the extraction of all its internal significations. Concepts in experimental reasoning serve as tools to specify *things* which are not given in the concept; the concept induces materialisation; it creates the conditions of the production of matter. Experimental sciences are neither speculative, aprioristic or rationalist, nor are they empiricist, inductivist or sensationalist; in them the classical opposition of the idea and the thing has no meaning.

(ii)

> Our ideas are only intellectual instruments which we use to break into phenomena (ibid., p. 41).

Theory is not deductive nor is it hypothetical. 'Hypotheses' in the experimental sciences are not constructions placed upon the phenomena which tremble as they consider the fate that awaits them in application and verification. Bernard's epistemology is different in essence from the positivist conception of science as a form of model building. 'Hypotheses' in Bernard's conception are the designs of experiments; they are 'instruments to break into phenomena'. In Bachelard's terms they are part of the phenomeno-technique.[29] 'Ideas' are neither proven nor disproven in experiments, rather they establish the conditions of experimentation and make experiments possible. They are more or less effective intellectual instruments of materialisation:

> We must change them when they have served their purpose, as we change a blunt lancet that we have used long enough (ibid., p. 41).

This conception has nothing to do with any relativist heurism. It does not install a doctrine of the equivalence of methods; methods which are more or less 'useful' to deal with certain problems, methods which function in so far as they yield results.[30] Methods are not equivalent, they are not pragmatically used or abandoned, their use is part and parcel of the experimental forging of better instruments. The principle of determinism excludes the possibility of any doctrine of relativism or fallibilism in respect of experimentation. Unsuccessful experiments are impossible because the practice of experiment is a material process of production which always constructs a real product:

> In fact, I have posited this principle: *there never are any unsuccessful experiments*; they are all successful in their own definite conditions, so negative cannot nullify positive results (ibid., p. 117).

There are no failed experiments because 'negative' results occur under definite and definable conditions which make possible further knowledge of the conditions of materialisation.

There can be no rational grounds for maintaining that an experimental result which contradicts another is a refutation of the previous experiment:

> Indeed, if a phenomenon appears just once in a certain aspect, we are justified in holding that, in the same conditions, it must appear in that way (ibid., p. 139).

Negative facts cannot exist since all phenomena have real conditions of existence; to argue otherwise is contrary to the principle of determinism. Contrary results are the products of experimentation under different conditions. Therefore experimental production is a continuous process within knowledge; it lends to the continuous

development of knowledge of the conditions of experimentation, to
more rigorous definitions of experimental problems and to the
refinement of experimental instruments. Experimentation produces
the reconstruction of its instruments. Experimental reasoning is no
idle metaphor; every stage of the experimental enterprise is interiorised within a rational materialism.

(iii) Bernard distinguishes between the means of production of
phenomena in experiment and their conditions of existence
(causes) in nature:

> In the knowledge that we acquire, we should distinguish
> between two sets of notions: the first corresponds to the
> *cause* of phenomena, the second to the *means* of producing
> them (ibid., p. 83).

He distinguishes between production and explanation. Experimental techniques are material causes which produce phenomena
in a mode whereby their conditions of existence (their cause) can
be explained. Experimental technique is not a technology. Experimentation is not governed by a pragmatism in which techniques
are created to produce given effects in which the separation of the
immediate cause and the causality in nature is of no importance
and for all practical purposes may be indistinguishable. It is not a
'result' but the explanation which matters. Hence experiments
must be designed in such a way that the effectivity of the instruments and the cause of the phenomena are separated.[31] Experimental techniques must be constructed so as to reveal causes. It
follows that experimental techniques as a material force obey the
laws of nature. It is therefore necessary that in order to know all
the conditions in experimentation the operation of experimental
instruments must be theorised. Scientific instruments must therefore be rationally constructed and become in themselves a product
of scientific knowledge. In Bachelard's terms the phenomeno-
technique of a science is different in essence from a phenomenology. Just as the relation of scientific theory to its object is not a
relation to given external phenomena so the relation of scientific
theory and its instruments is not an external relation but a relation
within knowledge.

(iv) Scientific theories are not proven *because* they produce
phenomena, or because they are able to replicate and reproduce
given appearances:

A fact is nothing in itself . . . when a fact proves anything, the
fact does not itself give the proof, but only the *rational*
relation which it establishes between the phenomenon and its
cause (ibid., p. 53).

Bernard means by a 'rational relation' a relation which conforms to
the principle of determinism. This relation is *rational* in that the
relation of cause and effect can only be known to be invariant
within the conditions of experimentation. Its rationality, its
invariance is not an observable given but a product of experimental construction. By the principle of determinism a materialised relation in experiment exists in conformity with the laws of
nature, but as natural laws are not givens they can only be discovered within scientific knowledge.

Experimental results do not validate experimental theories;
experimental theories validate experimental results. Experimental
results are questioned by 'reason' and by further experimentation.
Experimental proofs therefore consist in demonstrating the conformity of a result with the specified conditions of experimentation
and its invariance within those conditions.

Bernard's position is opposed to all conventionalist[32] conceptions of knowledge and proof. Science, for Bernard, does not consist in 'saving' the phenomena, of accounting for given appearances.
Conventionalism countenances the possibility of a multiplicity of
explanations and causalities for the given appearances. A conventionalist proof is the correspondence of an explanation with the
given, and equally plausible alternative accounts can be distinguished only by their elegance and economy of explanation.
Bernard, like Galileo, insists that there is only one valid explanation of a phenomenon. The relation of science and its phenomena is
not an external and descriptive relation but an internal and constitutive relation in which the phenomena are materialised under
controlled conditions by the sciences' operations. Phenomena are
knowable and invariant because they are produced by scientific
techniques under conditions specified by scientific reason (theory).
Experimental reasoning therefore requires the principle of determinism. The scientific process of production can only be conceived
by a materialist (determinist) epistemology; conventionalism
necessarily denies the real conditions of scientific knowledge.

(v) Science does not arise spontaneously from the 'facts', from its *discoveries*: 'If facts necessarily gave birth to ideas, every new fact ought to beget a new idea' (ibid., p. 33). The notion of *discovery* uncovers the essence of the spontaneist (empiricist) conception of knowledge. Knowledge is present in the real; the real has only to be *uncovered*, to be perceived, in order for the knower to know. Knowing is a passive operation and knowledge is the transparency of the given itself. All notions of spontaneous knowledge lead to that

> . . . . blind belief in fact which dares to silence reason [and] is as dangerous to the experimental sciences as the beliefs . . . of faith which also force silence on reason (ibid., p. 53).

Empiricism is an equivalent of faith because it admits of irrational facts, facts which have no cause but which merely exist. What is, is; reason is silenced because the very space of rationalism is denied. Knowledge is a given which the knower can only receive and accept.

In the *Introduction* Bernard strongly and repeatedly criticises four pseudo-scientific procedures which follow from conceptions of scientific knowledge alien to experimental reasoning:

(a) the construction of general 'systems' which relate all the 'given' phenomena of a certain domain to principles or essences which govern them, for example, the humoral theory of disease or vitalist biology;

(b) the pure empiricism of observing and noting all phenomena given to observation as facts of science, even if they contradict one another;

(c) statistical speculation, the establishing of relations between phenomena upon the basis of correlations or co-variance alone;[33]

(d) the reduction of problematic phenomena to forms which are explicable by means of the explanatory mechanisms of the already existing sciences.

Bernard argues that all of these procedures are unscientific in that they are unable to produce that rigorous determinism which establishes the causes of phenomena by producing them experimentally. They all lead to the contradiction of the principle that for each effect there is an invariant immediate cause and that if effects vary it is because their conditions of existence vary. All these methods entail either the existence of contrary effects of a single cause (as is the case in a, b, and d) or effects without an immediate and determinable cause (as is the case in b and c). All these procedures are not unscientific because they do not lead to performing of 'experiments' (some of them do so) but because they are unable to respect the principle which is necessary to experimental reasoning, determinism.

Bernard's definition of experimentation is a general definition, a philosophical definition; it holds good for all the sciences whatever their specific objects, methods or theories. The definition of experimentation and the principle of determinism are necessarily linked one to the other; without the specific practice of experimentation, determinism remains an empty position, for the conditions in which phenomena exist cannot be determined, and without the principle of determinism, experiment becomes a pragmatic technique rather than a means of the realisation of reason.

The Limits of Bernard's Epistemology

We have seen the character of the rupture with classical conceptions of epistemology produced by Bernard's definition of scientific determinism and experimentation. Bernard's position is unplaceable within the terms of the problematic of classical epistemology and his entry into the philosophical realm is marked by a profound indifference to established philosophical positions. But this philosophical enterprise, whose point of departure does not lie within classical philosophy, which does not have the character of a philosophical system, is not without, and is necessarily accompanied by, its theoretical errors, ambivalences and eclecticism. Bernard is in no way conscious of the revolution in epistemology which the *Introduction* represents and he lacks the conceptual means to recognise and carry through to completion that revolution. The *Introduction* is the complex and contradictory product of the conditions of its birth.

This spontaneous rational materialism which springs from scientific practice, and from the particular circumstances of physiology, has its limits. Bernard, whose position on scientific determinism and experimentation is both rigorous and revolutionary, is unable to produce an adequate conceptualisation of the nature of scientific theory, of how it is produced and of on what it is that theory works.[34]

Bernard's text is marked by the absence of a crucial concept, the rigorous distinction of the object of knowledge and the real object.[35] The text constantly returns to the site of this absence; it constantly seeks to recognise it and to abolish it. It is not the case that Bernard takes no account of the question which this distinction poses and resolves. The problem is glaringly present in the text but not its concept, its posing and its successful resolution. Consequently, without the aid of this concept Bernard seeks to resolve the problem by means of positions hostile in essence to its solution, for its solution abolishes them.[36] Bernard falls into the errors of treating the object of scientific theory as the real (even if it is not a given), and the nature of theory as *reason*, as an effect of the human mind. His errors are in turn empiricist and idealist, but they are not the errors of a simple eclecticism, the holding of essentially contradictory positions. Bernard uses empiricist and idealist positions, contradictory positions, to attempt to recognise and resolve a single problem. It is a problem that is not a problem internal to a rigorous empiricism or a rigorous idealism, but a problem that a rigorous idealism or a rigorous empiricism abolishes.

In conceiving the object of scientific theory as the real, Bernard is constantly led into fallibilist and falsificationalist positions:

> All the theories which serve as starting points for physicists, chemists, and . . . physiologists, are true only until facts are discovered which they do not include, or which contradict them (ibid., pp. 49–50).

It is all too easy on reading such statements to follow interpreters like Black (1949) and Kolakowski (1972) into arguing that Bernard's conception of the relation of theory and experiment is that of fallibilism pure and simple.[37] In this case theory vanishes from Bernard's position if it is considered as anything more than hypotheses. The role of scientific theory in constituting the object of a science (as distinct from real objects) is suppressed, and the object on which the science works becomes the real itself. As a consequence, experimental technique and experimental proof become a 'method' external to theory, and are themselves subject to no form of theoretical scrutiny or proof. Theory and experimentation are divorced and experimental technique becomes a given.

Bernard certainly adopts empiricist and fallibilist positions, particularly in some of his polemics against the vitalists and the system builders. His conception of experimentation is not that of falli- bilism or of a universal 'method'. First, Bernard's rigorous accept- ance of a fallibilist position would entail the abandonment of the conception of scientific work as a process of *construction* of nature and a continuous process of materialisation–realisation of reason. Second, Bernard defines the essence of experimentation in general, the elements of experimental practice common to all experimental sciences, but he does not produce a conception of a scientific 'method' which is universally and indifferently applicable to any object whatever. The definition of experimentation in general indicates that it does not exist *in general*, but only within the operations of a particular science. Experimental technique is not separable from the particular forms of reasoning of the sciences. If it were so, his distinction between production and explanation, his conception of the way in which experimentation is connected with the refinement and development of the knowledge of the con- ditions and means of materialisation within the science, would radically change its meaning and technique would become primary and reasoning secondary.

Moreover, while Bernard often appears to accept an empiricist conception of the refutation of particular experimental hypotheses, at no point does he even suggest that the basic concepts of any science, or of physiology, concepts like *milieu intérieur* or histo- logical unit, can be falsified or tested by experiments. These concepts are beyond question since it is they which define what it is on which science works:

> General physiology is thus shown to be the science of histological elements or of the ramifications of life (Bernard, 1878–9, pp. 99–100).

> Thus we have proved superabundantly that the physiologist can only modify the phenomena of life by modifying the organisation of life itself, that is, by attaining in the *milieu intérieur* the development of the functional properties of the histological elements (Bernard, 1867, p. 230).

General physiology in these *physiological* texts is not 'shown' or 'proved' to be what it is by testing or experimental proof. These 'superabundant proofs' are not proofs by experimentation, they are proofs of conceptual analysis and the theoretical critique of unscientific positions. Bernard never subjects these concepts to fallibilist conditions of proof because as *concepts* they define and make possible experimentation itself and they can only be proven or disproven conceptually. Bernard does not disprove vitalist theories in general by testing but by a conceptual critique that demonstrates that the object of vitalist theory is incapable of being the object of scientific theory.[38] In philosophy and in scientific practice Bernard's positions cannot be reduced to empiricism or fallibilism.

Bernard's idealist errors, for example, his falling into a 'cartesian' dualism, are not the result of a simple eclecticism but are an index of his attempt to separate the orders of the real and knowledge in the absence of the concept of that separation. Bernard poses the problem within the terms of the classical philosophical problematic of matter and mind. Bernard attempts to separate knowledge and the real in terms of the difference of the 'mind' of the subject and the cognition of real objects:

> As there are two kinds of functions in man's body, the first, conscious functions, the rest not, so in his mind there are two kinds of truths or notions, some conscious, inner or subjective, the others unconscious, outer or objective. Subjective truths are those flowing from principles of which the mind is conscious, and which bring it the sensation of absolute and necessary evidence (Bernard, 1865, pp. 28–9).

Bernard appears to adopt a dualist position. His separation of the relative intelligibility of the unconscious order of the objective and the absolute intelligibility of the subjective, the point of departure of certain idealist and neo-Kantian epistemologies which were developed in the nineteenth century,[39] is only an apparent one. Bernard argues that 'subjective truths . . . flowing from principles of which the mind is conscious' give it 'the *sensation* of absolute and necessary evidence'. This *sensation* is by no means certain knowledge but the appearance of a certainty which satisfies the subject. There is no certainty at all that this 'absolute and necessary evidence' is anything more than an illusion of the subject. Bernard makes this absolutely clear:

> The greatest truths, indeed, are at bottom simply a *feeling* in our mind; this is what Descartes meant by his famous aphorism (ibid., p. 29, our emphasis).

This is hardly what Descartes intended his aphorism to mean.[40] The 'greatest truths' in this passage are not scientific 'truths' as such but the truths of wisdom in general, of logic and of mathematics.

It should be noted that Bernard never argues that there is a philosophical guarantee of knowledge, nor that there is an objective correlate to which we may directly refer to test the validity of concepts. All theories of knowledge which reject empiricist guarantees or proofs, and which rely for their guarantees on the *a priori* or on a meta-knowledge entail either an infinite regress or subjectivism. Bernard does not attempt to create such an *a priori* guarantee; he treats the classic philosophical problem of knowledge as a non-problem. For Bernard scientific proofs are sufficient and necessary proofs. Bernard in dealing with the status of mathematical propositions argues as follows:

> We see now that all logical deductions in a piece of
> mathematical reasoning are just as certain as their principle,
> and that they do not require verification by experiment. That
> would be trying to place the senses above reason; and it would
> be absurd to seek to prove what is absolutely true for the mind
> and what it could not conceive otherwise (ibid., p. 29).

Bernard insists that mathematical propositions follow logically from their axioms and that experimental verification is unnecessary and absurd in respect of them. The truth of the axioms is absolute and universal; it cannot be effected by particular concrete conditions and to deny these axioms leads to absurdity; an absurdity we must presume which is either that of logical contradiction or of imagining things which *cannot* exist.[41]

What Bernard does not recognise and cannot recognise in the terms in which he has posed the problem is that the 'senses' and the 'reason' to which he refers do not have an equivalent location. 'Reason' as definite forms of scientific knowledge, in this case of mathematics, is not an attribute of the human subject, it is not equivalent to the 'mind'. The 'senses' can only be placed above 'reason' within the philosophical problematic which counterposes mind and matter in respect of the human subject. Bernard is absolutely correct to argue that mathematics' criteria of proof are internal to its theory. However, he appears to argue that mathematics is an *a priori* knowledge and that its certainty is an essential certainty entailed in the very nature of reason. But he does not argue this consistently:

> Mathematics embodies the relations of things in conditions of ideal simplicity. It follows that these principles or relations, once found, are accepted by the mind as absolute truths, i.e., truths independent of reality. . . .
>
> Still man must believe that the objective relations between phenomena of the outer world might attain the certainty of subjective truths if they were reduced to a state of simplicity that his mind could completely grasp (ibid., p. 29).

Mathematics, and potentially all scientific knowledge, are abstractions of the real which mirror its order in an ideal and absolute simplicity.[42] The essence of the real is an absolute stripped of all particular conditions and equivalent to the absolute truths of subjective knowledge in the conviction of certainty it generates in the subject. This position of mathematics as an ideal abstraction of the real would constitute a formalist empiricism. Founding the validity of this abstraction on its acceptance by the subject as a certainty would link this formalism of mathematical method with a guarantee which rests on a subjectivisim of internal sensations. But Bernard undercuts this combination of formalism and subjectivism:

> There seems to me only one form of reasoning: deduction by syllogism. The mind, even if it wished, could not reason otherwise, and . . . I might try to support my proposition by physiological arguments (ibid., pp. 49–50).

The ideal order of nature and the logical order of thought ultimately correspond because the form of human logical thinking is determined physiologically by the workings of the brain. Thought is incorporated into nature and is explained by natural science. The order of logical thought is determined by necessary physiological laws.

This argument which must lead either to a monist materialism[43] or to a conception of a creative intelligence in nature[44] is not developed any further by Bernard in the *Introduction*. Bernard's public position was based upon a developed critique of, and a rejection of, monist materialism and the idealisation of nature as doctrines inimical to science, which subordinate science to a proof of philosophical 'principles'. The function of the varying and often contradictory arguments about the nature of mathematics, of logic and of reason, is to reject an empiricist conception of knowledge, and the turns toward formalism and monist materialism indicate his attempt to demarcate his position from apriorism and idealism.

2

Bernard's Physiology

In this chapter we shall leave the purely philosophical terrain and enter the realm of physiology. However, our discussion of physiology will not be an exegetical or an historical one, it will deal with those elements of Bernard's physiology which are of relevance to his philosophical position and which are relevant to our analysis of Durkheim. It will not be our object to give a description of Bernard's scientific investigations, nor will it be our object to place him in the complex history of the biological sciences in the nineteenth century. These questions are beyond the scope of this work and we refer the reader to the specialist literature in the history of science.[1] The relevance of Bernard's physiological problematic to our discussion lies in the break it produces with the terms of the vitalism/reductionism couple. This structure of the idealist reference to essences, on the one hand, and the reductionist application of the normatised procedures of other sciences, on the other, was the predominant epistemological obstacle to the development of a scientific physiology. But it is not confined to physiology or to the biological sciences; it exerts a powerful influence in the social sciences – we shall encounter its effects in our analysis of *The Rules of Sociological Method*. A consideration of Bernard's break with and criticism of this structure will serve as a point of reference when we come to discuss Durkheim.

The Problematic of Bernardian Physiology

The Object of Physiology

> General physiology is thus shown to be the science of
> histological elements or of the ramifications of life; that is to
> say, it constitutes an experimental science which studies the
> properties of organised matter and explains the processes and
> mechanisms of vital phenomena (Bernard, 1867, p. 136).

The object of the new science of physiology is defined by
Bernard as the forms and conditions of existence of 'life'. The
notion of 'life' or 'vital properties' is most closely associated with
the unscientific or pseudo-scientific theories of vitalism in the
history of the biological sciences. The vitalist doctrines of the late
eighteenth and early nineteenth century[2] were under heavy attack
in the period when Bernard worked. A consistent reductionist
programme was formulated by Ludwig, Helmholtz, Brücke and du
Bois-Reymond, its object: 'We four imagined that we should constitute physiology on a chemico-physical foundation'.[3] Ultimately,
physiology would 'merge completely with the sciences and dissolve
into organic physics and chemistry'.[4] What then is the difference
between the 'life' which figured as a universal explanatory concept
in vitalist discourse and the 'life' the conditions of existence of
which were the object of Bernard's physiology? Bernard's difference from the vitalists did not consist in his denying the existence
of vital properties, nor in his adopting an agnostic, experimentally
provisional attitude towards them,[5] but in the mode in which he
conceptualised these properties in his scientific discourse.

We have already discussed certain of Bernard's criticisms of
vitalist doctrines;[6] here we will concentrate on their different conceptions of 'life'. In vitalist physiology and biology 'life' is at one
and the same time the object to be explained and the explanatory
mechanism:

> When an obscure or inexplicable phenomenon presents itself
> . . . physicians are in the habit of saying, 'This is life';
> apparently without the least idea that they are explaining
> darkness by still greater darkness. We must therefore get used
> to the idea that science implies merely determining the

conditions of phenomena; we must always *exclude life entirely from our explanations* of physiological phenomena as a whole (Bernard, 1865, p. 201, our emphasis).

Life is a *phenomenon* which must be problematised; it cannot be understood in its givenness because what it is cannot be determined until its conditions of existence are known. In vitalist discourse 'life', with its spontaneous and essential creative powers, is the primary explanatory concept, and its status is unproblematic. In the very nature of its questions the vitalist problematic already supposed its answers; its explanations were a mere mechanism for the repetition, the demonstration, of what it already 'knew':

Belief that the phenomena of living beings are dominated by an indeterminate vital force often gives experimentation a false basis and puts a vague word in the place of exact experimental analysis. *I have seen physicians submit questions to experimental analysis in which they took as their starting point the vitality of certain organs* (ibid., p. 202, our emphasis).

It was the *questions* the vitalists asked which condemned their explanations to the speculative and ideological mode. In the very definition of its object vitalism revealed the closure and ideological repetition which characterised its discourse; just as Bernard's scientificity did not rest upon his open-mindedness or upon his experimental 'tact', so the unscientific character of vitalism was not a function of its apriorism and its failure to conduct experiments.

The objects of theoretical problematics are objects conceived in theory and not objects given in the real:

It follows that the same body may be studied mineralogically, physically, chemically, etc.; but in nature there is really neither chemistry nor physics . . . there are only bodies to be classified or phenomena to be known and mastered (ibid., p. 144).

Nature cannot be studied naturally; Bernard's difference with the vitalists cannot be resolved on the plane empiricism–apriorism, but only 'mineralogically . . . chemically', etc. Just as the difference between physics and chemistry is a difference within knowledge and not a division of nature into separate realms, so the difference between science and ideology, between the scientific and the vitalist conceptions of 'life', is a difference in the form of theory, a difference in knowledge.

'Life', for Bernard, is neither a given fact nor is it an essential property which animates matter. Bernard, although he is opposed to vitalism, does not fall into the trap of dismissing life as a mere metaphysical illusion; life is a material and experimentally materialisable phenomenon, *an effect*, the nature and properties of which are known in so far as its conditions of existence are known. Life is the product of an organisation of matter under certain conditions. The laws of 'life', physiological laws, do not contradict the laws of the other natural sciences, they merely represent the action of those laws under specific conditions; those conditions are the object of a distinct science, physiology:

> Therefore . . . we must not set up an antagonism between vital phenomena and physico-chemical phenomena, but, on the contrary, we must note the complete and necessary parallelism between the two classes of phenomena. To sum up, living matter is no more able than inorganic matter to get into activity or movement by itself. Every change in matter implies intervention of a new relation, i.e. an outside condition or influence (ibid., pp. 78–9).

Bernard utterly rejects the vitalist's conception of life as a force in and of itself, a force of an essentially different nature from the 'matter' of the physico-chemical sciences. He rejects this essentialism which divides nature itself into qualitatively different domains of being.

Bernard's conception of life is not external to the nature of physiology as an experimental science; it is not a rival and equally speculative Naturphilosophie to that of vitalism. Life is defined by Bernard as an effectivity distinct from physico-chemical phenomena (although based upon them), but its specific characteristics can only be determined in the experimental practice of physiology. Life is nothing more than an effect which is produced in nature and experiment under certain conditions – its characteristics can therefore be known only through experimentation. It is, contrary to all the tenets of vitalism, not a cause, and it cannot therefore be known independently of a knowledge of *its* causes.[7] If we were to ask of Bernard what his conception of life means, what life 'is', he would be unable to answer directly, to define life as this or that substance.

'Life' is an open concept which provides for a concrete scientific content. Open as it is, it is not empty, it has a real function: to establish a space of investigation, a space whose bounds are not closed by the concept, and which is not subsumed by the other sciences. Vitalism fills this space with its own suppositions, and the reductionist programme cannot see this space, for it recognises only its opposed and mirror twin in the sciences of life. 'Life', as defined by Bernard, designates the object of physiology in a mode which makes its scientific penetration possible.

Life, as the product of certain conditions of existence, exists whenever and at whatever level those conditions are assured. Life is not a property essential to certain whole organisms, e.g. bears or molluscs, but a product of physiological conditions:

> It is doubtless correct to say that the constituent parts of an organism are physiologically inseparable one from another, and that they all contribute to a common vital result; but we may not conclude from this that the living machine must not be analysed as a crude machine whose parts also have their role to play in the whole (ibid., p. 89);

and:

> Life is fundamentally no more than a mechanism; it is maintained only by the balance of functional activity of all histological elements (Bernard, cited by Mendelsohn, 1963, pp. 425–6).

Vital properties can be produced and maintained in tissue elements separated from any organism under experimentally produced conditions of existence:

> Thanks to their organic self-regulation, we can also detach living tissues, and by means of artificial circulation or otherwise, we can place them in conditions where we can better study their characteristics (Bernard, 1865, p. 89).

The conception of life as a function of the whole organism, its parts being interdependent in their contribution to the result of the whole, has the effect of rendering whole organisms unanalysable and of preventing the experimental decomposition and variation of organic parts:

It is doubtless because he felt this necessary interdependence among all the parts of an organism, that Cuvier said that experimentation was not applicable to living beings, since it separated organised parts which should remain united. For the same reason . . . vitalists, have proscribed and still proscribe experimentation in medicine (ibid.).

General physiology breaks with these organicist notions because it has as its object the 'ramifications of life' – it studies first and foremost the smallest units in which matter is organised (histological units):

> The end which general physiology proposes to attain determines necessarily the direction which it is to follow in its procedure. . . . All physiological sciences have a procedure which is essentially analytical. . . . It is only progressively indeed, that the physiologist, in decomposing experimentally the complex phenomena of life, can succeed in reducing them to their active elements from which he afterward derives all the vital secondary actions and the explanation of all the particular physiological mechanisms (Bernard, 1867, p. 226).

Organic wholes must be decomposed if the phenomena of the histological level are to be analysed – it is at that level that the fundamental unity of physiological processes is to be understood. Unless these wholes are penetrated there remain as many fundamentally different species of being as there are wholes to be perceived and differentiated ('tree life', 'bear life', etc.). In the *Leçons sur les phénomènes de la vie communs aux animaux et aux végétaux*, his last important work, Bernard was able to demonstrate the unity of animate nature, not by reference to a life-force but to common experimentally determined properties.

The maintenance of the conditions of existence of life, of the functional properties of the histological units, depends upon regulation and nutrition – upon the production of a controlled environment for the tissue elements within the organism (the *milieu intérieur*). The reproduction and variation of the conditions of this *milieu intérieur* provide the experimental basis on which the conditions of existence of life are determined:

> The aim of experimental general physiology . . . is to conquer living nature and to work out the phenomena of life

scientifically. Thus we have proved superabundantly that the physiologist *can only modify the phenomena of life by modifying the organisation of life itself, that is, by attaining in the milieu intérieur the developmental or functional properties of the histological elements* (ibid., p. 230, our emphasis).

These functional properties cannot be determined by the analysis of organised matter into its elementary units; analytic knowledge is necessarily complemented by the synthesis which reproduces and varies the conditions under which these properties appear. Thus while chemistry and physics provide certain methods for physiology, it also has its own methods, in particular, the variation of the conditions of the *milieu intérieur*. This methodology relies on the reconstruction of organic totalities (viable environments for these histological elements in question and their relevant functions).

Thus while Bernard's physiology has no connection with any form of organicism or essentialist holism, it is not dogmatically opposed to all totalities in principle. Its totalities are constructed and known experimentally by determining the elements of which they are made up, the relations which unite them and the conditions of those relations.

The Milieu Intérieur

I think I was the first to urge the belief that animals really have two environments: a *milieu extérieur* in which the organism is situated, and a *milieu intérieur* in which the tissue elements live. The living organism does not really exist in the *milieu extérieur* (the atmosphere if it breathes, salt or fresh water if that is its element) but in the liquid *milieu intérieur* formed by the circulating organic liquid which surrounds and bathes all the tissue elements; this is the lymph or plasma, the liquid part of the blood which, in the higher animals, is diffused through the tissues and forms the ensemble of the intercellular liquids and is the basis of all local nutrition and the common factor of all elementary exchanges. *A complex organism should be looked upon as an assemblage of simple organisms that live in the liquid of the milieu intérieur.*

The stability of the *milieu intérieur* is the primary condition

for freedom and independence of existence; the mechanism
which allows of this is that which ensures in the *milieu
intérieur* the maintenance of all the conditions necessary to
the life of the elements. From this we know that there can be
no freedom or independence of existence for simple organisms
whose constituent parts are in direct contact with their cosmic
environment and that this form of life is in fact, the exclusive
possession of organisms which have attained the highest state
of complexity and organic differentiation . . .
The necessary conditions for the life of the elements which
must be brought together and kept up constantly in the
milieu intérieur if freedom and independence of existence are
to be maintained are already known to us: water, oxygen, heat
and reserve chemical substances.
These are the same conditions as are necessary for life in
simple organisms; but in the perfected animal whose existence
is independent, the nervous system is called upon to regulate
the harmony which exists between all these conditions
(Bernard, 1878–9, our emphasis).[8]

Milieu intérieur is the fundamental concept of Bernard's
physiology. This concept provided the basis upon which analysis
at the cellular level and the study of more complex organic functions could be united[9] – it made physiology a unified science rather
than a congeries of distinct and ill-related levels of research. The
concept of *milieu intérieur* underwent a long and complex development from its first formulation in 1857 to its fullest development in
the *Leçons sur les phénomènes de la vie* of 1878–9. This development
has been charted by Holmes (1963a) and we will refer here only
to the final formulation of the concept.

A complex organism consists of simple organisms; these simple
organisms have vital properties, and the 'life' of the complex whole,
the maintenance of the functional properties which sustain it,
depends on the survival of a sufficient proportion of the simple
organisms. These simple organisms live in the liquid internal
environment which sustains them.

The *milieu intérieur* defines the totality of conditions which must
be established within the organism if the tissue elements are to
have a stable environment; in summary form it consists of the
following aspects:

(i) The organic solids exist in the liquids of the blood which provide nutrition, temperature control and form the basis for exchanges and relations between tissue elements;
(ii) the blood is formed by internal secretions – the formation of the liquids of the *milieu intérieur* is controlled and regulated within the organism;
(iii) the regulatory mechanisms, which maintain the stability of internal conditions despite changes in the external environment and disturbing factors within, for example, the production of sugar by the liver[10] and the control of animal heat by the nervous system.[11]

The *milieu intérieur* provides the basis on which the histological units (cells-tissue elements) attain their functional properties. Like Virchow, from whom he accepted the cell theory, Bernard believed that cells were the primary active constituents of organisms,[12] the liquids and processes of the *milieu intérieur* forming the support and regulator of the cells' functional activity:

> Thus the cell theory as developed by Bernard became a complex system in which the cells, the fundamental physiological units, were in constant interaction with the fluid medium. . . . Bernard recognised that the constant environment produced had a single major function: 'the maintenance of all the conditions necessary to the life of the cellular elements (Mendelsohn, 1963, p. 429).

The more completely a constant internal environment is established in an organism, the less it is directly subject to the effects of changes in the surrounding milieu. Complexity is measured, in physiological terms, by the degree to which this independent milieu is attained and the degree to which its existence therefore depends upon regulatory mechanisms (e.g. the intervention of the nervous system). The more complex organism is therefore able to respond better to changes in its environment, but this does not mean that it is independent of its external environment:

> The phenomena of life, as well as those of inorganic bodies, are thus doubly conditioned. On the one hand, we have the organism in which vital phenomena come to pass; on the other, the cosmic environment in which living bodies, like

inorganic bodies, find the conditions essential to the
appearance of their phenomena. The conditions of life are
found neither in the organism nor in the outer environment,
but in both at once (Bernard, 1865, pp. 74–5).

Life is an independent phenomenon enclosed within the *milieu
intérieur* (in its developed forms), but it also depends for its
existence upon factors external to that milieu and which, beyond
certain limits, that milieu cannot control or compensate for.

Bernard's concept of the *milieu intérieur* is not reducible to a
variation of the notion of 'system' applied to physiology. 'Systems',
as purely formal constructs, can receive any given content (social,
biological, informational, etc.) and this content does not change the
form of the system or its properties. The systems approach is also
fully compatible with different forms of explanation of varying
degrees of validity.[13] The concepts 'system', 'function', and
'equilibrium', for example, are compatible with vitalist theories
and are present in vitalist explanations.[14] Calling the *milieu
intérieur* a 'system', therefore, tells us virtually nothing about its
characteristics or its validity as a scientific concept.

Bernard's use of the terms function and regulation in respect of
the *milieu intérieur* does not mean that he is constrained to adopt a
teleological mode of explanation. In Bernard's theory no function
can exist without conditions of existence and except as a definite
necessary effect or relation between phenomena. The destruction
of those conditions, the cessation of function and its effects are the
foundations of Bernard's theory of pathology. In physiology
functions, regulatory mechanisms, etc. cannot be defined independently of their experimental demonstration and proof. For
Bernard nothing is necessary but that which can be proven to
exist and its existence is always conditional on the presence of
certain conditions.

Histological Units

For physiologists, the truly active elements are what we call
anatomical or histological units (ibid., p. 73).

These units are the 'elements' of physiological analysis: the
most basic form of organised matter. As we have already seen,
complex organisms are combinations of these elements:

We can perfectly well picture to ourselves a complex organism
made up of a quantity of distinct elementary organisms,
uniting, joining and grouping together in various ways, to give
birth first to the different tissues of the body, then to its
various organs (ibid.).

Of course, the conditions of their combination are not given to the
elements; they are a specific function of the *milieu intérieur*.
Unlike Durkheim, Bernard does not conceive of association in itself
having any causal efficacy.[15]

The character of these 'elements' is determined by physiological
analysis – the elementary forms at which the analysis of organic
tissues terminates are what the histological elements are. Thus,
although after Bernard had assimilated the cell theory of Virchow
the meaning of the concept became the cell, and Bernard himself
considered the cell membrane to be the impassable frontier of
physiology, the concept is an open one and specifies nothing more
than the terminals of a physiological analysis which are capable of
supporting vital properties.[16] The notion of 'element' in physiology
has nothing to do with evolutionism or a reference to the origin.
The terminals are neither more primitive than the higher levels of
the analysis, nor are they prior to them in time.[17] The elements
exist coterminously with the other levels in a synchrony – their
elementariness is solely a function of their position in the analysis,
and their independent existence is an experimentally produced
condition internal to physiology.

Histological units with their different forms and characteristics
form what might be termed the 'elementary table' of physiology,
the invariant basis on which is constructed all the different complex forms of biological organisation. However, it should
not be thought that these histological elements are reducible
in their properties to chemical elements; it is a mistake to
consider them as a mere variant of the elements of the periodic
table:

Though we can succeed in separating living tissues into
chemical elements . . . still these elementary chemical bodies
are not elements for physiologists . . . tissues and organs
endowed with the most diverse properties are at times
indistinguishable from the point of view of their elementary
chemical composition (ibid.).

The elementary properties concerned in the case of histological units are *physiological* properties. Beyond the histological level Bernardian physiology ceases to operate, for it is here that the transition from organic to inorganic forms takes place.

Any physiology which does not depart from a specification of the units of composition of organic nature cannot reconstruct the conditions of life experimentally. Lacking this point of departure it is condemned to reason from the effects of already complex life processes:

> Real science exists, then, only from the moment when a
> phenomenon is accurately defined as to its nature and
> rigorously determined in relation to its material conditions,
> that is, when its law is known. Before that, we have only
> groping and empiricism (ibid., p. 74.)

Ideologies and the Sciences of Life

The consequences of the penetration of scientific theory and practice by ideologies are twofold:

(i) The deformation of scientific concepts and their transformation into the conceptual forms of ideology;

(ii) the displacement of the object of the science by the object of an ideological theory, and the transformation of the science's questions into the questions appropriate to that ideological object.

The main ideologies and ideological traps in the domain of physiology in Bernard's time were vitalism, materialistic reductionism, and anatomism. To illustrate the effects of these anti-scientific ideologies on scientific practice, to show what was at stake in Bernard's philosophical defence of the conditions of knowledge in physiology, we will give the following examples.

(i) *Vitalism*

The character and effects of vitalist doctrines have already been discussed in some detail; in this section some indication of the effects of vitalist ideology in respect of a specific physiological problem will be given.

Bernard had always given steady support to Pasteur in his

struggle to establish the germ theory of disease and the existence of
microbes. Pasteur was therefore shocked when, after the death of
Bernard in 1878, his notes on fermentation were published.[18] In
these notes on the theory of fermentation, which outlined a course
of experiments to determine that fermentation is the product of a
soluble chemical ferment, Bernard explicitly denied Pasteur's contention that there could be no fermentation without living yeast
cells, that fermentation could take place without air and that it
resulted from the decomposition of sugar molecules by yeast cells
in an attempt to obtain oxygen to support their life in the absence of
air. Pasteur was convinced that fermentation was a phenomenon of
life; that living organisms were essential to such processes as
fermentation. He sought to disprove Bernard's position by demonstrating that no alcohol was produced if grapes did not first come
into contact with air-borne yeast cells.

Pasteur had, however, entirely misconceived Bernard's position.
Bernard, in the posthumously published notes, had insisted that
Pasteur was right but that he had seen only one side of the question.
Bernard insisted that such phenomena as those Pasteur was concerned with must be explained in terms of the specific physico-
chemical processes from which they are built up. In the *Introduction*
(1865), Bernard maintained that 'life' could only have a scientific
meaning as a determinate effect of certain conditions:

> We must really learn, however, that vital phenomenon means
> only a phenomenon peculiar to living beings, whose cause we
> do not yet know; for I think that every phenomenon called
> vital today, must sooner or later be reduced to definite
> properties of organised . . . matter (ibid., p. 185).

Pasteur was mistaken in his belief that Bernard's position in his
posthumously published notes was in contradiction with the
positions he held during the major part of his life. In the *Introduction*, published thirteen years before the notes on fermentation,
Bernard stated:

> I emphasise this point, because I have seen chemists at times
> appeal to life to explain certain physico-chemical phenomena
> peculiar to living beings. Thus the ferment in yeast is an
> organic, living material which has the property of converting
> sugar into alcohol, carbonic acid and several other products. I

have sometimes heard it said that the property of decomposing
sugar was due to the life inherent in a globule of yeast. This
vitalistic explanation means nothing and explains nothing
about the action of yeast. We do not know the nature of this
property, but it must necessarily belong to the physico-
chemical order, and be as precisely defined as, for instance,
the property of platinum sponge which produces a more or
less analogous action that cannot be attributed to vital force
(ibid., p. 201).

In his lectures at the College de France in 1869 to 1870 he had
maintained the same position.[19] It is interesting to note that
Pasteur was a chemist and that Bernard's 1865 remarks attack
exactly the position that Pasteur was defending in 1878.

A conception of life like that held by Pasteur constituted an
epistemological obstacle to physiology. It prevented the determination of the conditions and processes of organised matter. These
conditions and processes obeyed physical and chemical laws and
could be analysed in terms of their constituent chemical reactions.
It was the task of physiological synthesis to reconstruct, experimentally, the effect of those reactions, and not to assert that effect
as a phenomenon in itself which contradicts the laws of chemistry:

> Certainly a special force in living beings, not met with
> elsewhere, presides over their organisation; but the existence
> of this force cannot in any way change our idea of the
> properties of organic matter. . . . In a word, physiologists . . .
> must seek to reduce vital properties to physico-chemical
> properties, and not physico-chemical properties to vital
> properties (ibid., p. 202).

This special force became an essentialist dogma unless its conditions were analysed.

(ii) *Reductionism*

> *Each science has its problem and its point of view which we
> must not confuse without the risk of leading scientific investigation
> astray.* Yet this confusion has often occurred in biological
> science which, because of its complexity, needs the help of the
> other sciences. We have seen, and we still often see chemists

and physicists who, instead of confining themselves to the demand that living bodies furnish them suitable means and arguments to establish certain principles of their own sciences, try to absorb physiology and reduce it to simple physico-chemical phenomena. . . . *In a word, biology has its own problem and its definite point of view; it borrows from the other sciences only their help and their methods, not their theories* (ibid., p. 95, our emphasis).

Here Bernard displays a clear theoretical conception of the episte-mological effect of reductionism – the abolition of the specific object of the science and its reduction to operations within another science. He demonstrates in this passage a clear conception that the object of a science is an object within knowledge and not an object given in the world. Bernard is defending this theoretical object and not the right of physiology to poke about in its patch of the real. He insists that the relation between the sciences is determined by the specific demands that are internal to each science and its object. Unlike Comte, he does not seek to order the sciences in a hierarchy which is external to them. He does not seek to determine the relation between physics and physiology on the basis that physics is a science of a higher order of generality; this order being deter-mined by philosophical criteria which are external to physics and physiology. Physiology does not adopt the *theories* of physics, either as normative models of a true generalising science or as specific explanatory mechanisms of physiological phenomena. To do so would be to pass beyond the specific theoretical level of physi-ology's own object. Physiology uses the other sciences' procedures as instruments, whose place and function as instruments is given by its own theory:

Each of the sciences possesses, if not an individual method, at least particular processes; and sciences serve as instruments for one another. Mathematics serves as an instrument for physics, chemistry and biology in different degrees; physics and chemistry serve as powerful instruments for physiology (ibid., p. 94).

The relation between physics and physiology is an internal one, within physiological practice and determined by the specific needs of physiology; it is not an external one, either of physics' reflection on physiology as a science of a subordinate order of generality, as one branch of its own knowledges, or of a philosophy's reflection on the order of all the sciences, as subordinate to its own meta-knowledge. Thus the reductionists and the philosophical meta-scientists, like Comte, are rejected in Bernard's insistence on the specificity of the object and theory of his science.[20]

In his response to reductionism Bernard has often been misconceived as a vitalist, just as his response to vitalism has been misconceived as reductionist. The basis of the charge of vitalism is his assertion of the object of physiology being a distinct object. Bernard's case that the biological has its own laws of organisation is theoretically sound, despite the relatively undeveloped state of the biological sciences at that time. The following passage indicates Bernard's conception of these laws:

> I should say: life is creation. . . . When a chicken develops in an egg, the formation of the animal body as a grouping of chemical elements is not what essentially distinguishes the vital force. This grouping takes place only according to laws which govern the physico-chemical properties of matter; but the guiding idea of the vital evolution is essentially in the domain of life and belongs neither to chemistry nor to physics nor to anything else. In every living germ is a creative idea which develops and exhibits itself through organisation. As long as a living being persists, it remains under the influence of this same creative vital force, and death comes when it can no longer express itself; here as everywhere, everything is derived from the idea which alone creates and guides; physico-chemical means of expression are common to all natural phenomena and remain mingled, pell-mell, like the letters of the alphabet in a box, till a force goes to fetch them, to express the most varied thoughts and mechanisms (ibid., p. 93-4).

This passage is wide open to a vitalist reading; indeed, the vitalist 'echoes' in this passage and others like it did not escape the ear of Bergson, who used Bernard as support for his notion of 'evolution créatrice'.[21] But this passage can be read in another way, a way which departs from the biological problem Bernard is trying to think in this passage. It can be read as an attempt to think the role of the laws of organic organisation without the guidance and insights of the theory of genetics. Indeed, certain aspects of this passage ('In every living germ is a creative idea which develops and exhibits itself through organisation', etc.) state the *place* and function of genetics in biological theory with the utmost clarity. They point to questions present in a problematic of the biological sciences which had not yet been formulated, for which the concepts that think them, which ask them, are not yet present as concepts.

They indicate the site at which these questions must be asked, but they do not provide the means to pose or answer them correctly.[22] Bernard's physiology, regional theory of the biological sciences, did not and could not provide the theoretical or experimental means to solve the problems of heredity and the development of complex organisms. In this area Bernard was speculating beyond the domain of his science.

(iii) *Anatomism*

Anatomists, we said above, try to invert the true method of explanation, i.e., they take anatomy as an exclusive starting point and propose to deduce directly from it all the functions solely by logic and without experiments. I have already protested against the pretentiousness of anatomical deductions, by showing that they rest on an illusion of which anatomists are unaware (ibid., p. 107).

Comparative anatomy has as its epistemological foundation taxonomies of organic and skeletal arrangements; its object is classificatory. But any attempt to make anatomy an explanatory science is doomed to failure. Anatomical deductions attempt to determine the functions of organs, etc. by reference to their structure. In essence such an anatomy maintains that functions can be recognised through forms. The functions and the forms are givens which are applied in this system of deductions; the basis of resemblance is not specified by concepts which are internal to anatomy. The basis of this system of resemblances is not a conceptual system which establishes a theoretical mechanism by which the equivalence of forms and functions can be thought. Its basis is analogy. Thus it starts from the fact that a certain (non-biological) structure has a certain function; this fact is determined by another science or form of thought, and anatomy asserts that another, a biological structure, which resembles it, has an analogous function. Anatomical deductionism asserts, in the last instance, a homology of form and function.

When this system of deductions is confined, for example, to precise mechanical structures and functions, the basis of equivalence is that of common mechanical properties. Thus joints are comparable to levers in structure and function because they have identical mechanical properties to levers.

But, once it departs from relations between structure and function which are determined by forms of reason external to it, anatomical deductionism becomes an ideology. It ceases to operate analogically and begins to assert a distinct theoretical position. It then entails a notion of a causality in resemblance. It asserts that a likeness of form implies a likeness of function.[23] There is no necessary relation between a given structure and a given function: any attempt to posit such a relation entails that causality be attributed to resemblance.

If the anatomical deductionist viewpoint and its 'object' are given primacy in the sciences of life, then these sciences are condemned to depend for their progress upon the external sources of the system of analogies, or, far worse, to be subordinated to an absurd 'science' based upon the causality of resemblance. But this order of relation between anatomy and physiology is absurd and impossible. The major source of these analogies in anatomy is physiology itself. Physiology determines the functions of the organs: .

> But, I repeat, dead anatomy teaches nothing; it merely leans on what experimental physiology teaches; and a clear proof of this is that, where experimental physiology has learned nothing as yet, anatomists can interpret nothing by anatomy alone. Thus the anatomy of the spleen . . . is as well known as the anatomy of a muscle or a nerve, and nevertheless anatomists are silent as to the uses of these parts (ibid., p. 108).

In the face of forms whose functions are not manifest, that is, which exhaust the repertoire of given analogies, anatomy is silent and waits for physiology to provide the knowledge which feeds its speculations: 'How indeed could the form of the nerve cell show us the nervous properties which it transmits' (ibid., p. 109). Thus anatomy is parasitic on physiology and adds nothing to physiological knowledge. All claims to the primacy of anatomical knowledge in physiological questions constitute epistemological obstacles to the science of physiology: 'In a word, anatomical deduction has yielded what it can' (ibid., p. 111).

(iv) Normality and Pathology – Physiology and Medicine

So that death came through death of the molecules of blood, or in other words by stopping their exercise of a physiological property essential to life (ibid., p. 161).

Bernard is here discussing the effects of carbon monoxide poisoning: the inhalation of this gas causes the displacement of the oxygen present in the blood cells and as a result destroys one of the conditions of their vital existence. This cessation of function of these histological units sets in train a series of reactions which destroy the conditions of vital phenomena in the whole organism. Pathology is the destruction of functional properties on the part of certain histological units by a change in their conditions of existence: '. . . death, in fact, can be understood only because some histological unit has lost its physiological properties' (ibid., p. 114). Disease is the malfunctioning of particular elements of a complex organism which has more or less widespread effects.

As a consequence all pathological investigation which is not founded on physiology has a fundamentally erroneous point of departure. Clinical rationalism, the observation of 'symptoms' and the deduction of the causes of diseases from their characteristics, is in essence speculative because it cannot produce the conditions governing these effects. The criteria by which phenomena are recognised as symptomatic are arbitrary in that these 'traces' have no scientifically determined and necessary relation to the causes of disease. In the absence of manifest symptoms diseases become essential entities without conditions:

But diagnosis became impossible in the case of diseases where changes were imperceptible with our present means of investigation. No longer able to find an anatomical relation, men then said that the disease was essential, i.e., without any lesion; which is absurd, for it amounts to acknowledging an effect without a cause (ibid., p. 113).

Clinical rationalism leads to the conception of disease as an entity (identified by a complex of symptoms) which enters the body and attacks it; lesions are the traces of the disease's presence. Disease becomes an object in itself as a result of this notion and pathology the science of this distinct class of phenomena.[24]

But disease, Bernard insists, obeys the same physiological laws as normality. It represents a specific change in the conditions of existence of organisms which is subject to the same means of investigation as vital phenomena under normal conditions:

> Diseases at bottom are only physiological phenomena in new conditions still to be determined; toxic and medicinal action . . . come back to simple physiological changes in properties of the histological units of our tissues (ibid., p. 198).

Pathology is not, therefore, the object of a science distinct from physiology:

> But for a man of science there is no separate science of medicine or physiology, there is only a science of life. There are only phenomena of life to be explained in the pathological as well as in the physiological state (ibid., p. 146).

Death is not a state different in essence from life, it is merely an effect different in character as the conditions which produce it are different in character from those which produce life:

> Physiological and pathological states are ruled by the same force; they differ only because of the special conditions under which the vital laws manifest themselves (ibid., p. 10).

Part Two

Émile Durkheim's Rules of Sociological Method

Durkheim's Epistemology

Scholars are so accustomed to apply the forms of philosophical thought to sociological matters that they are prone to see in this preliminary definition a kind of philosophy of social phenomena. They claimed that we were explaining social phenomena by constraint, just as Tarde explains them by imitation. . . . We proposed not to anticipate the conclusions of sociological science by a philosophical view but simply to indicate by what external signs it is possible to recognise the facts of which it must treat in order that the student may know how to detect them and in order that he may not confuse them with others (Durkheim, 1966, p. liii).

Durkheim, like Bernard, does not want a science of conclusions which are already given as deductions from philosophical principles, but a science of discoveries. The *Rules* is an instrument for the attainment of that end. Durkheim states the object of his treatise on method quite clearly: it is to distinguish the particular facticity of sociology from the facticities of the other sciences. Durkheim's *Rules* are founded upon their necessity for the recognition of a real object which is the space in reality of a science yet to come into being, a vacant space awaiting its science. The existence of this space must be demonstrated and distinguished before the science can begin its work of penetration and explanation. It must be distinguished to release it from the grip of discourses which deny its existence; the discourses of individualist metaphysics, of social 'common-sense', and of biologism and psychologism. The new 'science' must begin with a theoretical critique of the discourses which deny the very existence of the reality which is its object and with a set of rules which enable the as yet untrained practitioners of the infant science to 'recognise' the signs of the presence of this object. The origin of the science is the sighting, the recognition, of an existent real object hitherto obscured by the ideas which blind a true perception.

Durkheim sets out to complete the project laid down by Comte; to occupy the last space in knowledge created by the order of the real, a space which has always existed but for which until now man has been unready and unequal. But Durkheim sets out to complete Comte's project in opposition to Comte. He rejects the Comtian thesis that the positive philosophy is the basis for the completion of this project. He criticises Comte for an ideological conception of method, for rationalism. The positive philosophy installs in the space of the social a series of conclusions stemming from its principles. Comtianism is an obstacle to the true perception of the real object which is the object of the science of sociology.

Durkheim retains, however, the Comtian conception of the order of complexity of the real upon which the system of the different sciences is based. He retains also the position of the necessity of a recourse to the sciences nearest in that order of complexity to learn from them the rudiments of method:

> No doubt, when a science is in the process of being born, one is obliged, in order to construct it, to refer to the only models that exist, namely, the sciences already formed (ibid., p. 145).

The recourse to biology is founded, for Durkheim, on the fact that the realities of biology and sociology are similar in that they are distinguished from their immediate material substrata, the physico-chemical and individuals, primarily by reasons of their emergent properties as organised wholes:

> But it will be said that, since the only elements making up society are individuals, the first origins of sociological phenomena cannot but be psychological. In reasoning thus, it can be established just as easily that organic phenomena may be explained by inorganic phenomena. It is very certain that there are in the living cell only molecules of crude matter. But these molecules are in contact with one another, and this association is the cause of the new phenomena which characterise life, the very germ of which cannot possibly be

found in any of the separate elements. A whole is not identical with the sum of its parts. It is something different, and its properties differ from those of its component parts. Association is not, as has sometimes been believed, merely an infertile phenomenon; it is simply the putting of facts and constituent properties into juxtaposition (ibid., pp. 102–3). In a word, there is between psychology and sociology the same break in continuity as between biology and the physico-chemical sciences (ibid., p. 104).

Durkheim's epistemology takes as its point of departure the two problems which face this new science in the era of its birth:

(i) the necessity of a critique of the already existing ideological misrepresentations of the discrete reality which it claims for its object as a science;
(ii) the necessity of demonstrating that this reality is truly a *real* object and of developing the means to recognise it.

From this double necessity come the two primary constituents of the Durkheimian theory of knowledge: the theory of the epistemo-logical obstacle ideological thought presents to science, and the theory of the nature of social facts. From these two theories is derived the place and the role of the Durkheimian theory of cognition, the realist conception of scientific knowledge, in the dis-course of the *Rules*.

The form of Durkheim's theory of knowledge, and, in particular, its logical order (in contrast to its expositional order which is haphazard and confused), theory of ideology→theory of social facts →theory of cognition, is not merely derived from his borrowing or taking up theories of knowledge which are ready made and at hand, it is a form dictated by his point of departure and by the structure of his discourse as a whole.

The Theory of Ideology

This theory is developed primarily in chapter 2 of the *Rules*, 'Rules for the observation of social facts'. Durkheim does not begin in the *Rules* with the problem of ideology but with the definition of the social fact. However, this theory of the specific facticity of sociology is logically secondary to the general theory of the difference between the realm of ideas and the realm of facts (it should be noted that this is *not* a theory of the difference between real objects and scientific objects.

Chapter 2 is generally taken by sociologists to be a spirited rejection of the legitimacy of 'common-sense' conceptions as a point of departure for social investigations. It is taken as the statement of the necessity of eradicating preconceptions deriving from the reality to be studied for an objective study of that reality. It figures in sociological debates as a contribution to the question of the possibility or impossibility of an objective or 'value-free' social science. But far from being a mere thesis of objectivity, a gesture toward the purging of preconceptions, this chapter states, although not formally, a general theory of ideology, of its source, its function and its effect on scientific cognition.

The principal constituents of this theory of ideology will be presented in the form of four theses.

Thesis I : Ideology is Prior to Science

Ideology pre-exists science and all sciences have to come to terms with ideological thought in the period of their birth :

> At the moment when a new order of phenomena becomes the subject matter of a science, these phenomena are already represented in the mind not only by rather definite perceptions but also by some kind of crudely formed concepts. Before the first rudiments of physics and chemistry appeared, men already had some notions concerning physico-chemical phenomena which transcended mere perception, such as are found, for example, mingled in all religions. The reason for this is that thought and reflection are prior to science, which merely uses them more methodically (ibid., p. 14).

Ideology is not *mere* error but is the *first* and *basic* form of human experience of the world.

Thesis II : The Source of Ideology

Ideology is an original and necessary component of the existence of human subjects :

> Man cannot live in our environment without forming some ideas about it according to which he regulates his behaviour (ibid.).

Ideological conceptions are inextricably connected with the existence of human subjects. They are a condition of the subjects' existence in that they represent the subjects' immediate mode of relation to the real. Ideology is the spontaneous form of 'ideational' representation of the real:

> We cannot doubt their* existence, since we perceive it simultaneously with our own. Not only are they within us, but, as they are a product of repeated experiences, they derive from repetition and from the habit resulting from it, a sort of dominance and authority. We feel their resistance when we try to shake them off. We are bound to confer the character of reality on phenomena which oppose us (ibid., p. 18).

Thesis III : The Function of Ideology

> Those ideas or concepts, whatever name one gives them, are not legitimate substitutes for things. Products of everyday experience, their primary function is to put our actions in harmony with our environment; they are created by experience and for it (ibid., p. 15).

Ideology is the spontaneous form of experience by which human subjects adjust their relations to reality. This spontaneous experience/representation is necessary for the subject in order to have *a* relation to the real. A true perception of the real is never guaranteed and therefore ideology forms the essential way in which men relate to the world. However, these immediate forms of experience become givens; experience in these forms of immediate reflection becomes the automatic basis of the subject's relation to the world and his recognition of it. These forms of the organisation of experience become the datum of experience itself; these forms of representation of the world become the world for the subject:

> But, because these ideas are nearer to us and more within our mental reach than the realities to which they correspond, we tend naturally to substitute them for the latter and to make them the very subject of our speculations. Instead of observing, describing, and comparing things, we are content to

* 'Their', in this quotation, means common-sense representations of social life. But this statement applies equally to all 'ideas' which are not controlled by objectively (scientific) perceptions of the real.

focus our consciousness upon, to analyse, and to combine our ideas (ibid., p. 14).

Thesis IV : The Effect of Ideology

The effect of ideology is therefore the misrecognition of the real, and the misrecognition of the order of primacy between ideas and things. For real objects existing independently of thought, subjects substitute the representations of those 'objects' which are given in thought. The real becomes an effect of its being thought; a spontaneous product of will and consciousness:

> The ideas just mentioned are those *notiones vulgares* or *praenotiones* which he [Bacon] points out to be the basic ideas of all sciences, where they take the place of facts. These *idola*, which are illusions that distort the real aspect of things, are nevertheless mistaken for the things themselves. Therefore the mind, encountering no resistance in this *imaginary* world [our emphasis] and conscious of no restraint, gives itself up to boundless ambitions and comes to believe in the possibility of constructing . . . the world, by virtue of its own resources exclusively and at the whim of its desires (ibid., p. 17).

Thus ideological thought has the effect of establishing an *imaginary* world and the subject lives in an *imaginary* relation to the real. In the *imaginary*, the world is reduced to an effect of the subject's own will. Durkheim maintains that the effect of ideology is a spontaneous idealism.

In ideology the order of relations in the real is reduced to the order of association of our ideas. Ideology is not equivalent to 'common-sense' social experience. Durkheim conceives ideology as a general epistemological obstacle to science which is inherent in the nature of the human mind. For Durkheim, ideology is an essential and ever-present attribute and effect of the human mind: 'This procedure conforms so closely to the natural bent of the human mind that it is to be found in the beginnings of the physical sciences' (ibid., p. 16). Its effect is to bar the way to a true cognition of reality: 'Instead of a science concerned with realities, we produce no more than an *ideological* analysis' (ibid., p. 14, our emphasis). Ideology installs our epistemological autism with respect to reality. Durkheim compares ideology with the *idola* of Bacon; as presuppositions (*praenotiones*) which function as a veil between our cognitive faculties and the real objects ('things') which are the sole objects of science:

> By elaborating such ideas in some fashion, one will therefore never arrive at a discovery of the laws of reality. On the contrary, they are like a veil drawn between the thing and ourselves, concealing them from us the more successfully as we think them more transparent (ibid., p. 15).

The imaginary installs a field of spontaneous knowledge; a knowledge which is immediately given to the subject and in which the subject recognises only his own thoughts and will, his own spontaneously developed representations:

> If, therefore, reality can be thus understood at a glance, the study of present phenomenal reality is no longer of any practical interest. . . . Thus, an incentive is given to turn from the very subject of our science, namely, the present and the past, and to proceed at once to the future (ibid., p. 16).

This spontaneous knowledge leads to a conception of the immediate efficacy of the human will upon its own products:

> If men think they know what the essence of matter is, they immediately start to look for the philosopher's stone (ibid., p. 16).

> Indeed, social things are actualised only through men; they are a product of human activity. They appear to be nothing but the overt manifestation of ideas perhaps innate, contained in the mind; they are nothing but the application of these ideas to the diverse circumstances involving the relations of men (ibid., p. 17).

Ideology must be broken with if science is to come into being. The direction of this break is *away* from the illusions of the subject and toward the real. The real itself is the only sure foundation of science. The beginning of any science is the development of an objective mode of cognition of a 'new' reality, a reality which is new to man in that it was previously hidden from him by the blindness imposed by his own illusions.

Before we proceed with our discussion of the other constituents of Durkheim's epistemology a number of remarks are required to situate this remarkable conception of ideology.

First, Durkheim's discussion of ideology differs from *sociological* conceptions of ideology. Sociological theories of ideology are concerned to explain it as an element of 'social structure' or as the systems of ideas of social movements. For sociology, ideology articulates conceptions and interests that arise at definite locations in society. Durkheim's theory of ideology is not developed as a theory of his sociology but as a component part of his epistemology. The function of this theory in his discourse is to think the difference of the orders of the 'thing' and the 'idea'; to think the 'idea' as an obstacle to the cognition of the 'thing'. The theory of ideology effects the separation of these two orders by uncovering their difference in the mechanism of ideology: in the source of ideology in the subject's relation to the real and in the effect of ideology in its subjectivism and idealism. We know the difference of the 'idea' and the 'thing' in that we know ideology as an imaginary representation by the subject of the 'thing'. The theory of ideology is a general theory within Durkheim's epistemology; it is logically prior to any sociology.

Second, Durkheim's conception of the source and function of ideology is not in any sense sociological. Ideology is an effect of the existence of human subjects *per se*. *It is an effect of the nature of the human mind*. The status of this subject and this mind is treated as a given: the forms and conditions of their existence are never explained, but they are certainly not social. They are analytically prior to any sociology. In Durkheim's text the subject and the mind are merely distinguished from a reality which exists outside of them and independent of them. So far all that we know is that there are subjects with a constitution, 'mind', and objects which are independent of them, 'things', the constitution of which is not known. We cannot say that, because the *Rules* is a book about sociological method, the human subject which appears in its discourse must be a subject with a social constitution, for the subject is not *thought* as social in the logical form of the theory of knowledge of Durkheim. Indeed, as we shall see in greater detail later, in the *Rules* Durkheim never tells us the exact status of these subjects. In the *Rules* the 'individual' (whom we may equate with this subject) is taken as a given, and as something which is distinct from the 'social'. We can only conclude from the notions of the difference of the 'idea' (province of mind in general), and the 'thing' (province of the real in general), and the notions of the difference of the 'individual' (object of psychology), and 'society' (object of sociology), that the subject and ideology are not *thought* as social in the *Rules*.

The place of the theory of ideology in Durkheim's discourse is dictated by the points of departure of his theory of knowledge. The Durkheimian theory of ideology cannot be transposed into a sociological discourse. It should be noted here that the theory of 'ideology' in *The Elementary Forms of Religious Life* is quite different; the term ideology is not used in the *Forms*.* 'Ideology' in the *Forms* concerns representations that are social, representations of the social itself, and the subject which 'thinks' these forms is a different subject, the society – subject of the collective consciousness.[1]

In conclusion, the most notable aspect of the theory of ideology in the *Rules* is that it is based upon a thoroughgoing realism. Ideology is a misrepresentation of the real; it is an illusion, however real its representations may be to the subject, and however necessary it may be for the existence of the subject. Ideology for Durkheim is merely a given imaginary realm with which the sciences must break if they are to come into existence. Ideology is *unreal*. It is suspended unreality which is never anchored in the real itself; Durkheim never tells us anything more than that it is *different* from the real. Ideology has its source in the subject, but the subject is a given, the conditions of existence of which are never explained. This unconditional existence of the 'idea', this unconditional subject, which appears in the discourse merely counterposed to a realm of objects, whose condition of existence we are assured is that it is the very nature of 'things', is characteristic of the problematics of classical philosophy. The terms of these problematics, idea–thing, subject–object, are pre-given to the discourse of these problematics. These problematics merely reproduce these terms in discourse in certain relations of hierarchy, subject→object, object→ subject, according to whether the effect of this discourse is an idealist or empiricist position in philosophy. Durkheim's epistemology has not left the closed circle of classical philosophy.

* Hereafter, *The Elementary Forms of Religious Life* will be referred to as *Forms*.

The Theory of the Facticity of the Social

In spite of all these doctrines, social phenomena are things
and ought to be treated as things. To demonstrate this
proposition, it is unnecessary to philosophise on their nature
and to discuss the analogies they present with the phenomena
of lower realms of existence. It is sufficient to note that they
are the unique data of the sociologist. All that is *given*, all that
is *subject to observation*, has thereby the character of a thing
(ibid., p. 27, our emphasis).

Despite these remarks, as we shall see later, Durkheim *does* find
it necessary to philosophise, and he does find it necessary to draw
analogies with 'lower realms' of existence (biology). What is
remarkable here, however, is that Durkheim tells us that 'things',
realities are *given*. If we were to ask how is it that they are given,
we will only hear the answer that givens are 'subject to observation'. Durkheim proposes to reject all essentialist and ontological
arguments about the nature of reality apart from what is observable to us:

Our principle, then, implies no metaphysical conception, no
speculation about the fundamental nature of being. What it
demands is that the sociologist put himself in the same state of
mind as the physicist, chemist, or physiologist when he probes
into a still unexplored region of the scientific domain. When
he penetrates the social world, he must be aware that he is
penetrating the unknown; he must feel himself in the presence
of facts whose laws are as unsuspected as were those of life
before the era of biology; he must be prepared for discoveries
which will surprise and disturb him (ibid., p. xlv).

The nature of 'facts' concerns us only *methodologically*, only in so
far as we must establish that they exist and the method by which
we may recognise them. A naturalistic, that is, scientific, sociology
is not a metaphysical materialism:

We reject the term naturalistic if it is given a doctrinal
meaning concerning the essence of social objects – if, for
example, by it is meant that social objects are reducible to the
other cosmic forces (ibid., p. 141).[2]

Science cannot tell us why a thing exists; it can only discover the laws which govern its existence:

> Moreover, science is not concerned with first-causes, in the absolute sense of the word. For science, a fact is primary simply when it is general enough to explain a great number of other facts (ibid., p. 116).[3]

But how is it possible to establish the existence of, to delimit and 'subject to observation', a particular given reality? Any science must establish methodologically the field that is *given it* by nature or it cannot exist; it will never be certain of its relation to its real object and will fall subject to ideological illusions: 'Every scientific investigation is directed toward a limited class of phenomena, included in the same definition' (ibid., p. 34). The particular given field must be recognised and its givens must be uncovered in a form 'subject to observation':

> A theory, indeed, can be checked only if we know how to recognise the facts of which it is intended to give an account. Moreover, since this initial definition determines the very subject matter of science, this subject matter will or will not be a thing, depending on the nature of the definition (ibid., pp. 34–5).

First, therefore, at the beginning of our science, we must know by what properties we recognise a 'thing'. We must define the properties of 'things' in general:

> What, precisely, is a 'thing'? A thing differs from an idea in the same way as that which we know from without differs from that which we know from within. Things include all objects of knowledge that cannot be conceived by purely mental activity, those that require for their conceptions data from outside the mind, from observations and experiments, those which are built up from the more external and immediately accessible characteristics to the less visible and more profound. To treat the facts of a certain order as things is not, then, to place them in a certain category of reality but to assume a certain mental attitude toward them (ibid., p. xliii).

The most important characteristic of the reality which exists independently of us is that it is not subject to our will, its *resistance* to our subjective attempts to change it proves it to be an object which exists on the basis of conditions which are not those of our will:

> Indeed, the most important characteristic of a 'thing' is the impossibility of its modification by a simple effort of the will. Not that the thing is refractory to all modification, but a mere act of the will is insufficient to produce a change in it; it requires a more or less strenuous effort due to the *resistance* which it offers (ibid., pp. 28–9, our emphasis).[4]

Our definition of the 'thing', of the real object of our science, must be an objective and not an ideological definition:

> In order to be objective, the definition must obviously deal with phenomena not as ideas but in terms of their inherent properties. It must characterise them by elements essential to their nature, not by their conformity to an intellectual ideal (ibid., p. 35).

In the beginning of a science the sole basis for the constitution of its given field is that it departs from these characteristics of things which are given to perception (to a perception free of ideological illusions):

> Now, at the very beginning of research, when the facts have not yet been analysed, the only ascertainable characteristics are those external enough to be perceived (ibid., p. 35).

The function of the definition of the given, since it delimits what is to be, and what can be perceived, is heuristic: 'The sole function of the definition is to establish contact with things' (ibid., p. 42). Reality, although its external characteristics are given to perception, is not visible directly in its essence, it is only discovered through its traces in its visible phenomena, in its *external* characteristics: 'These characteristics are our only *clue* to reality; consequently, they must be given complete authority in our selection of facts' (ibid., p. 35, our emphasis). Knowledge of reality, in all its complexity, only proceeds through the successive refinements of our perceiving it, through successive approximations to the essence which we are never certain of uncovering: '. . . by successive approximations, to encompass, little by little, this fleeting reality, which the human mind will never, perhaps, be able to grasp completely' (ibid., p. 46).[5] (This apparent phenomenalism rather than realism in Durkheim's discourse has a function, which we shall see later, as a *moment* of his epistemology and does not exhaust the position of the epistemology as a whole.)

The relation between these directly perceivable characteristics, these 'clues' and 'symptoms', and the essence of reality is a real and objective relation because of the *principle* of causality:

> But, if the *principle* of causality is valid, when certain
> characteristics are found identically and without exceptions in
> all the phenomena of a certain order, one may be assured that
> they are closely connected with the nature of the latter and
> bound up with it (ibid., p. 43, our emphasis).

This *principle* has already taken us beyond pure phenomenalism. This principle is, for Durkheim, a necessary axiom or presupposition of all science, since it connects the visible traces of the real and the as yet undiscovered and deeper order of the real itself. The visible surface phenomena are the given forms in which deeper realities express themselves.

The facticities of all the sciences are constituted by a given visible field of phenomena which are expressions of the realities that underlie it. Sociology is no exception to this general rule of Durkheim's epistemology. We turn from the properties by which 'things' in general are recognised to the specific form of the given in the realm of social reality, social facts.

Durkheim poses the problem of the existence and character of the facticity of sociology by demanding the principle of its differentiation from the other sciences. If the common-sense definitions of what is social are accepted then everything that takes place in 'society' is a social fact and nothing is thereby constituted as a social fact:

> But on that basis, there are, as it were, no human events that
> may not be called social. Each individual drinks, sleeps, eats,
> *reasons*; and it is to society's interest that these functions be
> exercised in an orderly manner. If, then, all these facts are
> counted as 'social' facts, sociology would have no subject
> matter exclusively its own, and its domain would be confused
> with that of biology and psychology (ibid., p. 1, our emphasis).

How then are 'social facts' differentiated as a specific class of facts
which are exclusively the domain of sociology? By their partaking
of the general properties of all 'things'. That is, their objective
existence outside of 'us' and their resistance to 'our' will. By their
partaking of the specific characteristics of social things. That is, that
they are irreducible to biological and psychological phenomena and
that they are inexplicable by the sciences of biology and psychology.
These facts indicate a space in reality as yet unexplained by any
science; they are facts concerning humanity which are irreducible
to the biological constitution of the human species or the psychology of individual men. This latter argument is a variant of the
method of 'residues'.

In attempting to demonstrate that social facts are independent
of human wills and exert a coercive force upon them, Durkheim
lists a number of examples of the constraints that 'society' exercises
upon individuals. These are varied, and include the French
language, technical organisations of material production, moral
rules, laws and customs. Why these apparently heteroclite phenomena are social phenomena is not explained at this juncture, except
by the fact that they are prior to and constrain given 'individuals'.
He concludes:

Here, then, is a category of facts with very distinctive
characteristics: it consists of ways of acting, thinking, and
feeling, external to the individual, and endowed with a power
of coercion, by reason of which they control him. These ways
of thinking could not be confused with biological phenomena,
since they consist of representations and of actions; nor with
psychological phenomena, which exist only in the individual
consciousness and through it. They constitute, thus, a new
variety of phenomena; and it is to them exclusively that the
term 'social' ought to be applied. And this term fits them
quite well, for it is clear that, since their source is not in the
individual, their substratum can be no other than society,
either the political society as a whole or some one of the partial
groups it includes, such as religious denomination, political,
literary, and occupational associations, etc. On the other hand,
this term 'social' applies to them exclusively, for it has a
distinct meaning only if it designates exclusively the
phenomena which are not included in any of the categories

of facts that have already been established and classified. These ways of thinking and acting therefore constitute the proper domain of sociology (ibid., pp. 3–4).

The 'constraint' that a social fact exercises upon individuals may stem either from some sanction imposed by society upon certain acts of individuals or from the resistance which social organisation, as an organisation, offers to human wills:

> We thus arrive at a point where we can formulate and delimit in a precise way the domain of sociology. . . . A social fact is to be recognised by the power of external coercion which it exercises . . . over individuals, and the presence of this power may be recognised . . . either by the existence of some specific sanction or by the resistance offered against every individual effort that tends to violate it (ibid., p. 10).[6]

How are social facts to be recognised? They are recognised by the traces of their effectivity as facts; the application of sanctions and the resistance of organised social life. Social facts are embodied in perceivable realities:

> Social facts . . . qualify far more naturally and immediately as things. Law is embodied in codes; the currents of daily life are recorded in statistical figures and historical monuments; fashions are preserved in costumes; and taste in works of art. By their very nature they tend toward an independent existence outside the individual consciousness, which they dominate. In order to disclose their character as things, it is unnecessary to manipulate them ingeniously (ibid., p. 30).

Social facts are given. 'Generality combined with externality' (that is, coercion) are the two main criteria of their recognition, the generality of a phenomenon of human life indicates the presence of the social apart from purely individual manifestation (see p. 10 of the *Rules*).

The various expressions or crystallisations of 'social life', the various phenomena which embody its essence, vary from spontaneous social currents to articulated social structures:

> There is thus a whole series of degrees *without a break in continuity* between the facts of the most articulated structure

and those free currents of social life which are not yet
definitely moulded. The differences between them are,
therefore, only differences in the degree of consolidation they
present. Both are simply life, more or less crystallised (ibid.,
p. 12, our emphasis).

These forms exist 'without a break in continuity' because they are
expressions of a single essence which differ only quantitatively in
the 'degree of consolidation they present'. Articulated structures
are merely crystallised social actions and sentiments:

These 'ways of existing' are only crystallised 'ways of acting'.
The political structure of a society is merely the way in which
its component segments have become accustomed to live with
one another (ibid., p. 12).

Indeed, certain of these social manners of acting and thinking
acquire, *by reason of their repetition*, a certain rigidity which
on its own account crystallises them, so to speak, and isolates
them from the particular events which reflect them (ibid., p. 7,
our emphasis).[7]

Social currents of opinion are social facts no less than articulated
structures; they produce specific effects in the behaviour of individuals, but they are separable as social facts from their individual
manifestations. The basis of separation is the collective resultant of
the actions of individuals: 'The average, then, *expresses* a certain
state of *the group mind* [*l'âme collective*]' (ibid., p. 8, our emphasis).
Statistical codifications of these results remove the purely individual
element: 'But statistics furnish us with a means of isolating them'
(ibid., p. 8). But it is the articulated forms of sociality which are the
most objective basis for sociological observation since they are an
objective fixity separate from the individual and materialised in
'things' (see ibid., p. 30, quoted on p. 95). These objective sedimen-
tations of social life, legal codes, etc., furnish a stable, constant
standard for the investigation of social life which is not at all confused with individual manifestations. As they are 'merely social life
consolidated' it is possible to study the living being of society
through its objective expressions: 'Since, on the other hand, these
practices are merely social life consolidated, it is legitimate . . . to
study the latter through the former' (ibid., p. 45). Social life as such
is not a particular class of *material* objects in the simple sense; it is

not like rocks or tissue cells, although it may be embodied in material objects; it consists of *representations*:

> To allow our first proposition, that social facts must be treated as things, it is not necessary to maintain that social life consists of other than 'representations'; it is sufficient to postulate that the 'representations', individual or collective, can be studied scientifically only if they are studied objectively (ibid., p. xliv, footnote).

Social life consists of representations and these representations arise in, and are states of, the 'conscience collective'; the collective consciousness of 'society' which is distinct from the individual consciousness of its members. Sociology can only be a science if it recognises the particular modality of existence of its domain:

> This science, indeed, could be brought into existence only with the realisation that social phenomena, although immaterial, are nevertheless real things, the proper objects of scientific study (ibid., p. lvii).

Social facts are *real* but immaterial; their reality does not consist in their reducibility to cosmic forces but in the resistance that they offer to individual wills.

Durkheim's general theory of the domains of sciences, as 'givens' 'subject to observation', attempts to provide the basis and the proof for the existence and the validity of his characterisation of a particular 'given' domain, that of social facts. But the 'givenness' of these facts in general and in the social realm is quite spurious. These facticities are *given to us* by a definite theoretical system. Durkheim maintains in his general theory that we define a particular facticity by common external characteristics and that we work back by successive approximations to the reality which these characteristics embody and of which they are the phenomena. But, contrary to Durkheim's claim, this deeper reality must already be given for the immediate and visible 'facts' to be defined. It is given by the heurism of the definition of the field of the given. The definition of 'ascertainable characteristics . . . external enough to be perceived' is not a product of pure perception but a product of theory. The definition specifies which phenomena are perceivable and it depends on an already given characterisation of the deeper reality of which they are the phenomena. These phenomena are

'hand picked' by the theory which has already thought the existence
of that deeper reality. *The principle* of causality that apparently
links the phenomena with their as yet unknown essence is no more
than a smokescreen (and it could only be a presupposition, not
derived from perception, even if Durkheim's theory of the constitution of givens were true); it conceals the fact that the relation of
visible externals and the essence of the real is already pre-established in theory.

If we turn to Durkheim's particular theory of the 'social fact',
this becomes even more apparent. We already know the nature of
the essence of social reality which particular facts express. It
consists of representations which exist in the collective consciousness. The particular visible externals are 'hand picked' to fit their
role as phenomena of the collective consciousness.

Social facts are facts and are social because they constrain
'individuals'. But the nature of these individuals is taken as a given
in the theory: the most we can conclude from Durkheim is that
these 'individuals' are the individuals conceived by individualistic
psychology and common-sense representations in society. The
individual psychology to which Durkheim makes reference is an
elaboration of common-sense conceptions and need not concern us
at the moment. Let us try and determine the theoretical function of
these untheoretically 'given' individuals. If social facts constrain
individuals because a group of subjects x is subordinated to a
system of laws y, then all we know are the common-sense realities
of the experience of any subject; that there is law and that there is
punishment. If the individual is a social subject then necessarily he
is subject to society – all we have here is a tautology. But Durkheim
insists that individuals and individual manifestations are not social
facts. The realm of the social is distinguished from the individual
and it has a definite effect upon him and is external to him. These
given individuals separate from society are not the point of departure of a Robinsonnade; Durkheim is indifferent to the specific
constitution of these individuals; they are a means, a theoretical
device, by which the social is differentiated as a term in Durkheim's
discourse. The sole theoretical function of these 'individuals' is
that they are counterposed to the social and that they serve to
establish, in this difference, the existence of the specific realm of
the social. Durkheim's sociology is not an elaboration of an anthropology; he does not seek the essence of the social in the essence of

Man. 'Individuals' are beings external to society and its nature is not a direct result of their attributes.

Again, we are told that particular given facts, laws, houses, etc. are crystallisations of 'social life'. Social life or society is thus distinguished from the immediate and external facts which are expressions of it. But the nature of this essence, of which particular facts are the given manifestations, is itself a given. We know nothing of its constitution except that it consists of representations and that it exercises constraint upon the 'individual'. That laws and customs are phenomena which are in no way reducible to psychological or biological explanations tells us nothing about their constitution or of the type of explanation that will account for them. Constraint and irreducibility, the two main criteria of the differentiation and specification of sociology's own facticity, are not sufficient means to establish what 'social life' is.[8]

The sole function of the terms 'social life' and 'conscience collective' is to serve as foundations for the facts of laws, institutions and behaviour. These notions function to establish these 'given' facts as givens because they are expressions of a fundamental reality. These notions found the given field of sociology as laws, institutions and behaviour, in their manifest forms which we encounter in ordinary social experience. These entities merely shore-up phenomena which are ideologically given in 'common-sense' social experience. Thus codes of law become expressions of a social essence; they become necessary embodiments of 'society' as such. Far from being contingent, they become necessary by reason of their connection with the very order of things social. Thus these given social facts which are 'subject to observation' are the manifest phenomena of social experience and their visibility is not the visibility of a pure perception but the transparency of ideological givenness. Sociology is thereby assured a domain of facts it cannot help but 'see' and it is for this reason unnecessary to manipulate them ingeniously. Thus we see the trick of the 'initial definition'; far from installing a field of facts previously invisible because of ideological illusions, it installs the phenomena of ideology, or 'common sense', as a field of external and real facts ('things'). We thereby recognise the theoretical status of Durkheim's individualist and realist conception of ideology: it renders ideology a function of subjects in general and denegates the question of *social* ideologies and their connection with the 'facts' of society. The a-social individual becomes the source of misrecognition of the social. Durkheim's discourse denegates the questions that any sociological rationalism seeks to pose in respect of its object. Its structure renders impossible the question: by means of what concepts are these manifest institutions and practices demonstrated to be the object of the science of sociology?

Durkheim's realism denegates the theoretical character of his discourse. Thus while the 'given' facticity cannot exist without the theoretical system which gives (founds) it, that system has no function in the discourse but to reproduce the ideologically given, to underlie it and to shore it up. The two ends of the discourse are closed: theoretically-given givenness and theory as the mere reproduction of the ideologically given.

When Durkheim attempts to think the 'conscience collective' independently of its ideological function in his discourse, when he tries to pose its existence and its conditions as a distinct reality, its status in his discourse as a purely notional entity betrays him. The 'conscience collective' becomes, since it is the essence of the social itself and without conditions of existence, a mentalism, a society-subject. Collective representations become the representations, the thought and the images of a society-subject.[9] This mentalism is a necessary consequence of the structure of his problematic. The 'conscience collective' is the essence of reality and underlies the particular manifestations of social life. Its conditions cannot therefore be sought in the phenomena of social life since it exists beyond them. Durkheim is left with no option but to consign it to the place of the collective idea as opposed to the realm of given external things. In so far as it is a mental phenomenon, an idea, he faces the threat that it is an illusion, a misrecognition of the real. But since it is the order of the real itself, the society-subject can only be a subject without illusions, a subject whose ideas are pure knowledge. Thus knowledge is displaced into the real; it is made the order of the real itself. What is an ideological illusion in the individual subject becomes the rational character of the real itself in respect of the society-subject. The social world *is* the product of its representations. In Durkheim's theory the particular visible externals of social life have a necessary connection with its essence and that connection assures us that we can know 'the latter through the former' since the former are the phenomena in which the essence, which is knowledge in itself, expresses itself. It is no exaggeration to claim that through this mechanism of expression the real becomes the rational.

The articulation of Durkheim's discourse is as follows:

(i) *Foundation*

The relation essence→givens in which the initial (theoretical) definition of the domain of given facts (perceivable through external characteristics) establishes the givenness of that domain as a necessary rather than an arbitrary givenness. The essence, which is already contained in the initial (theoretical) definition, *underlies* the domain of given facts, and since they are necessary facts they are a fit object for science.

The contradiction that a theoretical foundation is necessary to constitute the supposedly *given* real object of the science is dene-gated by the realist theory of knowledge which is integral to Durkheim's problematic. The contradiction is not immediately visible since the very terms of the problematic, and the denegation of rationalism which they presuppose, do not provide the means internal to the theory to pose it as a problem (see pp. 110–13).

(ii) *Expression*

The relation essence → givens in which the essence 'surfaces' as the order of the given itself. The mode of explanation (causality) in this discourse is to refer the givens to the essence. The expres-sion of the essence in 'its' givens is the causality, the necessity, of the givens themselves. Since, however, the essence is both the condition of existence of the facticity and it exists without condi-tions in itself, the essence can *only* exist in the mode of expression. It can only be *referred to* as the order of the facticity behind the facticity. The given facticity is thus the sole '*clue*' to the existence of the essence. It is a *valid* clue by reason of the causality of expression and the nature of the essence as knowledge in itself. The *clues* are the solution since the phenomena of the essence contain the essence in the mode of expression. Thus the riddle is solved, the essence to which we refer tells us nothing but what we already know. It tells us that the given is the necessary order of things and that its relations are real relations. But, as we have seen, this given is not a pure given, subject to perception, it is an ideologically already given. The *content* of this given is not, of course, the manifest social world *in toto*. This given is the sphere of action of a process of selection. The elements that we selected to constitute the given social world are the elements selected by the practico-social ideology, the *political* ideology, to which Durkheim adheres. His theoretical discourse is an elaboration of that ideology.

This articulation is the necessary basis for the existence of both of its forms: the denegation (denial) of theoretically given givenness is the basis on which reference to the essence can appear as anything more than a tautology; the causality of expression is necessary in order that the theoretical foundation of the given can establish the given as part of the order of things. Thus although we are told that the nature of the facts concerns us only *methodologically*, that we are merely assuming 'a certain mental attitude towards them' we find that the methodological necessities of Durkheim's problematic drive him into an essentialism. It is to be sure, not the mechanical materialist essentialism Durkheim warned us against.

The role of this double articulation of Durkheim's discourse becomes even clearer in his attempts to explain particular social phenomena. As we shall see later, concomitant variation and correlation are the basis of explanation in Durkheim's sociology. Correlation, the mere co-existence of certain orders of facts defined and related by statistical operations, is, for Durkheim, a legitimate mode of explanation because it uncovers an order already existing in the real. Correlation reveals relations of facts in the same space, facts which are equivalent by virtue of their being alike expressions of the social essence. The unity of these particular facts, and of the given field of social facts in general is the unity of their common origin as phenomena of the essence.

In *Suicide*, Durkheim finds no contradiction in taking the phenomena of 'moral statistics', codifications of particular systems of judgment by coroners, etc., as given facts. For Durkheim, 'moral statistics' are a collective resultant, a state description, of the force and direction of the essential social sentiments. Durkheim's *Suicide* is apparently based upon the relation between the series of correlations, which, in themselves, can generate no causes for the phenomenon of suicide, and the explanatory 'concepts' of anomie, egoism and altruism. But these 'concepts' explain nothing since they are no more than redescriptions of the commonly attributed causes of suicides. These concepts do not explain the *rates* of suicide, merely the circumstances which may lead individuals to commit suicide. The 'suicidogenic current', which explains the particular force of the social sentiments which establish each year a certain contingent of voluntary deaths, is no idle metaphor. It is the particular form in which the notion of a society-subject's presence in 'its' phenomena comes to the surface in Durkheim's discourse. But the 'suicidogenic current', as the expression of an essence, has no substance as an explanation, and it can never be specified as an explanatory mechanism. Its presence behind the phenomena is merely *referred to* and the space of its presence is established by the way in which the phenomena are organised. For Durkheim, the rates of suicide are already 'things' as expressions of the essence before the essence is brought into play. The essence, 'social sentiments', justifies the 'given' phenomena as necessary phenomena; these phenomena then serve as the stage on which the essence plays its part as the *deus ex machina*.

Thus, in Bachelard's terms, Durkheim's sociology is a 'phenomenology'.[10] It is a theoretical mechanism for the reproduction of the 'given'. It is a device for 'saving' the phenomena of immediate experience: at one and the same time it promotes these phenomena to primacy ('the given') and it installs an essence behind their groundless existence.[11] The *stage* of Durkheimian sociology is peopled by the commonplace and that stage exists by virtue of the *theatre* of Durkheimian sociology and the fantastic of its theatrical machinery.

The Theory of Scientific Knowledge

Since objects are perceived only through sense perceptions, we can conclude: Science, to be objective, ought to start, not with concepts formed independent of them, but with these same perceptions (ibid., p. 43).

This extreme realist conception of knowledge demands that science: 'Ought to borrow the materials for its initial definitions directly from perceptual data' (ibid.).[12] It must base its concepts not upon ideological representations of reality but upon perceptions of reality itself:

> Science, then, has to create new concepts; it must dismiss all
> lay notions and extract the terms expressing them, and return
> to sense perception, the primary and necessary substance
> underlying all concepts. From sensation all general ideas flow,
> whether they be true or false, scientific or impressionistic
> (ibid., pp. 43–4).

All scientific concepts are representations of reality, as are ideological 'ideas'. Scientific concepts are different from ideological
'ideas' in that they are true to reality; they are representations of
the phenomena as they exist:

> Our ideas [representations] of physical things are derived
> from these things themselves and express them more or less
> exactly, so our idea of ethics must be derived from the
> observable manifestation of the rules that are functioning
> under our eyes. . . . Consequently, these rules, and not our
> superficial idea of them, are actually the subject matter of
> science, just as actual physical bodies, and not the layman's
> idea of them, constitute the subject matter of physics (ibid.,
> p. 23).

Science is a form of *perception*; its basis is sensation. Sensation can
only be a faculty of a human subject. Science is, therefore, the
perception of a given real object by a human subject. This subject
is an abstract subject reduced to a pure bundle of perceptual
faculties. Thus science can only be a *cognition* that reproduces the
order of the real itself and the order of the real must be knowledge
in itself. Science can only uncover or discover a knowledge that
already exists as a given in the real. Knowledge is displaced into
'things'. The scientific subject becomes little more than an accurate sensory apparatus which receives the true 'message' from
reality.[13]

For Durkheim, the object of each science is a delimited real
object which already exists in nature. Each science is grounded on
a distinct 'species' of reality which is its exclusive domain. There
are as many sciences as there are 'species' of reality and no more.
The system of the different sciences has always existed, at least
potentially, in the real itself. In an earlier text, his Latin thesis on
Montesquieu, Durkheim gave the clearest statement of this naïve
realist theory of the order of knowledge:

A discipline may be called a science only if it has a definite field to explore. Science is concerned with things, realities. If it does not have a definite material to interpret it exists in a vacuum . . . arithmetic is concerned with numbers, geometry with space and figures, the natural sciences with animate and inanimate bodies, and psychology with the human mind. Before social science could begin to exist it had to be assigned a definite subject matter (Durkheim, 1965, p. 3).

From this we may conclude that in mathematics, for example, zero exists in nature and that Euclidian space is a natural space.

It should be noted here that Durkheim is not an inductivist. His recommendations that 'all preconceptions must be eradicated' (Durkheim, 1966, p. 31) and his stress on the idealism of ideological thought merely lead to an extreme realism. It is on the basis of this realism that he rejects inductivism (and we may presume that the position he opposes is that of Mill). He rejects the notion that an exhaustive inventory of the phenomena of a particular class is necessary before any valid generalisation can be made about it:

It is not true that science can institute laws only after having reviewed all the facts they express, and can establish classes only after having described . . . the individuals they comprise. The true experimental method tends rather to substitute for common sense facts . . . *decisive* or crucial facts, which, by themselves and independently of their number, have scientific value and interest, as Bacon has pointed out (Durkheim, 1966, p. 79).

The real is an organised system, hence the knowledge of a part, one phenomenon in a definite relation with another, holds good for the whole. Durkheim does not share Mill's conception of the facts as particular and unconnected products of observation; the 'givens' 'subject to observation' are not atomistic assemblages of events but an already organised system.[14]

Durkheim further rejects the notion that causal relations are merely probabilistic constructions of relations between observed phenomena. He attacks Mill, like Bernard, on the basis of a determinist position. Durkheim maintains that Mill rejects causal relations which are anything other than a construction of the

relation of observed events in time; and that Mill argues that the
conception of a *necessary* relation between cause and effect is a
logically inadmissible extrapolation from the data observed.[15] To
this Durkheim replies:

> He [Mill] admits, in fact, that the same consequence does not
> always result from the same antecedent but may be due now
> to another. This conception of the causal bond, by removing
> all determinism from it, makes it almost inaccessible to
> scientific analysis (ibid., p. 127).

This arbitrary conception of causality as a temporal sequence is an
impossible conception for scientific practice:

> This supposed axiom of the plurality of causes is, in fact, a
> negation of the principle of causality. To be sure, if one
> believes with Mill that cause and effect are absolutely
> unrelated, there is nothing contradictory in admitting that
> an effect may follow sometimes one cause and sometimes
> another. If the relation which unites C to A is purely
> chronological, it does not exclude another relation of the
> same kind which would unite for example, C to B (ibid.).

The relation between cause and effect is what Durkheim calls a
logical relation, that is, it results from the very nature of things and
could not be otherwise:

> If . . . the causal bond is something logical, it could not be
> indeterminate. If it consists in a relation resulting from the
> nature of things, a given effect can maintain this relationship
> with only one cause, for it can express only one single nature.
> However, only philosophers have ever questioned the logic of
> the causal relation (ibid.).

Durkheim, like Bernard, insists that the notion of an arbitrary
relation between cause and effect posits a multiplicity of orders of
nature. This is intolerable to the scientist and undercuts the very
basis of his experimental practice:

> For the scientist there is no question about it; it is assumed
> by the very method of science. How could one explain
> otherwise both the very important role of *deduction* in
> experimental reasoning and the fundamental *principle* of
> proportionality between cause and effect? (ibid., our emphasis).

But in arguing in this way, from the standpoint of the experimental practice of the sciences, Durkheim's own realist theory of knowledge is contradicted, for he has suddenly introduced the 'role of deduction' in experimental reasoning and a 'fundamental principle'. Neither deduction nor principles are matters of sensation nor are they given in nature, unless, of course, nature *thinks*.

Durkheim discusses the role of experiment in quite a different vein. He defines experiment thus:[16]

> When they can be artificially produced at the will of the observer, the method is that of experiment, properly so called. When, on the contrary, the production of facts is not within our control and we can only bring them together in the way that they have been spontaneously produced, the method employed is that of indirect experiment, or the comparative method (ibid., p. 125).

Social scientists are not experimenters but observers, hence they must establish their causal relations by a less direct method:

> We have seen that sociological explanation consists exclusively in establishing relations of causality, that it is a matter of connecting a phenomenon to its cause, or rather a cause to its effects. Since, moreover, social phenomena evidently escape the control of the experimenter, the comparative method is the only one suited to sociology (ibid.).

The comparative method in sociology is the method of correlation:

> But the case is quite different with the method of concomitant variations or correlation. For this method to be reliable, it is not necessary that all the variables differing from those which we are comparing shall have been strictly excluded. The mere parallelism of the series of values presented by the two phenomena, provided that it has been established in a sufficient number and variety of cases, is proof that a relationship exists between them (ibid., p. 130).

The constant concomitance of two variables is sufficient to establish a law:

> The manner in which a phenomenon develops, expresses its nature. For two developments to correspond to each other,

there must also be a correspondence in the natures manifested
by them. Constant concomitance is, then, a law in itself (ibid.,
p. 131).

This law is more than a statistical relation, it is a law very different
from the 'laws' of Mill. Durkheim proceeds to indicate the tests by
means of which a chance concomitance can be guarded against (see
pp. 131–3 of the *Rules*). But he does not *prove*, against the strictures
of Mill, that these laws demonstrate anything other than the fact of
concomitance itself. He cannot give this proof for the very possibility of his method rests on the supposition that 'for two developments to correspond . . . there must also be a correspondence in
the natures manifested to them'. It is the role of the essence which
expresses itself in and which orders its phenomena which makes
the method possible. A correlation is a result of a certain form of
effect of the collective sentiments; it is a state description of
particular expressions of the essence in its phenomena. Correlations
are 'something logical', they consist in 'a relation resulting from the
nature of things', and that nature is already given by the theoretical
foundation of sociology's given field. Mill's scepticism would be
entirely justified in respect of Durkheim for the method of correlation is possible only as the condition that the nature of the reality
underlying the phenomena is already given in theory. Durkheim
never surrenders for a moment to this scepticism for he is 'certain'
of the results of his method in advance.

Durkheim's conception of method is destroyed by this assumption which is necessary to it; which guarantees its discoveries by
the prior possession of its conclusions. He cannot recognise that
scientific determinism, the production of causal relations in
experimental practice, does not depend for its existence upon any
assumptions about the 'real' but upon the activity of its phenomeno-
technique. His conception of the scientific object as a particular
'species' of given real object has nothing whatsoever to do with
experimental science. The objects of the sciences are internal to
their theories and experimental operations. The connection that
exists between theory and its object is an internal relation within
knowledge and not an external relation between a given 'real'
object and the cognition of a subject. Causal relations are logical
relations in science because they are relations established by a logic,
scientific theory, and not by a logic active in the 'real'. Determinism

is a valid *principle* in the sciences because theoretically defined phenomena are produced in relations determined by theory. Experiments are not, as Durkheim maintains, merely the 'artificial' production of already given objects. The experimenter does not 'will' what he has already 'seen'. Experiments can produce materialities specified by theory which have never been 'seen', and will never be seen or experienced by human subjects. Durkheim's philosopher's misconception of scientific practice is indicated by his conception of scientific instruments as 'precautions' necessary in view of the fact that 'sensation may be subjective' (see p. 44 of the *Rules*):

> thus the physicist substitutes, for the vague impressions of temperature and electricity, the visual registrations of the thermometer or the electrometer (ibid., p. 44).

No subject ever had vague impressions of 'temperature'. Temperature is a calibration of certain scientific instruments which measure the theoretically defined and experimentally produced phenomenon of 'heat'. The heat the subject feels when he approaches a fire and the heat measured in physics are in no sense equivalents.[17]

Durkheim's ultra-realist epistemology is the basis of his critique of the evolutionary theories of Comte and Spencer, and the economic theory of political economy. Durkheim criticises these theories for the fact that in them the 'idea' is dominant over the 'thing', for a discourse which remains an *argument* in the realm of ideas and is never a cognition of the realm of things:

> Thus although he [Spencer] claims to proceed empirically, the facts accumulated in his sociology seem to function principally as arguments, since they are employed to illustrate analyses of concepts rather than to describe and explain things (ibid., p. 21).

No doubt Durkheim is quite right to conclude that none of these theories are scientific theories, but he attacks them for the fact of their being *theoretical*; for *trying* to think the object of their scientific field. He thus cuts off the route to all genuine science. He cannot recognise that what is at fault in these theories is not that they are theoretical discourses, but rather the form of their theoretical discourse.

Durkheim's critique of political economy is a striking exemplifi-
cation of his realist position. However, in the process of his critique
Durkheim comes surprisingly close to an accurate assessment of
the *theoretical* errors of Mill and the other political economists.
According to Durkheim, Mill defines the object of political
economy as a facticity which is based upon a teleology; it consists
'of those social facts the *goal* of which . . . is the acquisition of
wealth' (Durkheim, 1966, p. 23). Durkheim then argues that:
'They are facts imagined by the economist as being related to the
above-mentioned end, and they are facts to the extent that he
recognises them as facts' (ibid., p. 24). Durkheim has uncovered
the fact that Mill's discourse is merely a mechanism for the reproduction of its own point of departure; the 'given' facts of ex-
changing, etc. It establishes this given object on the basis of an
anthropological assumption: that the desire for wealth, in the form
of commodities bought and sold for exchange, is a human need which
is an expression of human nature. This assumption, by means of
an anthropology which links human needs with a particular form
of exchange, establishes a field of facts in which men do seek wealth
as a necessary field. Individual desires and needs then underly and
explain the resulting economic activities – this is the basis of concepts such as 'utility' as explanatory concepts; they refer to an
essence beyond the field of given economic facts, the human subject as a subject of 'needs'. Durkheim, however, concludes his
critique by saying: 'Nothing, then, assures us in advance of the
existence of a sphere of social activity wherein the desire for wealth
really plays such a preponderant role' (ibid., p. 24). But, obviously,
something in Mill's discourse does do exactly this, the foundation–
expression relation we have already demonstrated in Durkheim's
discourse. Durkheim turns his scepticism on to Mill but he draws it
back at the point where it touches himself – Mill has not cut
through the veil of ideas to reach the thing. Thus this realist
critique of Mill denegates (represses) its own products. In Durkheim's problematic the source of Mill's error cannot be recognised
without the very structure of the problematic itself being called
into question by the recognition. Durkheim draws back into the
familiar territory of realism at the very point of his own theoretical
relation to Mill.

Durkheim's critique of political economy abolishes the
validity of all general concepts and all theoretical abstraction. He

attacks the economists' concept of production in the following
manner:

> For example, when [the economist] . . . undertakes the study
> of what he calls 'production', he thinks he can straightway
> enumerate and review the principal agents of that process. He
> does not, then, determine them by observing the conditions
> upon which the thing he was studying depends. . . . If, from
> the beginning of his research . . . he proceeds to this
> classification, it is because he has obtained it by a simple,
> logical analysis. He starts from the idea of production; in
> analysing it, he finds that it implies logically the ideas of
> natural forces, of work, and of tools or capital, and he likewise
> treats in their turn these derivative ideas (ibid., pp. 24–5).

He argues that the concept of production should be founded on a
description of observations of real processes of production. He is
arguing that production in general, as a concept, does not exist.
But any economist would gladly have told him that. No study of
particular operations, nail making, the fabrication of steam
hammers, etc., no observation of the particular actions performed
and of the particular instruments used, could ever generate the
concept of production. 'Production', for the pure observer, could as
well consist of fire, human sweat, a particular arm movement, etc.,
as of anything else. The constituents of the *concept* of production,
which Durkheim grotesquely transforms into 'the ideas of natural
forces, of work, and of tools or capital', enable us to think production as a theoretical generality. The concept establishes logically
what all production processes, as production processes, have in
common. It is an abstraction, production *in general*, which cannot
exist in reality; there are only particular processes of production.
But, for Durkheim, the only logic is the logic that is in the order of
the real itself.[18]

Durkheim's criticisms of the concept of value render his anti-
theoretical realism even more apparent:

> The most fundamental of all economic theories, that of value,
> is manifestly constructed according to the same method. If
> value had been studied as any fact of reality ought to be
> studied, the economist would indicate, first of all, by what
> characteristics one might recognise the thing so designated,

then classify its varieties, investigate by methodical inductions
what the causes of its variations are, and finally compare
these various results in order to abstract a general formula
(ibid., p. 25).

Durkheim is taking up here a more or less pure inductivist position,
although, as we have seen, he is not an inductivist in respect of his
own 'science' of sociology. How one could conceive value as a
'*thing*', as being in any sense amenable to observation, is beyond
possibility. A study of the various exchanges, of the given form of
commodities, of money, bills of exchange, etc., could never lead
us to the phenomenon of value. Value is the condition of existence
of these observable realities. He defines value as 'an object capable
of being exchanged' (see p. 25 of the *Rules*), but value is neither an
object, nor a visible property of an object. The value of a thing does
not inhere in it. Value is a social relation; it is the condition by
which the equivalence of certain 'objects', of a social usefulness
which is not equivalent, is established in commodity exchange.
The concept of value is part of a theoretical system which thinks
the form and condition of commodity exchange.[19] The object of
the theory of political economy is not a given which is visible in
'economic behaviour', it is the product of the theoretical operations
which define what the space is in which that 'behaviour' can take
place. Durkheim rejects any theoretical constitution of the object
of a science or theory.

Durkheim conceives theory as a stage in science which follows
from observation:

> Theory would be introduced only when science had reached
> a sufficient stage of advancement. On the contrary, it is
> introduced at the very outset (in economics). In order to
> construct economic theory, the economist is content to meditate
> and to focus his attention on his own idea of value. . . . To
> be sure, he confirms it by several examples. But, considering
> the innumerable facts such a theory must account for, how
> can one grant even the slightest validity to the necessarily
> limited number of facts thus cited at random? (ibid., p. 25).

This latter question could be flung back in Durkheim's face in
respect of his sociology. In fact, as we have seen, confronted with
'the innumerable facts' of 'social' behaviour Durkheim's observa-

tions could not have 'the slightest validity'. The domain of sociology is delimited by the heurism of the initial definition; which is supposed to depart from visible externals of the facts themselves. But the order he introduces into the facts comes in by the back door. It is a particular theoretical system, the dual relation of foundation and expression, which gives him his 'given'. Durkheim's whole discourse is based on this mechanism and the attempt to repress it. The contradiction of a 'given' 'subject to observation' that is an effect of a theoretical system is quite unsupportable. Sociologists tend to recognise in the *Rules* the positions they approve of or disapprove of, a sound 'value-free' basis for empirical social research, or a 'reifying' conception of social facts as 'things'. They pay very little attention to the discourse which produces these positions, and, since they exist only in that discourse, to the validity of these positions as products of that discourse.

Durkheim's differences with Bernard in respect of the theory of knowledge should be evident. Bernard's position is based upon the practice of an existing science, physiology. Durkheim's position, in effect, departs from a philosophical system in its attempt to found a 'science'. Durkheim, who was not a practising scientist, he was trained as a philosopher,[20] has no firm basis in the theoretical-experimental practice of the sciences. He has no conception of the rationalism entailed in the materialism of science, of the role of theory in the constitution of the objects of the sciences, or of the theoretical character of experimentation. Durkheim's system is based upon the erasure of the thought object; the abolition of the difference of concepts and 'reality'. Bernard, while he lacked a clear and consistent concept of that difference, returns to its site time and again in his discourse. Bernard is neither a consistent nor a simple realist.

It should be noted that neither Bernard nor Durkheim are exponents of the fallibilist doctrines in the philosophy of science which are so fashionable in our era. Durkheim rejects the *rationalism* of Comtian positivism, while Bernard rejects it because it is a philosophical 'system' and because of its effects on science. Durkheim is by no means a fallibilist since he accords so little of an independent role to theory, that the practice of posing and testing hypotheses, a practice which in a simple form does pose the difference of theory and 'reality', must appear to him as speculative and anti-realist.

The philosophical positions of these two thinkers can only be determined for what they are by a close reference to their particular problematics and the structure of their discourses. This indicated the necessity and the value of a reading of the kind which we have attempted in a preliminary form.

Pathology and Morphology

1. The Normal and the Pathological

Observation conducted according to the preceding rules
covers two types of facts which are very dissimilar in certain
respects: those which conform to given standards and those
which 'ought' to be different, in other words, normal and
pathological phenomena. We have seen that it is necessary to
include them both in the definition with which all research
must begin. But if their nature is in certain respects identical,
nevertheless, they constitute two different varieties of facts
which need to be distinguished (Durkheim, 1966, p. 47).

Durkheim maintains that this distinction must necessarily be
included 'in the definition with which all research must begin' in
order that the science studies the truly general and typical facts of
its domain and not irregularities and aberrations. But why is *this
particular* type of distinction, between 'two different varieties of
facts', necessary? It is not a necessary type of distinction in all
sciences: there are not normal and pathological 'varieties of facts'
in, for example, physics. Despite the reference to the 'definition
with which all research must begin', the necessity of *this particular*
type of distinction does not follow from the demands of scientific
explanation in sociology. It is a distinction which is given prior to
the science and which concerns the 'usefulness' of that science in
respect of certain given 'problems'. Thus, for Durkheim, the
scientific rationale for this distinction is a pre-scientific social
'need'; the very foundation of his 'social science' is subordinate to
the dictates of pragmatism. The character of the science is to be
determined by the pre-given applications of the science that are
required of it by extra-scientific factors.

In discussing the role of this distinction he makes reference to biology in such a way as to make clear this relation between scientific investigation and pre-given pragmatic needs. Durkheim, in effect, defines the *object* of biology as the production of medicine and therapy: 'The principal object of all the sciences of life, whether individual or social, is to define and explain the normal state and to distinguish it from its opposite' (ibid., p. 74). The scientific *object* of biology disappears into its practical effect; its scientific object becomes a practical end. The relation of the biological sciences and medicine, so clearly outlined by Bernard,[1] is thereby inverted.

The role of the definition of the normal and the pathological in respect of this pragmatism is made clear by a later passage in the *Rules*; it is to help society to steer a course between the extremes of pessimism and revolution:

If the social values are not subjects of observation but can and must be determined by a sort of mental calculus, no limit, so to speak, can be set for the free inventions of the imagination in search of the best. For how may we assign to perfection a limit? It escapes all limitation, by definition. The goal of humanity recedes into infinity, discouraging some by its very remoteness and arousing others who, in order to draw a little nearer to it, quicken the pace and plunge into revolutions. This practical dilemma may be escaped if the desirable is defined in the same way as health and normality and if health is *something inherent in the nature of things* (ibid., p. 75, our emphasis).

The task of sociology is to understand the causes of disease in the body social and thereby provide society with the technique of a cure: '. . . by revealing the causes of phenomena, science furnishes the means of producing them' (ibid., p. 48).

How then, are we to define health and disease in the body social? In physiology, as we have seen, the distinction is established on the basis of knowledge of the conditions of existence of life in general. Pathology, as a specific branch of physiology, is a consequence of the knowledge of these conditions. Disease is not a state different in essence from the normal functioning of an organism; it obeys the same physiological laws as normality and merely represents a specific change in the conditions of existence of the organism.

Pathology is founded on physiology; for a scientific pathology to exist, a scientific physiology must exist. Pathology is, therefore, an effect of scientific knowledge; scientific knowledge is not, however, an effect of any pre-given requirement for a pathology to meet the needs of medical technique.

For a social pathology to exist, a social science must exist and its object must be defined in such a way that knowledge of it generates a scientific pathology as a consequence. But Durkheim's 'social science', as he admits, is in its infancy, and, as we have seen, it has no scientifically constituted object and, therefore, it can have no scientific knowledge of the conditions of 'its' phenomena. How then can Durkheim produce a scientific pathology which is based upon a knowledge of the conditions which generate pathological forms? He cannot. In his sociology normality exists in and of itself as a given and so does pathology.

Durkheim's 'initial definition' of normality and pathology is entirely nominal: they are 'two different varieties of facts', 'those which conform to given standards and those which ought to be different'. Durkheim argues that health (normality) and pathology cannot be defined by their external manifestations in sociology any more than in medicine. Pain and death do not indicate pathology. Pain can be an aid to health; its absence signifies morbidity and it is also the accompaniment of the activities of a healthy organism. Death is a normal phenomenon in individuals, and, moreover, we cannot use death as an indicator of pathology in society because we cannot measure the moments of birth and death of a society. Pathology in the individual, or the social, cannot be defined by the probabilities of survival or the frequency with which it results in death.[2]

Thus the perceptible external characteristics by which we define normality and pathology in sociology cannot be of the above type. Health or normality *defines itself*. The norm, the standard, from which pathology deviates and to which it 'ought' to conform, exists as a given: 'We shall call "normal" those social conditions that are most generally distributed, and others "morbid" or "pathological"' (ibid., p. 55). Normality and pathology are different in kind and cannot have the same conditions of existence:

But it [pathology] is not grounded in their normal nature; it is not inherent in their ordinary constitution or bound up with the conditions of existence on which they generally depend (ibid., p. 58).

The healthy constitutes the norm for excellence and consequently can be in no way abnormal (ibid., p. 58).

It is inconceivable that pathology should be more widespread in society than normality since the norm is the healthy and its generality and frequency of manifestation is a proof of its superiority:

> It would be incomprehensible if the most widespread forms of organisation would not at the same time be, *at least in their aggregate* the most advantageous. How could they have maintained themselves under so great a variety of circumstances if they had not enabled the individual better to resist the elements of destruction. On the other hand, the reason for the rarity of the other characteristics is evidently that the average organism possessing them has greater difficulty in surviving. The greater frequency of the former is, thus, a proof of their superiority (ibid., p. 58, emphasis is original).

Survival defines the fittest. Normality and pathology are defined in a purely nominal and circular fashion; what is the norm is the given social practices and codes which are the average in a particular social species. The given standard from which pathological forms deviate is the established practices and codes of a particular society: 'The average, then, expresses a certain state of the group mind' (ibid., p. 8). Normality could in no way be abnormal since it is a function of the 'conscience collective'. The pathological could in no sense predominate since it consists in practices which offend the collective sentiments. In so far as the given social facts become necessary by reason of their being expressions of the collective consciousness so the *average* becomes necessary in that it is a given social fact.

The pathological is not merely an unfortunate and avoidable contingency, however. The pathological is a necessary effect of a certain constitution of the collective consciousness. No social structure is so completely articulated, no body of social sentiment so completely intensified and perfected, so as to prevent and proscribe all difference. The necessity of flexibility in social organisation, the necessity of adaptations to circumstances, the inability of

the collective sentiments to crystallise so completely that they
destroy all individual differences and absorb the individuals of a
society into an absolute social identity, entails the necessity of
pathological forms. But the reasons that Durkheim adduces for the
necessity of pathology existing in all social forms are neither
scientific nor rooted in the structure of society. On the one hand,
they are moralistic:

> Nothing is *good* indefinitely and to an unlimited extent. The
> authority which the moral conscience enjoys *must* not be
> excessive; otherwise no one would dare criticise it, and it
> would too easily congeal into an immutable form (ibid., p. 71,
> our emphasis).

The 'conscience collective' if it is too rigid and restrictive leads to
an illiberal and punitive society which unduly restricts the freedom
of individuals and has a lower capacity for adaptation. But the
'good' and the 'must' in Durkheim's passage refer only to his
wishes and his ethics; they do not represent social structural
limitations on the authority of the conscience collective.

On the other hand, they are psychologistic and biologistic
stemming from the a-social character of the individual:

> But a uniformity so universal and absolute is utterly
> impossible; for the immediate physical milieu in which
> each one of us is placed, the heredity antecedents, and the
> social influences vary from one individual to the next and
> consequently diversify consciousness. It is impossible for all
> to be alike, if only because each one has his own organism
> and that these organisms occupy different areas in space (ibid.,
> p. 67).

The space of freedom that allows the idealist and the reformer to
exist also permits the existence of the criminal. The existence of
crime has a positive function in respect of the collective sentiments;
the perpetuation of criminal acts 'tones-up' the collective sentiments and prevents them from atrophying by giving cause for their
exercise in condemnation and punishment.[3]

Durkheim's dialectics of morality, the necessary co-existence of
rules and deviations from them, his position that in a society of
saints deviations from the norm would still exist and outrage the

collective sentiments, so often considered by sociologists as a purely internal dialectic of the collective sentiments themselves, is, in fact, founded upon the extra-social constitution of the individual. It is founded upon the irreducibility of the biological and psychological nature of the individual to social forms and controls. Just as society is external to and constraining upon the individual so the individual is external to society and social constraint is necessary to control his extra-social 'will'.[4]

Durkheim's scientism and his sociological anti-individualism in fact depend upon morality and the individual being smuggled in by the back door. That which is the given average in society is, by its very nature as an expression of the collective consciousness, healthy. But the collective consciousness can be tyrannical and harmful if it suppresses the differences that inevitably stem from the existence of individuals. 'Society' has no conditions of existence; social life is the expression of an essence which underlies all its given phenomena; it has no structure and admits of no differences within its essential being. Durkheim's concept of social life, as we shall see later, is *vitalist* in conception. Essence has no contradiction within itself and there can thus be but one 'standard' *in society* to which all acts must conform.[5] But just as society is the expression of a given essence, so the individual is a given with an irreducible and a-social constitution. 'Society' has no contradiction within itself but it must not contradict that which is external to it, the constitution and needs of its human materials. Durkheim's doctrine of the normal and the pathological discovers the source and the necessity of pathology in the a-social individual. By individualising the *source* of pathology it de-socialises the pathological in society. Pathology becomes nothing more than the deviation from given social forms: its social existence is entirely negative, it is defined solely as the not-normal. Its necessity, its ineradicability in society, becomes an a-social necessity stemming from a source external to society. Thus the dangers of an over-punative society are dangers which can be recognised only by morality, and by a morality which seeks to enlighten and restrain the 'conscience collective'.

The definition of the normal and the pathological in Durkheim's sociology serves the epistemological function of maintaining a single space of equivalent social facts which are alike in that they are all expressions of a single essence. To admit of a social pathology with a *social* source would be to deny the existence of a single social facticity which is the unilateral expression of a single and unitary collective consciousness. For if Durkheim were to internalise pathology in society, given his mechanism for the establishment of a domain of social facts, he would then have to divide the collective consciousness within itself into a 'good' side and a 'bad' side.

For Durkheim, therefore, normality and pathology become different *states* which do not depend on the same conditions. Unlike the science of physiology, the 'science' of sociology requires different modes of explanation of the normal and the pathological. In that the normal is an expression of an unconditional essence the pathological cannot be a product of the same conditions and laws as social life in its normal state.

The pragmatic point of departure of Durkheim's doctrine is coupled with its epistemological function in respect of the theory of social facts. That theory, as we have seen, makes the contingent necessary. But if the 'contingent' is unconditionally and ever-always necessary then the sole function of sociology is to accept the given to its last detail. The doctrine of the normal and the pathological introduces a way out of this impasse. In so far as society is composed of individuals, the 'problems' of society stem from its relations with its external material conditions, for example, with individuals. This introduces the epistemological space of sociology's pragmatic role. Sociology respectively takes the part of 'society' and the 'individual'. It reasons with the collective consciousness through the medium of the individuals that compose society on behalf of the individual. It takes the part of the collective consciousness in speaking to individuals about the dangers of untrammelled individualism. In that the collective consciousness exists apart from individuals there is always the problem of its effective presence in the individuals who form the material vessels of its embodiment. In that the collective consciousness exists apart from individuals there is always the problem of its neglect of their 'needs' and conditions of existence. The double givenness, of individuals and of society, in Durkheim's epistemology is no unfortunate accident, it is the condition of the pragmatic effectivity of sociology itself. It establishes the space which gives sociology its 'play'; its role as a go-between. Contrary to the claims that Durkheim's sociology is 'sociologistic', the individual is necessary to it.

It should be noted, however, that the content of this mediation which forms the basis of its pragmatism is not an effect of sociology's scientific knowledge. It is an effect of pre-existing 'common-sense' questions, 'problems' and modes of reasoning in society.

2. Social Morphology

We know that societies are composed of various parts in combination. Since the nature of the aggregate depends necessarily on *the nature and number of the component elements and their mode of combination*, these characteristics are evidently what we must take as our basis; and we shall see from what follows that it is on them that the general facts of social life depend. Moreover, as they are of the morphological order, one could call the part of sociology which has for its task the constitution and classification of social types, 'social morphology' (ibid., pp. 80–1, emphasis is original).

For Durkheim, the necessity of a systematic social morphology, a system of classification of social types, stems from the fact that the normal or pathological character of a social fact or the function of a social institution can only be determined in relation to a given social species.[6] A social morphology is a necessary part of a scientific sociology in that it provides a means for resolving a classic methodological dilemma. By defining particular social species as the primary units of analysis it avoids the abstract and *a priori* philosophical analysis of humanity in general (Comte), and the relativism and descriptivism of a purely monographic approach to given societies (ethnography):

It seems, then, that social reality must be merely subject matter of an abstract and vague philosophy or for purely descriptive monographs. But one escapes from this alternative once one has recognised that, between the confused multitude of historic societies and the single, but ideal, concept of humanity, there are intermediaries, namely, social species (ibid., p. 77).

Neither of these two approaches enables sociology to assess the function of particular social facts or institutions since they are unable to specify the real units of social analysis, particular social forms or types.

Any valid classificatory system must be based upon a rigorous initial definition of the elementary units of composition of the phenomena classified and the forms of the combination of these units one with another to produce those phenomena. Durkheim rejects purely speculative classificatory schemes which lack this rigorous foundation for the equivalence and comparability of their phenomena. Social morphology is not an abstract discipline independent of social 'physiology'.[7] The initial definition in morphology cannot be an *a priori* definition which is developed abstractly and in isolation from the 'physiological' analysis of the nature and conditions of existence of social life:

> We must, then, choose the most essential characteristics for
> our classification. It is true that we can know them only when
> the explanation of the facts is sufficiently advanced. These
> two parts of science are inseparable, and each progresses
> through the other (ibid., p. 80).

Thus in the *Rules* the analysis of morphology follows the chapters in which Durkheim presents his conception of the nature of social facts.

Durkheim's conception of social morphology is presented by means of analogies with chemistry, biology and geology; the very language of the text is scattered with such terms as 'aggregate', 'element', 'protoplasm', etc. It revolves around two basic notions, that of elements, irreducible atoms of social life, and the combination of these elements into 'aggregates'. It should be noted that, for Durkheim, all social elements have the same composition, unlike chemical elements, and that there is no equivalent of *chemical* compounds, only mixtures, or fused substances.[8] The units of composition of a social 'aggregate' are simpler societies which form its component parts:

> The principle of this classification can be given even greater
> precision. We know, indeed, that the constituent parts of
> every society are societies more simple than itself. A people
> is produced by the union of two or more pre-existent peoples.
> If, then, we understand the most simple society that has ever
> existed, to make our classification we should only have to

follow the way these simple societies form compounds and
how these compound societies combine again to form complex
wholes (ibid., p. 81).

Durkheim is thus vigorously opposed to any form of reductionism
to the individualist or evolutionist forms of explanation in which
the social is generated from the non-social. Society is ever-already
present; there is no pre-social moment in sociological analysis. The
simplest societies are the irreducible elements of sociality itself,
and they are *elements* in that they cannot be reduced to non-social
conditions of existence.[9]

It is necessary to give a most exact definition to the term
'simplicity' which denotes the basic units from which social types,
and the classificatory system in sociology, are built-up. Spencer,
although he understood the basis of methodical classification in
general, was unable to give a scientific definition of simplicity and
therefore unable to establish a scientific system of classification:

> Unfortunately, to put this principle into practice it would be
> necessary to begin by defining with precision what is meant
> by a simple society. Not only does Spencer omit this
> definition, but he believes that it is almost impossible to make
> it. The fact is that simplicity, as he understands it, consists
> essentially in a certain crudity of organisation (ibid., pp. 81–2).

Durkheim defines simplicity as follows:

> The definite meaning of the term 'simplicity' can be no other
> than that of the complete absence of parts. A simple society
> is, then, a society which does not include others more simple
> than itself, and which not only at present contains but a single
> segment but also presents no trace of previous segmentation
> (ibid., p. 82).

The basic element, from which all more complex societies, and,
therefore all classifications, are built-up, is the 'horde':

> The 'horde', as we have elsewhere defined it, corresponds
> exactly to this definition. It is a social aggregate which does
> not include, and has never included, within itself any other
> more elementary aggregate, but is directly composed of
> individuals. The latter do not form, within the total group,
> special groups differing from the whole; they are in atomic

juxtaposition. Plainly a simpler society is impossible; the horde is thus the protoplasm of the social realm and, consequently, the natural basis of classification (ibid., p. 83).

More complex societies are merely particular forms of the combination of these irreducible elementary units:

> As many fundamental types will be distinguished as there are ways for the horde to combine and give birth to new societies and for the new societies to combine among themselves (ibid., p. 84).

The basis of classification of social types is the *mode* in which the elements combine to form more complex societies:

> Social phenomena vary not only with the nature of the component elements of society but also with their mode of composition; they will especially be very different according to whether each of the subgroups keeps its local life or is drawn into the general life – in other words according to the degree of concentration (ibid., p. 85).

The classificatory system generates a finite number of types since the different social species are only variations on the theme of the same basic elements and there are morphological-structural limitations of compatibility to the number of types of combination which can be generated by the clustering of elements:

> *We have seen that societies are only combinations of one and the same original society.* Now the same element can combine only with others like it; and the compounds which result can, in their turn, combine only among themselves by following a limited number of combinations, especially when the compound elements are few, as is the case with social segments. The gamut of possible combinations is therefore finite, and consequently most of them will necessarily appear repeatedly (ibid., pp. 86–7, our emphasis).

It should not be thought that Durkheim is proposing a diffusionism in reply to evolutionism. The statement 'societies are only combinations of one and the same original society' means only that all societies have their origin in the combination of simpler forms whose morphological characteristics are identical. The finitude and the repetition of social forms makes possible and requires a morphological branch of the science of sociology; it is not confronted with an infinite variety of unique individuals.[10] Even if a form appears only once, its characteristics are still those of the morphological order, and it remains a species although it includes only one individual.[11] This is the burden of Durkheim's answer to historical relativism.

Social species exist for the same reasons as do biological species:

> There are social species, then, for the same reason that there are biological species. The latter are due to the fact that all organisms are merely varied combinations *within one and the same anatomical unit* (ibid., p. 87, our emphasis).

Social species, like animal species, are the different forms that the original and basic elements of social life take as a result of different environmental pressures, and of different conditions of adaption to those pressures which force those elements to combine together in different modes.[12] These different 'social species' *'are of the morphological order'*; Durkheim's classificatory system is not founded upon any teleology or necessary evolutionary order. The classificatory system thinks the different species as existing in the same space. This space is constituted by the equivalence of the elements which make up the species and the difference of their particular modes of combination. Different forms or species are recognised as variations on a theme; 'societies are only combinations of one and the same original society'. The variations, in the conditions of their appearance, are contingent; they obey no pre-given evolutionary 'Law'. The variations are, at the same time, systematic; they have an order, but it is not an evolutionary order. While the number of social types is finite, it is not necessary that all the possible types exist and be represented by concrete societies. While, 'most of [the types] will necessarily appear repeatedly', it is not the case that the character of this repetition will be that of teleological evolutionism; that is, that each concrete society will, in turn, necessarily pass through each of the successive 'stages' of an evolutionary scheme. The 'species' are not stages; their systematic order is a classificatory and not an evolutionary order. Repetition is a contingent matter; its only necessity stems from the fact that, as the number of species is finite, the 'multitude of historic societies' will include several members of the same species.

The character of the *order* of social species is the character of the classificatory system itself. This order is the product of classificatory *thinking*. It is the classificatory system which brings the particular species together as a system. Durkheim certainly regards classification as a genuine theoretical activity.[13] This is because the order of social types is not an order which is immediately and necessarily given in the real; it is not the order of an evolutionary necessity which arranges the types in the lineality of its progress. Since this order is not directly given it must be constructed and this construction is a task of social science. The classificatory system is not, however, imaginary; it is not a product of purely speculative thinking. It is based on the perception of given realities; the elementary units and the particular species or types, which are combinations of them, exist. As we have seen, morphology is founded on physiology, and, according to Durkheim, the givens which are subject to observation have already been defined in the theory of social facts.

The difference between social and animal species consists in the fact that the characteristics of animal species are fixed by the biological mechanism of heredity which ensures the reproduction of offspring with the same *species* characteristics as their parents:

> In animals there is an exclusive trait which lends to their
> characteristics a fixity and permanence which is not found in
> the social species, namely, the capacity to reproduce (ibid.,
> p. 87).

Heredity preserves the characteristics of the species by a strict biological law; animal species do not respond automatically to each and every environmental pressure. This is because of the 'reserve vitality' which heredity imparts to the organism: There is an internal force, heredity, that keeps them constant in spite of the structural stimuli which oppose it' (ibid., p. 87).[14] Social species lack this 'internal force', the 'reserve vitality' of heredity, and are therefore far more open to the external environmental pressures of the other societies to which they relate and to extra-social factors. Thus the reproduction of a society is almost invariably the birth of a new social type.[15]

In a note to the second edition of the *Rules*, Durkheim makes it quite clear that the relative fixity or permanence of social species

can only be established by a classificatory system which defines
the most basic characteristics as the key characteristics of social
species.[16] If morphological analysis were to concentrate on the
'surface' phenomena of society then it would be the inevitable
consequence that a given individual society might appear to differ
completely in its characteristics in a short period of time, and,
therefore, appear to have changed its species:

> Since its origin, France has passed through very different
> forms of *civilisation*; it began by being agricultural, passed
> to craft industry and to small commerce, then to manufacturing,
> and finally to large scale industry. Now it is impossible to
> admit that the *same collective individuality* can change its
> species three or four times. A species must define itself by
> more constant characteristics (ibid., p. 88, our emphasis).

The characteristics which form the basis of the classification must
be so defined as to offer a considerable measure of stability.
Economic and technical organisation, artistic and scientific culture
are far too variable to form characteristics for such a classification:

> The economic state, technological state, etc., present
> phenomena too unstable and complex to furnish the basis
> of a classification. It is even very probable that the same
> industrial, scientific and artistic *civilisation* can be found in
> *societies* whose heredity constitution is very different. Japan
> may in the future borrow our arts, our industry, even our
> political organisation; it will not cease to be a different *social
> species* from France or Germany (ibid., p. 88, our emphasis).

Durkheim appears to have made a simple confusion in these
passages by pressing the analogy with biology beyond its limits.
Individuals of particular animal species cannot change their species
because these very species' characteristics are part of the condition
of existence of the animal itself. Therefore, it seems Durkheim is
arguing, an individual society cannot change its species without
ceasing to exist as that society. Durkheim appears to have abolished
social development, as we know it. Feudal France and the France
of the Third Republic become one and the same social entity, and
the changes that have occurred in that period are secondary matters
of *civilisation*. This calls to mind the excesses of the English
'constitutional' historical school which traces the origins of the

modern English constitution in the feudal period. However, this
position of Durkheim's is founded on something far deeper than
the mere over-extension of a biological analogy, or a merely conservative and continuist bias; it is rooted in his very conception of
sociology.

For Durkheim, social morphology does indeed depend upon
social physiology, upon the nature of social facts. His social types
are in no sense similar to the structural types of modern sociology
('industrial society', etc.); his types do not define mere complexes
of institutions. Social types are concerned with the essential forms
of social life and not with the mere 'surface' phenomena of *civilisation*. Durkheim's definition of characteristics is not an arbitrary
definition which is based upon the selection of elements which
stress social continuity over and above social change in the interests
of a conservatism. The definition is connected with the very kernel
of his method.

Durkheim's opposition between *civilisation* and *collective
individuality*, his stress upon cultural entities (France, Germany,
Japan), recalls the opposition and emphasis of Tönnies, and the
German historical school. Durkheim is not merely opposing
Kultur to civilisation, or cultural entities to technical and artificial
social relations, in the interests of the recovery of the national
'spirit', the preservation of the 'race', or the romantic rejection of
modern capitalist society, as many of the German conservatives
openly and avowedly did. There are elements of these themes in
the work of Durkheim, an element which is most evident in his
discussions of the disintegrating effects of the competitive capitalist
economy and of the dangers to the moral collectivity of untrammelled individualism. This element is most strongly evident in
such texts as *Professional Ethics and Civic Morals* and *Socialism and
Saint Simon*. These positions, however, have their source in a
logical and not merely an *ideological* system, particularly in the
Rules. We should note that ideologies are not simply positions
which appear in the text by reason of certain 'interests' which are
announced by or which are attributable to its author. The author
and the text are not equivalents and the author's social life and
opinions cannot be the measure of the text. Ideological positions
in a text are the products of a certain form of discourse. Theoretical
texts are not a matter of 'policy'; they are not the continuation of
ideological interests by other means pure and simple. It is in the

logical consequences of his theoretical position that we must seek the source of Durkheim's conception of social types.

The classificatory system, the social morphology that Durkheim proposes in the *Rules* is a continuation of his social physiology. We have seen that all particular social currents and institutions are only more or less 'crystallised' expressions of social life. We have seen that, in the *Rules*, Durkheim lacks a concept of social structure as anything more than a vessel for the collective sentiments.[17] We shall see that his conception of social life is vitalist in character.[18] The whole, for Durkheim, is a real entity or essence which exists distinct from its parts, and that the parts are *pars totalis*, that is, particular expressions of the whole which in their particular existence reflect its essence. Social life is an entity and the whole is the effective presence of this vital principle.

From this conception of social 'physiology' follows social morphology. Societies which include only more 'simple' societies can only be a product of the combination of these original and irreducible elements of social life: 'The horde is thus the *protoplasm* of the social realm and, consequently, the natural basis of classification' (ibid., p. 83, our emphasis). The elements of social life are essential, since they exist unconditionally. They cannot be reduced to their non-social components, nor can they be defined as certain effects of the *organisation* of these components, since they have no internal organisation. The notion of the horde as the '*protoplasm* of the social realm', as the essential irreducible and indivisible elementary matter of society, is essential to Durkheim's classificatory system. The horde is without parts or organisation, and all social structures are merely different combinations of hordes. Thus all more complex social forms are merely elaborations of this given essential element. The character of the horde is unproblematical; it is given, unconditional and impenetrable. The character of all more complex forms is unproblematical; they are built up by the joining together of hordes. The character of the 'givenness' of social facts is thereby preserved in the theory of social types.

All more complex social organisations are combinations of hordes. Organisation is therefore an external connection of these elements. The formation of hordes into complex wholes must be the product of factors external to the horde. Complex social wholes lack internal 'reserve vitality' since their organisation depends on external linkages of their elements, unlike the internal unity of the organs or characteristics of an animal. Larger units formed by the fusion of hordes are, in effect, larger hordes. Wholes formed by the combination of hordes are a unity because of the commerce between the hordes on the one hand, and, on the other, of the creation of a more general 'conscience collective' which is reflected in the particular consciousnesses of the elements. The unity of complex wholes is a unity of external interaction and mutual coercion of the elements, and, a 'mental' unity of the more general collective consciousness (a unity which is itself *external* to each element but which is reflected in its own consciousness).[19] In the last instance coercion, of both an objective and a moral kind, not only binds the individuals to the collective, but the parts of the collective to each other.

The Durkheimian social whole has two aspects; it is built up by the linkage of the irreducible elements and it is bound together by the moral unity of the 'higher' collective consciousness. The whole is either the relation of its pre-given parts in response to necessity external to them or an essential and spiritual unity which is the protoplasmic unity of the original parts writ large. This latter aspect becomes increasingly dominant in Durkheim's sociology; notably in the *Forms*. To conceive the whole in any other way than as an irreducible essence or a combination of such essences is impossible in Durkheim's sociology for it poses a challenge to the givenness of its constituents and the form of its organisation. It poses a problem which the foundation-expression relation of Durkheim's theory of social facts cannot think. It requires the posing of the question of a rationalism; which parts, institutions or activities compose the whole, and how is it that they are articulated together into a whole? It removes from sociology its realm of given facts for it requires that their very character as facts be specified by theory.

It is by posing the problem of social types in this way that we can begin to uncover the theoretical source of that extraordinary 'fable' by which mechanical solidarity is transformed into organic solidarity in another and earlier text of Durkheim's, *The Division of Labour in Society*.* The analysis of the theoretical structure of the *Rules* enables us to uncover the problem from which this 'fable' is built up. In the *Division* the 'fable' has neither time nor location; the scene that the 'fable' recites is an imaginary scene, a

* Hereafter this text be cited as *Division*.

construction in thought whereby Durkheim thinks out what is essential in this transition.

In the *Rules* the epistemological status of the horde is left as an open question by Durkheim:

> Once this notion of the horde . . . has been established –
> whether it be conceived as a historic reality or as a hypothesis
> of science – we have the *support* necessary for constructing the
> complete scale of social types (ibid., p. 84, our emphasis).

But this 'openness' of the question is quite spurious; the horde is a theoretical device, a theoretical *support* on the basis of which the classification system can be generated. The existence of the notion of the horde is essential to the system whatever its status as 'historic reality' or 'hypothesis'. If it is not an 'historic reality' it still remains a theoretical necessity. The horde is a 'fiction' (it is not illegitimate because it is a fiction); a fiction similar in character to the fictions of the natural man and the social contract by which Rousseau thought the necessity of sociality for man's existence. Durkheim's praise of this theoretical mechanism in *Montesquieu and Rousseau* is not accidental, for the mechanism is similar to Durkheim's own mode of thinking in the *Division*.[20]

The 'fable', which is the kernel of Durkheim's explanation in the *Division*, is the primary means by which he explains the development of organic solidarity out of mechanical solidarity. Mechanical solidarity is incapable of generating any other social form from within itself:

> We saw how the organised structure, and, thus, the division
> of labour, develop as the segmental structure disappears.
> Hence, either this disappearance is the cause of this
> development or the development is the cause of this
> disappearance. The latter hypothesis is inadmissible, for we
> know that the segmental arrangement is an insurmountable
> obstacle to the division of labour, and must have disappeared
> at least partially for the division of labour to appear. The
> latter can appear only in proportion to the disappearance of
> the segmental structure (Durkheim, 1964, p. 256).

As a form of society with identical and morally equivalent segments, and without internal sources of division, mechanical solidarity is necessarily a static and fixed form:

But the disappearance of this type can have this consequence (the loss of individuality of the social segments) for only one reason. That is because it gives rise to a relationship between individuals who were separated, or at least, a more intimate relationship than there was. Consequently, there is an exchange of movements between parts of the social mass which, until then, had no effect on one another. The greater the development of the cellular system, the more are our relations enclosed within the limits of the cell to which we belong. There are, as it were, moral gaps between the various segments (ibid., pp. 256–7).

The sources of transformation are external to the form of solidarity and they force, by reason of 'environmental' pressures, adaptive changes on the social organism. The increase of 'dynamic density', the increasing concentration of social life and the 'struggle for survival' this forces upon the undifferentiated segments and individuals of the mechanically solidaristic society, stem from factors external to the form of solidarity itself. Concentration has its source in the realm of 'civilisation' and technique which creates a greater and more concentrated population in both density and volume.[21] The causes of this concentration of social life are not simply pressures of increased biological reproduction; Durkheim's theory does not rely on a 'law' of population.[22] But 'civilisation' is not, as we have seen, a primary social factor; it is something which is external to the essential form of society. The effect of this 'environmental' pressure on social solidarity is to destroy the forms of coercion and regulation by society of its extra-social constituents and conditions, individuals.[23] The institution of a division of labour, the distribution of social segments and individuals into different functions, reduces the threats that moral density poses to organised social life. It is an adaptive response to 'environmental' pressures which handles the dangers posed by the 'struggle for survival' between individuals and social segments to the control of individuals and sub-units by the 'conscience collective'.

It is necessary for Durkheim to go outside the unity of expression and identity of mechanical solidarity to find the sources and pressures of this social transformation. This is a 'special' explanation quite different from the explanation of the function or place of any social fact within the social whole. The Durkheimian theory of 'social facts' explains why those facts are necessary parts of a common field. The theory of solidarity, the province of 'normal' explanations of social facts, cannot explain the transformation of the form of solidarity itself, since its theoretical function is to render that solidarity essential and necessary. The 'special' explanation places great stress on the effect of those factors of 'civilisation' on the individuals who compose a society and are by no means entirely social individuals with entirely social needs.

The division of labour and organic solidarity produces a more complex relation between 'society' and extra-social forces. The resolution of the problems of increasing dynamic density is achieved only at a price. Organic solidarity does not provide the social organism with an effective 'reserve vitality' any more than does the mechanical form. Rather, it tends to weaken the very order of the moral collective and moral coercion. The interdependence of individuals, their objective necessity one to another, tends to become preponderant and the moral unity of the 'conscience collective' secondary. The division of labour installs the forces of 'civilisation' in a more central place in the social order of organic solidarity than in that of mechanical solidarity. 'Civilisation' becomes an important component of solidarity itself. The organically solidaristic social order, by instituting a diversity in the social positions of individuals, opens the door to the forces of individual-isation. The 'conscience collective' becomes increasingly generalised in relation to the positions specific individuals occupy and the values of individualism become a significant element of the collective representations.[24] Individuals become increasingly separated from the collective moral controls of the collective sentiments, and these sentiments become less effective in controlling, and less effectively mediated to, the individual.

Organic solidarity, in its extreme forms, generates the pathological forms of unrestrained individualism and the anomic division of labour. It threatens, in these pathological forms, the very bond between the collective consciousness and the individual.[25] Hence the necessity of binding the individual to the collective order through the medium of social sub-groups which express in a concrete form the morality of the more general 'conscience collective'. In *Professional Ethics and Civic Morals* Durkheim proposes the mechanism of occupational groups of a morally binding character which strike at the very roots of anomic technicism in the sphere of economic activity.[26] The occupational group thus becomes a *pars totalis* which is a specific expression of the collective sentiments of the social whole. By this means the dangers of a pathological individualism, of the failure of society to regulate and coerce the extra-social element within it, individuals, are overcome. The unity of expression of the social whole, a unity present in its most primitive form in the horde, is thus restored on a new level.

Durkheim's social morphology, to the mind of the contemporary sociologist a rather quaint doctrine, is no mere by-product of the more curious by-ways of the nineteenth century 'mind'. It is systematically connected with his general epistemology and his theory of the nature of social facts. Durkheim's definition of his object requires such a conception of the nature of the different forms of society.

Individualism and Holism: Purpose, Function and Social Facts

Humanism and Anti-Humanism[1]

> Most sociologists think they have accounted for phenomena
> once they have shown how they are useful, what role they
> play, reasoning as if facts existed from the point of view of
> this role and with no other determining cause than the
> sentiment, clear or confused, of the services they are called to
> render (Durkheim, 1966, p. 89).

It will be recalled that Durkheim conceives social facts as 'givens'
'subject to observation' which exist in and of themselves. Social
facts require no *raison d'être* in human terms; it is vain for human
reason to question the existence of these facts, for social facts are
realities, no more and no less, than the facts to which physics and
chemistry apply themselves. Durkheim's critique of explanations
of social facts which confine themselves to divining the purpose or
end these facts serve is a critique of the anthropocentric and
rationalist conception of society from which they derive.

Durkheim recognises that, in this conception, the ends social
facts are presumed to serve are human ends and that the measure
of the utility of these facts is that of their utility for human individuals. This conception of sociology represents the needs, desires
and wills of human subjects as the condition of existence of social
facts; all social facts must therefore have a human utility or be
unreal or irrational. But, just as water does not turn into wine
because we desire it, or drought cease because it is inimical to
human life, so the forms of social organisation do not necessarily

change, or modify their effects, to meet the desires and needs of their human subjects:

> But this method confuses two very different questions. To
> show how a fact is useful is not to explain how it originated
> or why it is what it is. The uses which it serves presuppose
> the specific properties characterising it but do not create
> them. The need we have of things cannot give them existence,
> nor can it confer their specific nature upon them. It is to causes
> of another sort that they owe their existence (ibid., p. 90).

This separation of the functions certain phenomena may perform for man and the causes of the existence of those phenomena follows logically from Durkheim's conception of all facts as *things*, but it also presupposes the separation of the social and the individual as distinct domains of reality; a separation in which the social is the superior domain. The social realm is external to the individual, just as nature is; it may or may not fulfil his needs or grant his wishes, but it exists prior to and independent of those needs or wishes and so it cannot be created or destroyed by them. There is a discontinuity between the two realms:

> But since each one of them (social facts) is a force superior to
> the individual, and since it has a *separate* existence, it is not
> true that merely by willing to do so may we call them into
> being (ibid., p. 90, our emphasis).

Social facts owe their existence to causes within their own distinct domain of reality and to no external cause whatever, be it individual wills or cosmic forces.[2] If social facts do meet human needs or fulfil human purposes this relation between the two realms can be no more than a contingent and external relation, and never a necessary one, except in so far as it stems from causes internal to the social realm itself.

Durkheim's position is not reducible to the banalities of the superiority of the 'group' to the 'individual'; his separation of the two domains as distinct realms of reality, distinct domains of nature, is central to his conception of the sciences.[3] Durkheim's position is a sociological *anti-humanism*; it insists that the human subject is neither the author of society nor a purely social being. This anti-humanist position is central to his critique of the anthropocentric fallacy and the teleological forms of explanation which follow from it. Durkheim must oppose any anthropologically founded sociology; his general epistemology and his theory of social facts are in direct contradiction with such a conception of sociology. Likewise anthropological theories are rigidly opposed to the Durkheimian conception; as his phenomenological, existentialist or personalist critics conceive it, Durkheim's conception is 'sociologistic' and 'reifying'.[4] But just as Durkheim's conception is not the product of a misanthropy but of an epistemology, so the anthropological conception is not the product of love for mankind and it also has a theoretical source. The unity of human ends and social existence can only be the product of a theoretical conception which makes social nature an extension of human nature and sociology an extension of anthropology. And, since, except for the most panglossian of doctrines, this unity can never at any given moment be a perfect and unproblematic unity, the anthropological conception generally entails as a consequence an evolutionist or historicist conception of society. It is this mechanism of the necessary future, or of the gradual realisation of human nature, that equates human needs or purposes and their fulfilment in social existence.

Durkheim's critique of the 'sociology' of Comte and Spencer, and, by implication all previous 'sociology',[5] is no piecemeal or *ad hoc* critique, but a confrontation of two quite different conceptions of the object, and therefore the method, of sociology.[6] Durkheim's critique is a rejection of these anthropological and evolutionist sociologies from a consistent anti-humanist and anti-rationalist position. It is a critique of the reductionism, the reductionism with respect to his own realist conception of the object of his science as a 'thing' *sui generis*, which humanism installs in the realm of the social. Durkheim traces the effects of this conception in relation to his own object; he examines the logical consequences and errors of this conception as a form of discourse, and he analyses its source.

If it is accepted that social facts exist because they are the product of human wills, and that they fulfil the ends to which these wills are directed, then our explanation of social phenomena is by no means complete; it is necessary to investigate the nature of these wills in themselves. Human wills are as varied as the individuals who will; human ends are as varied as the individuals who project them and the individual circumstances which give rise to them:

> Where purpose reigns, there reigns also a more or less wide
> contingency; for there are no ends, and even fewer means,
> which necessarily control all men, even when it is assumed
> that they are placed in the same circumstances (ibid., p. 94).

The effect of this multiplicity of human wills could only be the
multiplicity of the social forms which they produce and the
multiplicity of the social forms which function to fulfil the ends of
which these wills are the supposed servants:

> If, then, it were true that historic development took place in
> terms of ends clearly or obscurely felt, social facts would
> present the most infinite diversity; and all comparison should
> be almost impossible (ibid., p. 94).

The result of this multiplicity of ends would be an infinite series of
discrete facts, each so different in its origin and substance as to be
incommensurable with another. Social species could not exist. The
average social conditions, the collective resultant of individual acts
each directed by a common collective force, could not exist.
Normality in society would have no basis and pathology could not
be defined because of the absence of the norm. Social life would
present the spectacle of the most anarchic diversity.[7]

But, argues Durkheim, this an absurdity which contradicts the
logic of the facts; social facts exist and they are ordered phenomena which present themselves as definite regularities which are
comparable and classifiable:

> To be sure, the *external* events which constitute the *superficial*
> part of social life vary from one people to another, just as
> each individual has his own history, although the bases of
> physical and moral organisation are the same for all. But
> when one *comes into contact* with social phenomena, one is, on
> the contrary, surprised by the astonishing regularity with
> which they occur under the same circumstances (ibid., p. 94,
> our emphasis).

> This wide diffusion of collective forms would be inexplicable
> if purpose or final causes had the predominant place in
> sociology that is attributed to them (ibid., p. 95).

We have already noted Durkheim's opposition to relativism and
we have seen how this social morphology is founded upon the

epistemological necessities of his theory of social facts. But we should also note that the above statement of the existence of regularities of social organisation is only as well founded or as unfounded as his theory of social facts. Durkheim's answer to relativism depends on the notion that these regularities are 'givens' 'subject to observation'. That is, it depends upon the acceptance of Durkheim's realist contention, that the existence of these regularities is a matter of perception.[8] Doubtless, most contemporary sociologists accept, as a matter of the practical common sense of their discipline, the existence of social types, but it is not a logically unquestionable contention.[9] On what basis is it evident that certain 'events' are 'external' to the essential constitution of social facts and therefore 'superficial'? On the basis that 'one comes into contact with social phenomena' which present themselves in this way as givens. Consistent relativist positions maintain exactly the opposite, that what is given to perception is an innumerable variety of unique phenomena. Durkheim's answer to relativism is, in this respect, an answer that is acceptable only to those who have already rejected the premises of relativism itself. It is Durkheim's opposition to theory, his insistence that the nature and order of the social realm is given to perception, that leads him into an impasse in the face of positions which are consistent but which operate from different premises about the nature of social existence. This impasse is a very real one, for Durkheim can only state the adverse effects of the opposing conception in relation to his own position. It is not possible, as Durkheim wishes to do, to refer these opposed conceptions to an independent tribunal; to the 'facts' themselves. The facts are an ambiguous arbiter in the case because the case itself is premissed on the predominance and priority of certain types of facts, and both positions can uncover ample empirical 'confirmation' for their premises.

Relativisim is only one possible variant and theoretical effect of the humanist or anthropocentric conception of sociology. Evolutionism was the primary target of Durkheim's criticisms and these social evolutionist theories were by no means relativist. Durkheim's criticisms of evolutionism are far sounder than his critique of relativism, since, in effect, they are confined to the form of discourse and the logic of this position. Durkheim confines his critique to the 'psychological' variants of evolutionism, that is, to a theory which seeks the origin and direction of the evolutionary tendency in the constitution of man; in an evolutionary process which is the product of human acts and intentions which realise human ends, and in which these ends are the necessary consequence of a specific nature of humanity. Such theories, Durkheim argues, are unquestionably teleological. This form of evolutionism was present, Durkheim maintains, in the work of the two most influential representatives of such theories in nineteenth-century sociology, Comte and Spencer. Durkheim does not deal in any direct or significant way with other variants of evolutionism. Biologistic theories are obvious non-starters in the question of *social* evolution, which, even in its simplest sense, must entail the development of 'higher' and more complex forms of technique, intellectual culture, and of man's relations to his kind. Biological needs and man's biological nature cannot generate a process of social evolution because the basic biological needs of man can be met in the most simple and primitive socio-technical organisation as well as they can in the highest and most complex. Durkheim criticises the notion of innate human attributes and the validity of race as a factor in social explanation,[10] this is the closest he comes to dealing with biologistic theories of social evolution.[11] Durkheim never directly deals with the Hegelian theory of history, with the theory of the historical process as an effect of a transcendental subject, but his attitude to such historicist conceptions is clear from certain of his remarks on Comte.[12] Durkheim's critique of Comte and Spencer contains the outlines of a rejection of all evolutionist and historicist conceptions.

If we accept that social evolution had its origin in the 'psychological' constitution of man then we have to presume the internality of the causes and of the direction of that process itself in the human mind. It is within man himself that the ends and intentions which are realised in the evolutionary process must be contained if that process is to be a necessary effect of human nature. An essential constitution, already pre-given, in which is stored the whole future history of humanity is the necessary condition of such a theory:

If social evolution really had its origin in the psychological constitution of man, its origin seems to be completely obscure. For we would then have to admit that its motivating force is some inner spring of human nature. But what could this be? Is it some sort of instinct Comte speaks of, which impels man more and more to express his nature? But that is begging the question and explaining progress by an innate 'tendency toward progress' – a metaphysical entity of the very existence of which there is no demonstration (ibid., p. 109).

Such an inherent teleology is absurd and unthinkable:

For, unless we postulate a truly providential and pre-established harmony, we cannot admit that man has carried with him from the beginning – potentially ready to be awakened at the call of circumstances – all the intentions which conditions were destined to demand in the course of human evolution (ibid., p. 92).

But such is the logical necessity of any attempt to explain human development as a systematic process which represents the realisation of the necessary ends of man. If such a harmony between human intentions and human needs under different conditions does not exist, if intention is neither necessary nor spontaneous, then intentions must arise as a result of circumstances which are neither foreseen nor created by these intentions, and the causes of those circumstances cannot therefore be given in the intentions themselves:

Apart from the fact that they cannot, in any case, make something out of nothing, their actual intervention, whatever may be its effects, can take place only by means of efficient causes. A deliberate intention can contribute, even in its limited way, to the production of a new phenomenon only if it has itself been newly formed or if it is itself a result of some transformation of a previous intention (ibid., p. 92).

It is necessary to explain the causes of those circumstances, and the role they play in the resultant effects, apart from any reference to intentions. The product or resultant in which intention may play a part is therefore not reducible to the intention itself and exists apart from it. Thus, even if Spencer's conception of a tendency toward greater happiness with the progress of civilisation were true, it would still not be possible to ascribe this tendency to the motivating urge of humanity toward greater happiness except on the condition of accepting a purely teleological explanation.

Durkheim is arguing that such theories represent a case of *histoire raisonnaire*; a construction of a pattern or tendency in

events, perhaps real and perhaps not, and the motivating force of
this tendency is ascribed to the direction or end which has been
divined in it:

> Thus [Comte's] . . . famous law of the three stages of history
> has no relation of causality; if it is true, it is, and can be, only
> empirical. It is a bird's-eye view of the elapsed history of the
> human species. It is entirely arbitrary to consider the third
> stage as the definitive state of humanity (ibid., p. 119).

The tendency or law thus established is not a causal law for it can
only be an effect, an effect which is produced and reproduced by
conditions existing concurrently in relation one to another. *Past*
events can have no causal effects in the present and they cannot
explain the existence or persistence of present phenomena:

> The principal causes of historical development would not be
> found, then, among the concomitant circumstances; they
> would all be in the past. . . . The present events of social life
> would originate not in the present state of society but in prior
> events from historical precedents; and sociological
> explanations would consist exclusively in connecting the
> present with the past.
> . . . But it is impossible to conceive how the stage which
> civilisation has reached at a given moment could be the
> determining cause of the subsequent stage. . . . We understand
> that the progress achieved at a given epoch . . . makes new
> progress possible; but how does it predetermine it? (ibid., p.
> 117).

The pattern we divine in history can at best be only a rational
reconstruction or *account* of events; it is therefore logically inadmissible to ascribe to this pattern its own causality. To attribute
causality to such a pattern, a pattern which spans different time
periods and different conditions, can only mean that it is attributed
to something which exists through those periods and conditions,
humanity, as an entity, or a transcendental subject. It involves a
construction of history as a biography of the being whose successive
acts are the products of its ends and will and have a common
source as acts of that being.

The logical absurdities and errors of evolutionism are no
accident; they are the necessary effects of the psychologistic or

teleological method that follows from an anthropological conception of sociology:

> At the same time that it is teleological, the method of
> explanation generally followed by sociologists is essentially
> psychological. These two tendencies are interconnected with
> one another. In fact, if society is only a system of means
> instituted by men to attain certain ends, these ends can only
> be individual, for only individuals could have existed before
> society (ibid., p. 97).

The 'humanity' of Comte and other evolutionists can only exist if it is displaced into the individuals who compose it; humanity is a being that cannot exist in and of itself. Such evolutionist conceptions share a common method with more limited psychologistic and individualistic explanations of particular social institutions and practices. Social facts and society as a whole, are, for this humanist conception, a product of individual needs and wills:

> From the individual, then, have emanated the needs and
> desires determining the formation of societies; and, if it is
> from him that all comes, it is necessarily by him that all must
> be explained. Moreover, there are in societies only individual
> consciousnesses; in these, then, is found the source of all
> social evolution (ibid., pp. 97–8).

Thus it follows, as the necessary consequence of the anthropological conception, that sociology is merely a derived branch of psychology, that sociological explanations are reducible to explanations in terms of individual actions and that these actions derive from the general constitution of the human mind:

> Hence, sociological laws can only be a corollary of the more
> general laws of psychology; the ultimate explanation of
> collective life will consist in showing how it emanates from
> human nature in general, whether the collective life be
> deduced from human nature directly and without previous
> observation or whether it must be related to human nature
> after the latter has been analysed (ibid., p. 98).

The object of sociology becomes humanity or Man:

> 'Since', says he [Comte], 'the social phenomenon, conceived
> in its totality, is fundamentally *only a simple development of*

*humanity, without the creation of any special faculties
whatsoever . . .'* (ibid., p. 98, emphasis in original).

Thus humanity, which must necessarily be displaced into the
individual, reappears as the condition of existence of the individual.

The object of sociology, as Durkheim conceives it, is abolished by
such a conception. The existence of society itself becomes problematic, and, if that existence is accepted, it must be explained in a
manner consistent with the reductionist method.[13] Such a conception of sociology entails, at least logically even if the proposition
is not deduced,[14] a well-known and well-rehearsed 'fable', the
pre-social existence of humanity. This 'fable' is generated by the
theoretical priority of the object, Man, in this conception. This
fable may take two forms: either, that society is an unfortunate
necessity forced on humanity by its inability to reconcile the con-
flicting demands of individual wills in the pre-social state, or, that
man is *by nature* spontaneously social and needs society.[15] These
two doctrines, two different conceptions of the generation of
society from the nature of the individual, have a long history. It is
a history which begins in the seventeenth century, the former with
the critical political philosophers, the latter with the philosophers
of natural law and the political economists. Durkheim maintains
that the 'sociology' of Comte and Spencer is a continuation of the
latter tradition.

Durkheim describes the *source* of these theoretical positions, and
all humanist conceptions by means of his theory of ideology.
Humanism and anthropology are effects of the spontaneous
idealism of the experience of the human subject. Humanist conceptions derive from the fundamental misrecognition of ideology
in which the subject recognises the world as an effect of his will and
thought. In both cases of the 'fable', the former and the latter, the
source of these anthropocentric conceptions is an aspect of the
social realm itself apprehended in a partial and distorted form. The
former doctrines stem from spontaneous representations of the
reality of social constraint, the latter from the recognition that
social life is natural and spontaneous. In both cases these anti-
sociological doctrines are an intellectual elaboration of an ideological representation of the superior being of society by the
subjects who exist in relation to it and for whom it forms an external

world of experience and perception. Anthropological thought is
merely a rationalised form of the common-sense experience of
social subjects. Theoretical anthropocentrism is a mirror-image of
the anthropocentrism of ideology. As such these doctrines are, in
their very character, stamped with the traces of society; these
doctrines, apparently so anti-sociological, are living proofs and
confirmations of the effectivity of the social being on its human
subjects.[16]

In opposition to this 'fable' Durkheim insists that, as far as man
is concerned, society ever-already exists:

> Moreover, as all societies are born of other societies without
> a break in continuity, we can be certain that in the entire
> course of social evolution there has not been a single time
> when individuals determined by careful deliberation whether
> or not they would enter into the collective life or into one
> collective life rather than another (ibid., p. 105).

Man himself cannot be imagined without social attributes except in
his specifically individual aspect, in terms of his biological and
psychological constitution.[17] Man in this specifically individual
aspect is not reducible to society; the individual is a distinct reality
external to society. But no concrete individual ever existed prior to
or in isolation from society. The 'fable' of the pre-social existence
of humanity is a fable and a fable which serves only to reproduce
elements of social life as attributes of man. The theoretical necessity of humanism, the theoretical priority of man to society, is
contrary to the order and priority of *things* in nature. Humanism is
an idealism.

Individual and Social Effectivity

Durkheim's critique of humanist doctrines is not based upon an
absolute sociologism which reduces the individual to an effect of
society, but, rather, upon the separation of the individual and the
social as two discrete realms external one to another. We have
already seen that the existence of the individual external to society
is necessary for Durkheim's conception of society itself and that
the interaction of social organisation and human needs is a crucial
part of his explanation of the transformation from one form of

solidarity to another. In this section of the *Rules*, however, Durkheim adds a most revealing passage on the nature of the relation between the two realms:[18]

> If the collective life is not derived from individual life, the two are nevertheless closely related; if the latter cannot explain the former, it can at least facilitate its explanation. First, as we have shown, *it is indisputable that social facts are produced by action on psychological factors. In addition, this very action is similar to that which takes place in each individual consciousness* and by which are transformed the primary elements (sensations, reflexes, instincts) of which it is originally constituted. Not without reason has it been said that the self is itself a society, by the same right as the organism, although in another way; and long ago psychologists showed the great importance of the factor of association in the explanation of mental activity. (ibid., p. 111, our emphasis).

Previously we have seen Durkheim maintain that the decisive proof of the existence and the power of society is the constraint and coercion it exercises on individuals. This constraining force takes two forms: first, social life becomes embodied in material realities, it becomes an external world constraining the individual in the same way as physical nature does; second, the force of direct and primitive coercion against individuals whose acts or sentiments offend the collective conscience. Now is this coercion a purely external force acting upon the individual which he learns from experience to fear and which he avoids offending through prudence hardened into habit? Such would be the individual's reaction to a dangerous but predictable wild animal. The collective conscience is not a creature of this kind. However much the individual may *experience* society as a purely external and punitive force, it is a moral and rational being whose relation to the individual is much more complex.

The above passage enables us to see with greater clarity the form of relation to and action of the collective upon individuals. It is the interaction of distinct domains which have the same general nature; society and the individual are not as utterly different in character as man and the wild beast. Society and the individual share the same essence of being domains of consciousness.[19] It is thus possible to understand the mode of effectivity of the collective

upon the individual. It is through the insertion of the representations of the collective consciousness into the individual consciousness, through the possibility of the collective representations being
recognised by the individual and being transformed by the mental
activity of the individual into recognisable ideas and suggestions,
that the social realm is able to act upon the individual realm.
'Social facts are produced by action on psychological factors' and
'this very action is similar to that which takes place in each individual consciousness.' If social facts were 'things' of the same order
as stones or thunderstorms their effectivity in respect of the individual could only be a purely *physical* effectivity. Social facts are
internalised in the individual consciousness and they have a life in
the individual because they possess an aspect which corresponds
to the nature of the individual; they are facts of consciousness.
Thus a relation between the *laws* of psychology and sociology is
possible; they are both laws of consciousness which explain
different locations and forms of consciousness of differing causal
effectivity. It is thus possible to understand the strict parallelism
that exists in the separation of the two realms.

It would be a mistake, however, to imagine that this parallelism
provides a bridge by which the two realms may be united. The
relation of the two realms is contingent in that neither is the necessary cause of the other. Both realms represent certain necessary
conditions of existence each for the other; the individual is the
necessary material embodiment of the social, and the social must
not destroy the conditions of existence of the individual. But the
character of the relation between them is determined by causes
internal to each realm itself; each realm has a specific nature and
specific causes of existence which are not given it by the other. The
relation remains an external and problematic relation, and it is in
the space of the discontinuity between the two realms that most of
the problems of the social order arise and also the vicissitudes
which beset the individual.

The individual realm is a *given* to sociology; it must accept it as
an external facticity which cannot be incorporated in its own. The
internal characterisation of this external but related realm is not
the task of sociology but the task of a distinct science, psychology.
Durkheim accepts psychology's definition of its object, its methods
and its mode of explanation as a datum *given* to sociology. Thus
Durkheim's *sociological* anti-humanism, his rejection of humanist

reductions of the object of sociology, is not a thoroughgoing anti-humanism. Durkheim does not question or overthrow the category 'Man' as such, he merely refuses to found sociology on an anthropology. 'Man' remains within his own sphere. Durkheim does not argue that the individual or psychological realm is *unreal*. We have seen that ideology is unreal, but the unreality of ideology is a function of perception and interpretation. The same psychic laws operate in the case of false and true recognitions of reality. Ideology concerns a specific kind of *relation* to the real, and not an essentially ideological and unreal subject. Thus Durkheim's rejection of the psychologistic character of anthropological explanation is not a rejection of all psychology. Far from it; it is an enthusiastic acceptance of the now 'objective' and 'empirical' psychology of the latter part of the nineteenth century. This new psychology escapes the rationalism and speculation of earlier anthropological conceptions, but it retains the same object as those conceptions, man's consciousness and reason. It is a continuation of humanism in a scientistic form.[20] Durkheim's anti-humanism is a rejection of anthropology's claims in respect of his own sphere, but the humanist conception of man as a being of consciousness, separated into its own given realm, is central to his conception of sociology.

Social Needs and Social Functions

Thus far, we have dealt with Durkheim's separation of function and cause as a separation of the functions social facts perform for individuals, which must necessarily be varied and relative, and the causes of existence of these facts, which, by reason of the principle of determinism, must be singular and constant. Teleological explanations of social facts are wrong because individual wills are insufficient to bring social facts into being to fulfil the ends they suppose. But are the functions of social facts confined to meeting individual or human needs? No, they are not; the social organism also has its own needs:

> *The determining cause of a social fact should be sought among the social facts preceding it and not among the states of the individual consciousness.* Moreover, we see quite readily that all the foregoing applies to the determining of the function as well as the cause of social phenomena. The function of a social

fact cannot but be social, i.e., it consists of the production of socially useful effects. To be sure, it may and does happen that it also serves the individual. But this happy result is not its immediate cause. . . . *The function of a social fact ought always to be sought in relation to some social end* (ibid., pp. 110–11, emphasis in original).

We use the word 'function', in preference to 'end' or 'purpose', precisely because social phenomena do not generally exist for the useful results they produce. We must determine whether there is a correspondence between the fact under consideration and the general needs of the social organism, and in what this correspondence consists, without occupying ourselves with whether it has been intentional or not (ibid., p. 95).

It is not the case that 'social phenomena do not generally exist for the useful results they produce' because these results merely concern human individuals, or, that, in respect of its own needs, the will of the collective being is insufficient to fulfil them. The separation of function and cause is a rigid separation. It is based on Durkheim's general epistemology. Like Bernard, Durkheim insists that there can be no necessary relation between a function and an organisation:[21]

It is, moreover, a proposition true in sociology, as in biology, that the organ is independent of its function – in other words, while remaining the same, it can serve different ends. The causes of its existence are, then, independent of the ends it serves (ibid., p. 91).

If the function a social organ performed were its cause of existence, since it is possible that the organ may serve, successively, different ends or several ends at once, then we would have to admit that a single phenomenom could have several causes or be due to different causes at different times. This contradicts the very nature of determinism and would abolish causal explanations in sociology.

Moreover, social facts are in their nature neither purposive nor projective. These facts are results or effects of the action of the 'conscience collective'. The 'conscience collective' is not teleological'; it is not teleological, even in the only sense in which it is legitimate to consider the individual consciousness teleological, that is, in its aspect of making plans for the future, having wishes, and striving to accomplish them. The 'conscience collective' is *regulative* in its action; it controls, coerces and limits individual thought and behaviour. Society is not a being which lives through time independent of its material embodiments, individuals; it lives *through* them and through its effects on them. *Past* social relations cannot affect present social relations – the continuing effectivity of the collective consciousness is a result of its being reproduced and of its conditions of existence being secured within each successive set of existing conditions. Society may have 'needs', but these needs are only met on the basis of certain conditions and these conditions are not a product of these needs. The existence of the social realm is not guaranteed; societies may exist but this is due neither to the human need for them nor to their own needs.

'Survivals' are a further proof of the separation of function and cause; institutions, practices and representations may continue to exist long after their functions have ceased and without new ones because they are reproduced through habit and no other force has been engendered sufficient to cause their disappearance. There is in this question of survivals, however, the basis of a definite link between function and cause:

> Indeed, if the usefulness of a fact is not the cause of its existence, it is *generally* necessary that it be *useful* in order that it may maintain itself. For the fact that it is not useful suffices to mark it harmful, since in that case it *costs effort* without bringing in any returns. If, then, the majority of social phenomena had this parasitic character, the budget of the organism would have a deficit and social life would be impossible (ibid., p. 97, our emphasis).

There are two possible explanations of this curious passage. First, that the burden of useless facts makes the reproduction of social life more elaborate and difficult; in particular, it overloads the institutions and individuals who are the transmission belts by which such reproduction takes place. Second, that it undermines the regulative basis of social life in that it leaves a large measure of doubt as to the representations and practices which are necessary to be upheld and followed, and those which are 'superficial' and 'external' to the essential constitution of society. Thus the accumulation of functionless social facts breaks down the distinction

between the normal and the pathological; it undermines the basis
and givenness of normality itself. Such societies encumbered by
such an accumulation of dead and sclerosed tissue are morbid and
ritualistic; they undermine the mechanisms of the regulation of
individual behaviour and complexify the problems of the reproduction of social forms to an impossible degree. Social facts therefore
appear to be 'useful', in so far as they contribute to the survival of
the society, and 'harmful', in so far as they are inimical to it.[22] The
dangers to survival posed by these harmful social facts appear to
centre on the question of society's reproduction and its relation to
individuals. Its cohesion at a given moment in time does not appear
to be problematic. Consequently Durkheim's statement that:

> It is necessary to show how the phenomena comprising it
> combine in such a way as to put society in harmony with
> itself and with the environment external to it (ibid., p. 97).

is somewhat ingenuous since, in its 'normal' state, society's
'harmony with itself' is given.

This is confirmed by the fact that at no point does Durkheim
define what the 'needs' of society in general are in any concrete
sense. Doubtless, this is something of a blessing to a generation of
sociologists who have suffered from a surfeit of 'functional pre-
requisites'. But this absence is indicative of a general aspect of
Durkheim's theoretical system we have noted several times before.
It is in fact impossible for him to specify these 'needs' because he
has no genuine concepts of social structure and also because the
attempt to do so must expose and undermine the character of the
'conscience collective', its existence as an essence in the mode of
expression, and its theoretical role in the reproduction of the
'given' as a necessary given.

Individualism and Holism:
Vitalism and the Social Milieu

The Law of the Transformation of Things

We saw above (pp. 136–46) that in his critique of the humanist conception of the object of sociology Durkheim denounces the psychologistic reductionism inherent in that conception; a reductionism which, he claims, inverts the given order of relations in nature. Humanism reduces sociology to an extension or variant of psychology. So far Durkheim's critique has remained on the familiar ground of his realist epistemology and on the firmer ground of his analysis of the teleological form of explanation which is part and parcel of the humanist discourse. But in chapter 5 Durkheim also confronts a variant of reductionism which presents a more serious threat to his position and forces him to change his mode of argument against reductionism.[1] This variant of reductionism takes a consistent realist or empiricist epistemological position as its point of departure in opposing 'holist' conceptions of society. It poses acute difficulties for Durkheim because it takes exactly the same epistemological position as he does and he cannot refute it by reference to 'givens' or by attacking idealism.

This variant of reductionism follows the mode of argument we have previously encountered in our discussion of Bernard and the question of reductionism in the biological sciences. Durkheim makes explicit reference to the debate in the biological sciences in his presentation of this particular reductionist position; he is aware of the analogous character of these reductionist arguments in both disciplines:

> In a word, there is between psychology and sociology the same break in continuity as between biology and the physico-chemical sciences (ibid., p. 104).

Reductionism in biology maintains that 'life' is not a tangible entity, that what are called 'living beings' consist only of matter and certain properties of matter (motion, heat, etc.), and therefore that any notion of 'life' as something unique and different is a metaphysical absurdity which posits an existence which is not given to the senses and to observation. These objections to the notion of 'life' in biology can be applied equally well to the notion of 'society' as an existence different from individual thought and behaviour. These objections are the stock in trade of the philosophical position we now call methodological individualism.[2] It is argued that 'society' as a phenomenon *sui generis* does not exist because all that we can observe are particular individuals and their actions.

Durkheim's reply to this argument is not in the terms of the usual arguments he deploys to prove the existence of the social realm: the arguments of the constraint society exercises upon the individual and the inefficacy of human wills in producing or changing social phenomena. He continues to insist on the irreducibility of social phenomena to effects of individual phenomena but in doing so in this context he introduces a philosophical position concerning the emergent properties which stem from all forms of association in the different realms of nature. This position appears at first sight to be a repetition of the vitalist critique of biology.[3] Durkheim recognises the threat of reductionism to be similar in both disciplines: the science of the organic faces exactly the same epistemological challenge from physico-chemical reductionism as the science of the social faces from individualistic reductionism. This challenge is nothing less than the denial and destruction of their real objects, of the existence of their subject matter, 'life' and 'society'. The existence of these objects cannot be defended by reference to their effects since not only are there effects but the existence which produces them is at question. Durkheim is forced to give general philosophical arguments for the *possibility* of the existence of these forms:

> But, it will be said that, since the only elements making up
> society are individuals, the first origins of sociological
> phenomena cannot but be psychological. In reasoning thus,
> it can be established just as easily that organic phenomena
> may be explained by inorganic phenomena. It is very certain

that there are in the living cell only molecules of crude matter. But these molecules are in contact with one another, and this association is the cause of the new phenomena which characterise life, the very germ of which cannot possibly be found in any of the separate elements (ibid., p. 102).

This represents a very drastic mutation in the form of Durkheim's argument. Far from asserting that society is a 'given' 'subject to observation', he is now defending the existence of that 'given' by postulating a general 'law' of association[4] which has the same effects in all the realms of nature. In the Preface to the second edition of the *Rules* he recognises this mutation in a remark that accepts that he is arguing in as 'idealist' a way as the defenders of the existence of psychological phenomena do against the physiological determinists:

Since it has been customary to think of social life as a logical development of ideal concepts, a method which makes social evolution depend on objective conditions will perhaps be judged crude and will possible be termed 'materialistic'. Yet we could more justly claim the contrary designation. Is not the essence of idealism contained in the idea that psychological phenomena cannot be immediately derived from organic phenomena? Our method is in part only an application of this principle to social facts. Just as the idealists separate the psychological from the biological realm, so we separate the psychological from the social; like them, we refuse to explain the complex in terms of the simple. (ibid., p. xxxix).

Durkheim has been upstaged in his own realism by this empiricist reductionism and has been forced to openly adopt a vitalist/idealist position. This mutation in the form of argument brings to the surface the nature of social life as essence that Durkheim's realist epistemology serves to denegate. The nature of social life and the essentialist conception of 'life' in vitalist biology are rather similar.

If we return to the substance of Durkheim's argument the nature of the change in its terms will become clearer. Life in the cell or in society is a real phenomenon which is a product of their both being organised wholes. The association of certain given elements into a whole gives rise to properties which are not present in these elements and which are emergent from the combination of these elements into a larger entity:

> A whole is not identical with the sum of its parts. It is something different, and its properties differ from those of its component parts. Association is not, as has sometimes been believed, merely an infertile phenomenon; it is not simply the putting of facts and constituent properties into juxtaposition (ibid., pp. 102–3).

In the biological realm, association, and the different forms of association, juxtaposition and combination, gives rise to all the differences which exist between organisms. This fact of association must be the sole source of these differences since all the organisms are combinations of one and the same elementary matter:

> [Association] is the source of all the innovations which have been produced successively in the course of the general evolution of things. What differences are there between the lower and higher organisms, between highly organised living things and protoplasm, between the latter and the inorganic molecules of which it is composed, if not differences in types of association? All these beings, in the last analysis, resolve themselves into the same elements, but these elements are here in mere juxtaposition, there in combination, here associated in one way, there in another (ibid., p. 103).

But these emergent properties of association are not peculiar to the biological realm, they are a general phenomenon of nature and obey the same general laws. Association is the universal source of the difference and transformation of things. All the different forms of existence in each of the major realms of nature, the physico-chemical, the organic and the realm of consciousness, are products of the different organisations of the elementary matter of each of these realms:

> One may even enquire whether this law does not apply in the mineral world and whether the differences separating inorganic bodies are not traceable to this same origin (ibid., p. 103).

> What we say of life could be repeated for all possible compounds. The hardness of bronze is not in the copper, the tin, or the lead, which are its ingredients and which are

soft and malleable bodies; it is in their mixture. The fluidity
of water and its nutritional and other properties are not to be
found in the two gases of which it is composed but in the
complex substance which they form by their association (ibid.,
p. xlviii).

It appears that, not content with the support afforded him by the
vitalist position in biology, Durkheim has embroiled himself in an
incipient Naturphilosophie. This philosophy of nature consists in
the generalisation of the character of vitalism, the ascription of
properties such as those of 'living beings' to all complex phenomena in nature. Obviously, Durkheim does not maintain that
bronze is an animate substance, but that its relation as a whole to
its component elements is similar to the vitalist conception of the
relation between an organism and inanimate matter. Durkheim's
position is not a simple variant of holism; it is a general theory of
the sources of change and difference in nature and matter. It
suffers from the idealist conception of the whole or organism we
find in vitalist biology but it generalises this conception to the
whole of nature. Vitalism is an idealist doctrine because it conceives certain properties to be essential.[5] Vitalism can provide no
explanation of the conditions of existence of the phenomenon of
'life'; life exists as an essence in itself and without any conditions
of existence but itself. It makes life a property of organisation, of
the organism, but the vitalist whole is not structured; it is the
essential and indivisible unity of life itself.[6] Durkheim's conception
of the emergent properties of organisation is vitalist in this respect.
We have seen that the only two levels in his analysis are a whole
with certain properties and the basic elementary matter which the
whole transforms, and which does not possess in itself the properties of the whole. These properties are then ascribed to the
whole as a given; they become effects of its 'wholeness'. Thus a
society is a whole over and above the individuals who form its
elementary matter, and complex societies are aggregates of 'parts',
which are simpler societies identical to the 'complex' whole in their
internal composition.

Naturphilosophie and Scientific Theory

We can begin to see in this example the difference between such
philosophical conceptions and scientific theories. Durkheim ascribes

a causal function to the whole itself; he turns the whole into the source of certain effects and into its own spontaneous cause. This mechanism of ascription is like that of vitalist theories in biology. Vitalism takes as its point of departure the common-sense conception of 'life'; a conception rooted in the human subject's experience of itself as a 'living' being and which follows the human subject's extension of its own experience of 'life' to other bodies in nature which it recognises as sharing elements of its own nature. Beings like dogs or trees are 'alive' or 'possess life'. Vitalism turns this phenomenon of life into an essence, the vital principle, which explains the phenomenon. Life is a state which is its own cause. Vitalist explanations are condemned to the repetition of their premisses, taken from common-sense, in the form of answers. 'Life', the object to be explained, is the source of the explanation.[7] Vitalism merely reproduces its own presuppositions as its explanations; it is therefore incapable of generating further theoretical forms.

Bernard's conception of the object of physiology is, as we have seen, quite different. The object of Bernard's physiology is to explain the conditions of existence of 'life', but the Bernardian conception of its object is quite different from the vitalist conception. 'Life' in the Bernardian conception is thought only as a specific effect of certain conditions of existence; the result of certain combinations of physico-chemical processes which secure these conditions. What 'life' is can only be known by determining what kind of effect it is. Thus, for Bernard, life is never a given which science seeks to explain. Life is an intra-scientific product; we know what it is only through the procedures of analysis and synthesis in physiological science.

Bernard would disagree with Durkheim's statement that:

> Life could not thus be separated into discrete parts; it is a unit, and consequently its substratum can be only the living substance in its totality and not the element parts of which it is composed (ibid., p. xlviii).

He would detect in it the very essence of vitalism, that is, the conception of life as an indivisible and essential property of certain given organisms, an essentially 'cell life', 'dog life' or 'tree life'. The life effect of any organism, be it a dog or a cell, is neither essential nor impenetrable. It is useless to repeat that the 'inanimate particles of the cell do not assimilate food, reproduce, and, in a word, live',[8] if one cannot explain the processes by which food is assimilated or reproduction takes place.

The concept of histological unit is the means by which Bernard thinks the elementary forms in which the conditions of existence of life are secured by the physico-chemical processes and exchanges which cause and maintain this effect. This concept establishes the point at which this analysis of life into its inorganic components takes place. There is no equivalent of this concept in vitalist biology or in Durkheim's sociology. There is for these idealist theories nothing but a given elementary matter and the properties of the whole, *sui generis*. There exists an untraversable space of difference between the elements and the whole. This space only serves to indicate an essential difference in quality in these two forms of existence. This space is central to the conception of the whole as an essence, for it renders any connection of the two levels impossible and any causation of the properties of the whole, but that of the whole itself, impossible. Vitalism is the mirror image of reductionism and merely counterposes its terms.

Complex organisms are, for Bernard, no less penetrable and analysable than histological units. The concept of *milieu intérieur* is the means by which Bernard thinks how it is that these complex organisations can exist as combinations of histological units: how the physico-chemical conditions of the regulation and control of the internal environment make possible the exchanges between histological units from which all the more complex processes, which give rise to the life 'effect' in the organism, are produced. Organisms, as we have seen, are not mere assemblages of organs interacting one with another, they are also combinations of processes which create these organs and make their relations possible. The *milieu intérieur* makes possible the control of the internal conditions of the organism. This is why Bernard maintains that morphology is not a sufficient basis for biological science and why physiology is necessary to explain the facts of morphology itself. Durkheim's sociology has no such conception of structure. In Durkheim's sociology, morphology and physiology are identical, they are alike manifestations of the essence of social life. As we shall see below, Durkheim's notion of the 'social milieu' is only a repetition of his previous position on the nature of social facts and social morphology and is in no sense a new concept in its content.

Transformations in the Realm of Consciousness

Durkheim's general 'law' of association as the source of the difference and transformation of things operates in the realm of consciousness as it does elsewhere:

> By reason of this principle, society is not a mere sum of individuals. Rather, the system formed by their association represents a specific reality which has its own characteristics. Of course, nothing collective can be produced if individual consciousnesses are not assumed; but this necessary condition is by itself insufficient. These consciousnesses must be combined in a certain way; social life results from this combination and is consequently, explained by it. Individual minds, forming groups by mingling and fusing give birth to a being, psychological if you will, but constituting a psychic individuality of a new sort (ibid., p. 103).

Society is the product of the fusion of individual consciousnesses into a larger collective entity. The existence and the forms of social life are explained by this 'mingling and fusing' of 'individual minds'. Society is not a product of the mere juxtaposition of individuals, a series of external exchanges and interactions between them, it is a being created by combination with a distinct nature and a distinct existence from its elements. Nevertheless, the terms in which Durkheim has presented his position seem to imply that society is, indeed, generated from individual consciousnesses. The parallelism which we noted earlier between psychological and social laws would appear to be more than a parallelism; society is the psyche writ large and sociology is the psychology of this collective psyche. It would appear that while the collective consciousness is a phenomenon distinct from the sum of the individual consciousnesses it is no different from them in essence. This appears to be a real retreat on Durkheim's part, for society is again connected genetically and ontologically with the psychic by the terms of this argument. Durkheim attempts in a footnote to qualify this position and to prevent possible misreadings of it by psychologistic and individualistic interpreters, but all he succeeds in telling us is nothing more than he asserted many times before, that the collective consciousness is supra-individual:

In order to justify this distinction [between the collective and the individual consciousness], it is not necessary to posit for the former a separate personal existence; it is something special and must be designated by a special term, simply because the states which constitute it differ specifically from those which constitute the individual consciousnesses. *This specificity comes from the fact that they are not formed from the same elements.* The latter result from the nature of the organic psychological being taken in isolation, the former from a plurality of beings of this kind (ibid., p. 103, note 18, our emphasis).

In the Preface to the second edition of the *Rules* Durkheim returns to this question and attempts to settle it once and for all with a categorical statement of his position.[9] Social facts 'have a different substratum' from psychological facts; they are the phenomena of a different order of consciousness. Society is not reducible to its elements, individuals, because it exists in and of itself as a distinct reality which is the result of the association of the elements:

> If . . . this synthesis constituting every society yields new phenomena, differing from those which take place in the individual consciousnesses, we must, indeed, admit that these facts reside exclusively in the very society which produces them, and not in its parts, i.e., its members. They are, then, in this sense external to individual consciousnesses, considered as such, just as the distinctive characteristics of life are external to the mineral substances composing the living being. These new phenomena cannot be reduced to their elements without contradiction in terms, since, by definition, they presuppose something different from the properties of these elements. Thus we have established between psychology, which is properly the science of the mind of the individual, and sociology (ibid., pp. xlviii–ix).

We are back on the terrain of realism. The collective consciousness, for which Durkheim can produce no explanation but the spurious 'law' of association, is a given fact of nature. Psychological reductionism, by displacing the social into the individual, ignores a given reality. The effect of this displacement is identical to the error, within the psychological domain, of ascribing the thoughts of one man to another.[10]

Durkheim has been arguing that the relation of the individual and the collective consciousness is like the relation of the inorganic to the organic. But, in fact, this analogy with the biological realm conceals an important difference. Durkheim's critique of empiricist reductionism relies on a general theory of the effects of association. He claims[11] that the effects of all the transformations produced by association are identical in that they give rise to a whole, distinct from its elements. On the basis of his own argument, however, this is not the case in respect of the individual consciousness and the collective consciousness. The effect of association in the realm of consciousness is not to change the nature of the realm itself, but merely to produce a new being within that realm. Individual psyches are transformation effects of the nature and properties of the physico-organic elements of which they are composed, just as biological organisms are transformation effects of physico-chemical matter. It is the individual psyche which is the origin point of the whole realm of consciousness. Without it the collective consciousness could not exist for it would lack the elementary matter appropriate to its nature as a being of consciousness. Individuals are not merely physical or biological supports of the social realm; it is necessary that they be beings of consciousness if the collective consciousness is to be carried in and through them. Without this *prior* transformation in nature, the social consciousness could not exist for it would lack the materials from which it is formed: 'nothing collective can be produced if individual consciousnesses are not assumed'.[12]

Thus while the collective consciousness has an existence external to, and exerts a force superior to, any given individual consciousness, or to the sum of the individual consciousnesses, it is not, logically or existentially, *prior* to the realm of consciousness itself. This realm has its origin in, and is created in, the individual psyche. The social is not reducible to the individual, but it is inconceivable without it. Durkheim never explains the source of the generation of the social; he certainly never claims that it arises in response to any need of, or action by, the individual. That is to his credit, but, in consequence, the conditions of existence of the social realm remain a mystery. We can only conclude that the social is a given fact which exists. The introduction of the general 'law' of the effects of association does not change the terms of Durkheim's argument presented in his theory of the nature of social facts. All it achieves is to weaken the realist and empiricist epistemological cover of this 'theory' of social facts. This new argument adds nothing because in it the production of the transformation effect of association is unexplained and inexplicable. The whole creates these effects but it is itself an uncreated essence whose conditions of existence are nothing but itself in another guise.

The existence of the collective consciousness does not create a new realm of nature, but merely produces a transformation within a realm already created by the individual consciousness. The difference between the collective and the individual consciousness, to use Durkheim's own argument, is similar to the difference between bronze and copper in the physico-chemical realm. Bronze cannot exist without copper; it is a different and more complex metal than copper, but a metal none the less. Bronze and copper are both the subject matter of a branch of the physico-chemical sciences, metallurgy. Sociology and psychology are both sciences of the realm of consciousness. Psychology is, however, the more general and the primary science. Sociology is a collective psychology and the processess of the collective consciousness obey the same laws of consciousness as those of individual psychology. This is the inescapable conclusion of Durkheim's position.[13]

In vitalist biology the living cell and inorganic matter can be represented as essentially different forms of existence. The space of difference, between the collective whole and its individual elements, is, in Durkheim's sociology, constantly traversed by the parallelism of sociology and psychology. This space is unstable because of the parallelism of the substance of its two poles and the parallelism of the explanations of that substance. Durkheim is caught in a contradiction between his assertion of the difference between the collective and the individual consciousness; a difference which he demarcates in a vitalist fashion, and his conception of the collective as a being of consciousness, a position constantly reinforced by his inability to develop any concept of social structure. This produces the unstable combination of a conception of society as a being, *sui generis*, irreducible in essence to the individual and the psychic, and a conception of the *content* of that being as a consciousness obeying psychic laws. This is why Durkheim's critique of empiricist reductionism cannot rely on the mere restatement of vitalist notions in respect of the social and the psychological but produces their generalisation in a theory of the effects of association in nature as a whole. Even so, in the terms of his own argument, a real difference emerges between the vitalist conception of the relation of biology and the inorganic realm, and the relation of sociology and the psychological realm.

The Social Milieu

> Since the facts of social morphology are of the same nature as physiological phenomena, they must be explained by the principle just enunciated (ibid., p. 112).[14]

Morphological and physiological phenomena are 'of the same nature' because they are both social facts, common products of social life. The social milieu is a phenomenon of the morphological order in society. Association, and its different forms, is the primary determining condition of all social phenomena:

> In fact, the determining condition of social phenomena, is as we have shown, the very fact of association, the phenomena ought to vary with the forms of that association, i.e., according to the ways in which the constituent parts of society are grouped (ibid., p. 112).

Association is the source of difference and change in the social realm as it is in and between all the different realms of nature. Explanations of morphological facts in society are explanations which seek the particular characteristics of these facts in different forms of association.

The social milieu, the internal environment of a society, is formed by the way in which its elements combine into a whole:

> Since, moreover, a given aggregate, formed by the union of elements of all kinds which enter into the composition of a society, constitutes its internal environment (just as the aggregate of anatomic elements together with the way they are disposed in space, constitutes the internal milieu of organisms)[15] we can say: *The first origins of all social processes of any importance should be sought in the internal constitution of the social group* (ibid., pp. 112–13, emphasis in original).

This milieu is composed of two kinds of elements, residues or objectified products of social life, and persons: 'The elements which make up this milieu are of two kinds: things and persons' (ibid., p. 113). The material objects incorporated into society and the immaterial but real residues of social life cannot explain the transformations which take place within the social realm; they cannot explain why particular social facts exist nor the genesis of the different forms of social aggregates. They are not the living tissue of society; they are products of past social life and have, as a consequence, no motive power in themselves:

> But it is clear that the impulsion which determines social transformations can come from neither the material nor the immaterial, for neither possesses a motivating power. . . .
> They are the matter on which the social forces of society act, but by themselves they release no social energy. As an active factor, then, the human milieu remains (ibid., p. 113).

This 'human milieu' is the immediate source of social energy, of the living forces of society. The human milieu consists of the relations between persons which arise in the internal environment of society. Social energy is produced by the interaction of individuals as a result of their being brought together in the internal social environment. Different forms of association, different social milieus, give rise to different intensities of social interaction depending on the extent to which they force individuals into social and moral contact with one another.[16] Different milieus generate different forms of social energy; a result of the degree to which they force the molecules of society to interact. In these terms Durkheim's notions of organic and mechanical solidarity seem to resemble the kinetic theory of gases. Social energy is generated by the density and the degree of friction of the social molecules.

Sociological explanations are primarily explanations in terms of different effects produced by the different distributions of individuals, different human milieus, within the internal environment or social milieu:

> The principal task of the sociologist ought to be, therefore, to discover the different aspects of this milieu which can exert some influence on the course of social phenomena. Until the present, we have found two series of acts which have

eminently fulfilled this condition; these are: (1) the number
of social units or, as we have also called it, the 'size of a
society; and (2) the degree of concentration of the group, or
what we have termed the 'dynamic density' (ibid., p. 113).

Durkheim recapitulates the theses of the *Division*.[17] The different
types of social associations generate different dynamic densities and
volumes of social life. The lower the degree that the social segments
are insulated from one another, the greater are the intensities and
frequencies of moral interaction of individuals, and the more
intense and vital the human milieu. In mechanically solidaristic
societies the potential social energy is dammed up by the insulation
of individuals within the respective social segments. Organically
solidaristic societies by reducing this insulation, by uniting the
parts into a more integrated whole, create a human milieu of
greater density and volume of human social exchanges and
relations.

The different morphological forms of the social whole, and the
internal environments they produce, give rise to human milieus of
a different volume and intensity. Morphology, by the very fact of
the differing arrangements of parts, generates physiological processes and explains their differing force and intensity:

> The constitution of the social milieu results from the mode of
> composition of the social aggregates – and *these two expressions
> are essentially synonymous* – we now have the proof that there
> are no more essential characteristics than those assigned by us
> as the basis of sociological classification. (ibid., p. 120, our
> emphasis).

Unlike Bernard, who insists that 'dead anatomy teaches nothing'[18]
it is Durkheim's contention that association is 'not merely an
infertile phenomenon'.[19] The reason why Durkheim considers
morphology to have an active role, and not merely the status of a
'dead anatomy', is not to be found in his conception of the emergent
properties of association but, rather, in an unconscious subterfuge
in the terms of his argument. The social wholes he is discussing
in this section on the social milieu are not merely combinations
of human individuals, they are, by the theses he has developed in
chapter 4, complex wholes which are combinations of simpler
societies. The different forms of association, the different internal

environments he is discussing here do not refer to the simplest societies but to 'complex' societies which are already combinations of given simpler societies. The terms mechanical and organic solidarity do not refer to the simplest societies. Thus the 'elements' of social morphology are not individuals but already living social wholes. Social morphology is not a 'dead anatomy' for Durkheim because it is concerned with the forms of combination of already given elements of social life. Morphology can give rise to different physiological processes because its forms are organisations and associations of parts which are already imbued with life. Physiological phenomena are already present in the morphological order. Morphology and physiology are interchangeable because physiological phenomena are presumed in the morphological order right from the start.

If the passages in which Durkheim treats of the social milieu were considered in isolation, one might think that he had come close to demonstrating the source of social energy and, thereby, of social 'life'. One might consider the solution to this problem to be that different forms of social environment give rise to forms of human interaction which produce different amounts of social energy, and that the source of social energy in general was the effect of the collective upon the relations of individuals, bringing them together and generating the living forces of society by friction, as it were. The problem with this construction of Durkheim's position is that he cannot analyse the process of the creation of social energy in general. He can give a more or less plausible account of the effects of the different forms of social solidarity, but he cannot explain the conditions of social solidarity as such. Mechanical solidarity, the existence of simpler societies in juxtaposition, and organic solidarity, the combination and fusion of the social segments, both entail the pre-existence of simpler societies. The kinetic theory of the generation of social energy presupposes the social forms in which it takes place; it therefore presupposes an energy or force which creates those forms. He cannot explain how the simplest societies come to exist and how they survive as societies. The simplest societies are without parts, and their energy or vital force must exist independently of the individuals who live in them, or otherwise this energy would be an effect of those individuals themselves. If we consider Durkheim's conception of the simplest society it becomes evident that its motive power can come neither

from combination or juxtaposition, nor from the effect of these
different forms of association upon individuals. The elementary
societies are the primitive, essential and indivisible, protoplasm of
social life. Social life remains an essence, and the very conception
of the social milieu is predicated on its existence.

Durkheim's whole discussion of the 'social milieu' is based upon
a play on the word 'element'. In the beginning of this discussion he
treats the social whole as a simple unity without social parts whose
'elements' consist of 'things and persons'. But when he comes to
discuss the different effects of the forms of association, combination
and juxtaposition, he is discussing what he previously called
'complex' wholes, and the 'elements' of those wholes are not 'things
and persons' but 'simpler societies'. The 'essential characteristics'
of his theory of classification are the different combinations of the
elements, combination and juxtaposition, but they are combinations of *simpler* societies, not of things and persons. It is by means
of this switch of levels, and by means of the change of the nature
of the component 'elements', that Durkheim avoids the question of
the genesis and nature of social life and social energy. The 'persons' who are forced into contact, like molecules in a gas cloud,
are already in a social milieu. The internal environments that give
rise to the action of these molecules are already composed of
societies. The simplest societies are irreducible units of social life
and must contain it in essence. Social life is presupposed in the
analysis of the social milieu rather than explained by it.

Conclusion: The Rules of Sociological Method and Durkheim's Sociology

It has been the object of this work to show that Durkheim's attempt to create a scientific sociology could not but be a failure. Durkheim's sociology is as impossible as the epistemology on which it is founded, and, far from being a science, it is a mechanism for the rationalisation of phenomena given to it by political and social ideologies. Our analysis has been largely confined to *The Rules of Sociological Method*, the text in which this project of creating a scientific sociology is most developed and most clearly articulated. This concentration on one text may appear to have its defects. It may be objected that, even though the *Rules* is a failure, the Durkheimian project is fulfilled elsewhere, that the problems and contradictions of the *Rules* are overcome in Durkheim's substantive works or in other of his methodological writings. There are good reasons why this should not be the case. In the introduction the intellectual space in which Durkheim's project is confined was specified: for Durkheim to escape the parameters of the subjectivism/positivism couple, to constitute an object which is not pre-given by ideology, he would have had to shatter the boundaries of sociology as we know it. What works are possible candidates for this status? Clearly, there are none. Sociologists will not be satisfied with this; it is an answer predicated on the impossibility of a scientific sociology. But if the sociologist does believe that there is a Durkheimian sociology distinct from the *Rules*, a sociology which avoids its worst failings, we will try to show him otherwise. We will attempt briefly to argue the unity of Durkheim's sociology, to argue that the *Rules* is its logical expression.

Sociologists tend to believe that the 'empirical' covers a

multitude of theoretical sins. It may be thought that, beyond the
arid realm of epistemology, in the positive investigation of the real,
Durkheim's sociology *does* exist and *is* viable. Durkheim's sociology,
like all real sociology, is to be found not in methodological tracts
but in his 'empirical studies'. But this empiricism, which is happy
to forego epistemology and sets little store by logic, has forgotten
itself; where are these Durkheimian studies of the real? *The Division of Labour in Society? Suicide? The Elementary Forms of
Religious Life?* In what sense are these studies of the concrete?
Each of these works, each 'positive investigation', is really nothing
but the *Rules* in a different form, each is an argument for a scientific
sociology and in each the 'empirical material' is deployed as a
means of illustration and persuasion.

Suicide is an exercise in method; a proof of the value and via-
bility of the method by its application to a familiar object in French
social research. *Suicide* is a brilliant exercise in 'saving the phenomena', of explaining facts which were already elaborated and well
known. Suicide rates can appear to be a given object only if the
Durkheimian theory of social facts is accepted, otherwise, far from
being given, they can be recognised as the product of definite processes of evaluation, collection and compilation. No more 'given'
than racing form books. The relation between the suicide rates and
the causes which are supposed to explain them is a relation possible
only if the Durkheimian essentialist causality, the Durkheimian
conception of the social fact as the phenomenal expression of an
essence, is accepted. That less Catholics than Protestants, per
thousand of the population, commit suicide, that members of the
liberal professions take their own lives more than the desperately
poor, are correlations which in themselves can tell us nothing; the
relation between the 'facts' and their 'explanation' is a relation of
parallelism, a saving of the phenomena – and others are possible,
unless one accepts Durkheim's realist epistemology. And does the
empiricist need an arcane epistemological criticism to tell him that
Suicide is not truly a study of the concrete. Do we not have empiricist critics like Jack Douglass to tell us exactly that? That empiricism can never be the basis of a science is not the issue here; what
is pertinent is that Durkheim's sociology can never be the science
empiricism wants.

For *The Division of Labour in Society* to count as an 'empirical
study', Hobbes's *Leviathan* and Rousseau's *Essay on the Origin of*

Inequality Among Men would have to be counted also. Hobbes's and Rousseau's problems and explanations are no more and no less fabulous than Durkheim's. Durkheim's explanation of the transformation from mechanical to organic solidarity, as we have seen, involves a fable, and the types themselves are no less characters in this fable. Mechanical and organic solidarity are only possible if the presupposition of Durkheim's social morphology is accepted – no empiricist sociologist has yet found a mechanically solidaristic society.

In addition to the empiricist position, which seeks to found scientific practice on the given, beyond theory, there is another argument which attempts to separate the *Rules* and other elements of Durkheim's work. This position is based upon the periodisation and division of Durkheim's *œuvre*, upon the argument that Durkheim's later works, *The Elementary Forms of Religious Life* and *Primitive Classification*, entail a quite different epistemology from the earlier works. The classic case for such a division between Durkheim's earlier and later works is made by Talcott Parsons in *The Structure of Social Action*. Parsons contends that the 'sociologistic positivism' of the *Rules* was subsequently replaced by the 'idealism' of the *Forms*. The insights of his early empirical work, which made possible the posing of the problems of the voluntaristic theory of action, were never developed by Durkheim. 'In fact Durkheim in escaping from the toils of positivism has overshot the mark and gone clean over to idealism' (Parsons, 1949, p. 445).

In part two of this work we have argued that Durkheim's position in the *Rules*, far from being 'positivist' is *realist*, and that it involves an essentialisation of the social not unlike that which Parsons calls 'idealist' with regard to the *Forms*. Here we will briefly examine the epistemology entailed in the project of *The Elementary Forms of Religious Life* in order to see how it compares with the *Rules*.

What is the object of the *Forms*? The object of the *Forms* is twofold: (i) the determination of the most primitive form of religion, in order to comprehend the essence of religious belief, and (ii) the analysis of the fundamental categories which ordered thought presupposes, the 'ideas of time, space, class, number, cause, substance, personality, etc.' (Durkheim, 1915, p. 9).

Concerning the first of these two objects, why should this

investigation of the *elementary forms* be so crucial in the determination of the essence of religion, or of any other form of belief or practice? The very project of the *Forms*, contained in this notion of elementarism, tells us that we have not in any way left the terrain of the epistemology of the *Rules*. Elementarism enables us to penetrate to the essence, because in the simplest forms the essence is revealed; it is simply present in its phenomena: 'Primitive civilisations offer *privileged* cases, then, because they are *simple* cases' (ibid., p. 6). This notion of the privileged nature of the elementary reveals the profound continuity between the epistemology and the social morphology of the *Rules* and the *Forms*. A continuity in *realism*: simplicity is privileged because it makes the essence *visible*, simplicity of the object perceived makes perception a direct perception of the nature of reality. Hence to find the essence of a phenomenon one must return to its simplest form, strip off the dross of secondary complexification to reveal the simple core which is the essential. A continuity in *social morphology*: all more complex social forms are merely combinations of simple social forms; the simple is privileged because the complex is secondary to it; as it is merely the combined and juxtaposed form of the simple, the complex can tell us nothing more about the essence of social life. Hence the reduction which makes the essence visible is possible; the complex can be taken apart into its elements.

Religion is defined according to the rule: '*The subject matter of every sociological study should comprise a group of phenomena defined in advance by certain external characteristics*' (Durkheim, 1966, p. 35). As in *Suicide* Durkheim purports to define religion by the common external resemblances which all the diverse forms of religion share. The very universality of these visible externals gives a clue as to the essence of this social fact: 'But these external resemblances suppose others which are profound' (Durkheim, 1915, p. 5). It is no accident that not all religious beliefs entail the notion of a God, and that this notion is absent from the most primitive – this absence reveals an important clue as to the nature of religion. The common external characteristics of religion, the characteristics which define it are the division of things into the *sacred* and the *profane* in religious belief, and the existence of *rites* concerning the sacred objects; religion is '*a unified system of beliefs and practices relative to sacred things*' (ibid., p. 47). As in *Suicide* this initial definition of the nature of the phenomena in question determines the whole nature of the enquiry. The real, the visible external characteristics, defines the object of the enquiry, the nature of the problems posed, and, therefore, the nature and direction of the enquiry. This relation phenomenon/essence, a relation in which the essence is present in the visible phenomena which it gives rise to, is familiar to us from the *Rules*.

Concerning the second of these two objects, Durkheim's attempt to determine the origin of the fundamental categories of thought is an attempt to settle an epistemological problem by means of a positive sociological investigation. Durkheim tries to show that these necessary logical categories have an extra-logical origin. Durkheim rejects both of the opposed positions in philosophy as to the origin and nature of these categories. For *apriorism* the categories are innate and exist prior to and independently of experience; they are part of the constitution of the human mind. For *empiricism* the categories are the product of experience; they are constituted from elements of experience and this combination is effected by the perceiving individual subject. Neither empiricism nor apriorism can account for the origin of the categories. Apriorism is condemned either to rationalism or to theism; either to asserting that the capacity to order and transcend experience is given in the human intellect, which explains nothing, or to deriving the powers of human reason from divine reason, which involves either blind faith or an infinite regress. Empiricism is condemned to irrationalism; experiences are particular, a-conceptual and of themselves can never give rise to general categories; as a result, either a faculty of reasoning must be posited, which involves a contradiction, or men are capable of nothing which transcends individual and immediate sense-perceptions, which is absurd. It is the opposition which is false; both reason and experience are essential. Empiricism denies the existence of general categories which transcend individual human subjects, but these categories are constitutive of logic and reason. Apriorism gives a metaphysical answer to the question of the origin of the categories, but this is unacceptable since it is not susceptible to empirical proof and, therefore, a non-metaphysical origin of the categories has to be found.

Durkheim's explanation of the categories must respect certain conditions which derive from his critique of the philosophical explanations, these are: (i) that the categories must have a non-metaphysical, that is, a material foundation; (ii) that this foundation must be subject to empirical proof; and (iii) that the categories, thus materially grounded, must transcend the individual and be common to human subjects.

What is the origin of the categories? It is *social*, says Durkheim. These categories are presupposed in the elementary forms of religious beliefs: 'Now when primitive religious beliefs are systematically analysed, the principal categories are naturally found' (ibid., p. 9). Religious representations are collective representations; they express collective sentiments and collective facts:

> Religious representations are collective representations which express collective realities; the rites are a manner of acting which take rise in the midst of the assembled groups and which are destined to excite, maintain or recreate certain *mental* states in these groups. So if the categories are of religious origin, they ought to participate in this nature common to all religious facts; they too should be social affairs and the *product of collective thought* (ibid., p. 10, our emphasis).

Religious representations, in which the categories are presupposed, derive from the social – it is in the phenomena of social life that the origin of the categories is to be found; space exists as materialised social space, the space of the social groups and the spaces of its internal divisions, class in the division of the social group into classes, etc. These conceptions are developed further by Durkheim in the essay he wrote with Mauss, *Primitive Classification*. It is in the reality of the social, in its divisions and forms, that the material basis of the categories is to be found. This significant materiality, this materialised social significance, is given the form of ideas/beliefs in the collective representations. Religion, the dominant form of collective representation in simple societies, creates certain *mental* states in its participants. Religion provides those in whom such states are engendered with the categorical forms that are presupposed in it.

The transcendent nature of the categories, their supra-individual character, is explained by the fact that they are social; they are phenomena of the collective consciousness:

> From that one can understand how . . . reason has been able to go beyond the limits of empirical knowledge. It does not

owe this to any vague mysterious virtue but simply to the
fact that according to the well-known formula, man is double.
There are two beings in him: an individual being which has
its foundation in the organism and the circle of whose
activities is therefore strictly limited, and a social being which
represents the highest reality in the intellectual and moral
order that we can know by observations – I mean society.
This duality of our nature has as its consequence in the
practical order, the irreducibility of a moral ideal to a
utilitarian motive, and in the order of thought, the irreducibility
of reason to individual experience. In so far as he belongs to
society, the individual transcends himself, both when he
thinks and when he acts (ibid., p. 16–17).

Experience and reason are both saved and assigned their place in
nature. Experience is a property of the individual, of his extra-
social cognitive and sensory apparatus. The categories which
make logical thought possible are social in origin. Man is able to
reason because he is provided with the elementary means of logical
thought by the social – the collective consciousness is constitutive
of the rationality of the individual consciousness.

Here again we see that Durkheim posits an extra-social individual and conceives the essence of the social to be the collective
consciousness. The individual is a being of consciousness; for
mental states to be created in him he must have a *mind*; for the
categories to become the basis of ordered thought an individual
mental apparatus must exist which is capable of internalising and
using those categories. Like the empiricists Durkheim has impli-
citly presupposed a faculty of reasoning in the individual subject.
The social is the point of origin of the *content* of the categories; it is
not and cannot be the point of origin of the *capacity* for and the
means of complex thought as such.

Durkheim claims that his solution of the question of the origin
of the categories means that 'the problem of knowledge is posed in
new terms' (ibid., p. 13). Far from it, classical epistemology has its
revenge. Durkheim's project, far from being 'idealist' in the simple
sense in which the word is used, that is, rationalist, is a variant of
the empiricist project – to find an extra-logical origin for logic.
Logic is secreted in the real, in the social and in collective representations – which *is* idealist, in the sense of the realisation of the

idea. In this sense Parsons is correct, but in this sense also the *Rules* is no less idealist; realism involves the materialisation of the idea in its supposition that the real is a rational order. The *Forms* does not depart from Durkheim's realist epistemology – the social is a rational order; its essence consists in collective representations, real but immaterial, which exist in the collective consciousness, and it is accessible to understanding through perception. Logic is inscribed in the individual – without *mind* and the *capacity* to reason, the categories supposed in religious beliefs would be no more intelligible to men than they are to dogs. The individual is a being of consciousness and it is only thus that it can function as the support or carrier of the collective consciousness.

Society imposes its fundamental categories on men. These cognitive means are a necessary element of social cohesion and social control:

> If men did not agree upon these essential ideas at every
> moment, if they did not have the same conception of space,
> time, cause, number, etc., all contact between their minds
> would be impossible, and with that, all life together. Thus
> society could not abandon the categories to the free choice of
> the individual without abandoning itself (ibid., p. 17).

The categorical *content* which is imposed upon individual minds is a content which is not so much necessary to thought, to consciousness, as such, but to the making of the individual consciousness a fit carrier for the collective consciousness.

Durkheim's attempt to give the logical an extra-logical, *social* foundation leads him into impossible contradictions. *Contradiction 1*: If logic has its origin in the collective consciousness it is imprisoned in that consciousness; the individual subject cannot interiorise it unless a capacity for logical thought is presupposed in that subject. *Contradiction 2*: If logic is purely social in origin, if society must impose its categories on individuals as a necessary means of its own existence and social control, then how is a social science possible? Are its most basic assumptions not derived from the society in which it exists? The only escape from the first contradiction is an absolute sociologism which submerges the individual, which determines even his biological capacities – this sociologism was adopted by Mauss after Durkheim's death. This means of escape from the first contradiction exacerbates the second;

scientific knowledge is impossible. The only escape from the second
contradiction, to suppose that the perceiving subject is not reducible to society, that by freeing himself of preconceptions he can
perceive the rationality of the real (the position of the *Rules*)
exacerbates the first contradiction; it supposes an epistemologically
extra-social rational perceiving subject.

Durkheim has not escaped from the epistemology and the
epistemological problems of the *Rules* in *The Elementary Forms of
Religious Life*. The method of the *Rules* is reproduced in the *Forms*.
In the *Forms* the problems of a realist knowledge are sharpened in
trying to anchor logic in social life. Durkheim's work is a unity, a
unity not of science but of epistemological contradiction and of
ideology.

Notes

Introduction

1 Positivism and subjectivism form a unity; they are variant positions within a single epistemological space. Positivism gives to the knowing subject a central place in its theory of knowledge and it in no way precludes the object of 'scientific' enquiry being human subjects with meaningful behaviour, nor the object of sociology being inter-personal or inter-subjective relations. Indeed, because positivist epistemologies conceive the object of valid knowledge as an object given to experience, positivist sociologies necessarily tend to reduce the social to given observables, to behaviour, interaction, etc., and to measurable and controllable reports of experience, attitudes, statements of value, etc. on the part of human subjects. Subjectivism conceives the relation between the knowing subject and the known in a no less empiricist fashion than positivism – meaning is a given which is recognised by the subject.

It is in the light of this that we can see that the other two major projects of constructing an epistemological foundation for a sociology, the work of Max Weber and Talcott Parsons, are less of a radical departure in their conceptions of the type of knowledge of society they wish to create than Durkheim's. Weber's positions, complex, contradictory and ambivalent as they are, have a straightforward epistemological origin. They stem from the positivistic problematisation of the *Geisteswissenschaft* conception of 'understanding' and the nature of historical knowledge. Parsons continues this project of an essentially positivistic knowledge of human meanings and actions. Both Parsons, at least in *The Structure of Social Action*, and Weber conceive the social as ultimately reducible to or intelligible in terms of inter-subjective relations, in terms of the meaningful action of individual human subjects.

2 'The *will* is a kind of causality belonging to living beings in so far as they are rational, and *freedom* would be this property of such causality that it can be efficient, independently of foreign causes determining it; just as *physical necessity* is the property that the causality of all irrational beings has of being determined to activity by the influence of foreign

causes' (Kant, *Fundamental Principles of the Metaphysic of Morals*, T. K. Abbott (ed.), 1883, p. 65).

3 Bachelardian concepts will be explained in the notes to chapter 1 as they are introduced; references to the relevant works will also be given there.

4 It should be noted that the Willers' conception of scientific knowledge differs radically from that of Bachelard and Althusser; they have a correspondence theory of knowledge in which science is the abstract and rational form of the real.

5 Idealist scepticism questions and problematises the possibility of an experience of objects which is certain – see note 25 of chapter 1.

6 Durkheim's theory of knowledge is *realist* in that it conceives nature to be a structured and rational order, whose phenomena obey invariant laws and are determinate. True knowledge is the unprejudiced cognition of nature's plan; such knowledge is based upon experience, all non-experiential 'knowledge' is ideological and gives rise to metaphysical speculation, and an experience purged of preconceptions. This a-theoretical experiential knowledge can be a knowledge of the *essence* of things (and not merely of their appearances) because the external forms of phenomena are determinate expressions of the essence; the essence is present in its given phenomena. Hence it is possible to work back from phenomena given to experience to the essential cause of those phenomena. Nature is therefore knowable through experience and this knowledge is not limited or provisional, but, provided the perception is free of preconceptions, absolute and certain.

We have called this conception *realist*, developing Bachelard's concept of realism in order to differentiate it from other forms of empiricism.

The difference from the English empiricist tradition of Hume and Mill should be evident. This position supposes that valid knowledge is possible only through experience, but no suppositions can be made beyond the facts of experience about its nature; knowledge is necessarily always provisional and uncertain because sensations can be misleading and it is to go beyond the facts of experience to suppose that nature is a rational order. Generalisations from past experience are legitimate but provisional, since there is no guarantee that they will not be contradicted by future experience. Nothing is certain, not even individual sense-perceptions. Realism differs from this in that it is founded on the supposition that nature is a rational order which is intelligible through experience.

7 The notion of 'saving the phenomena' is a central part of the conventionalist theory of scientific knowledge developed by Pierre Duhem – see note 32 of chapter 1 for a brief explanation of his position.

8 See Althusser, 'On the materialist dialectic' (1969) and Althusser and Balibar, 'From *Capital* to Marx's philosophy' (1970), particularly the latter chapter which problematises the empiricist notion of reading and argues for a theoretical practice of reading.

9 The concept which differentiates *langue* and *parole*, which inscribes the

linguistic totality (*langue*) in definite practices which articulate it in a
partial form and which depend upon it, has its origin in the work of the
Swiss linguist Ferdinand de Saussure. It is from Saussure's pioneering
Course in General Linguistics (1966) that modern structural linguistics
has developed (ibid., pp. 7–20).

Chapter 1   Claude Bernard's Epistemology

1 For a thorough summary and discussion of Bernard's scientific work
   see Olmstead (1939); on glycogenesis see Bernard (1865), pp. 163–8
   and Larner (1967); for the concept of *milieu intérieur* see Holmes
   (1963a) and (1967).
2 For Bergson's assessment of Bernard's philosophy, see Bergson (1913),
   an address to the Academy on the centenary of Bernard's birth.
3 Where concepts of Bachelard's are used they are explained in the notes
   to the text. Bachelard's most accessible work is *The Philosophy of No*
   (1968). For an excellent account of the key concepts of Bachelard see
   Lecourt (1969).
4 By 'classical' philosophy we do not mean the philosophy of classical
   antiquity. 'Classical' philosophy refers to the system of problems and
   concepts which has dominated formal and academic philosophy since
   the seventeenth century. Its objects are the forms and the conditions
   of the knowledge and the conduct of the human subject, and the nature
   of the constituents of the universe. 'Classical' epistemology in both its
   sensationalist and its rationalist forms conflates the knowledge of
   human perception or reason with scientific knowledge – it is rigorously
   anthropological and anthropocentric. 'Classical' metaphysics attempts
   to determine the nature of the universe autonomously from the science
   and as a universal science. Cartesianism is the point of origin and union
   of these two disciplines in the modern age.
5 See Lecourt (1973), Part 2, p. 106, for a discussion of what he calls,
   following Canguilhem, 'scientific ideologies'.
6 E. H. Haeckel (1834–1919) was Professor of Zoology at Jena University', See Haeckel (1908) for a popular exposition of his theories.
   Rádl (1930), chapter 12, discusses his theories in the context of evolutionism and Darwinism.
      E. Mach (1838–1916) was Professor of Mechanics at Vienna
   University; For examples of Mach's works in English see Mach (1902)
   and Mach (1959). Bradley (1971) provides a sympathetic account of
   Mach's theories and his epistemology.
7 Engels's construction of a 'dialectical materialism' as the philosophical
   complement of historical materialism, the transformation of Marxism
   into a universal philosophy/science of dialectics valid in all realms of
   nature, is an analogous practice. See Engels (1954) and Engels, 'Ludwig Feuerbach and the end of classical German philosophy' (1886), in
   Marx and Engels (1962), vol. II, pp. 358–402.
8 The literature on this 'crisis' is large and varied; for readily accessible
   English versions of the texts of certain key participants, see: H.

Poincaré (1913); E. Mach (1959); P. Duhem (1954, and 1969). Rey's most important text in this context is *La Théorie de la physique chez les physiciens* (1907).

Kolakowski (1972), chapters 5 and 6, is a good general introduction to the epistemologies of Avenarius, Mach, Poincaré, and Duhem; see also Lecourt (1973), particularly on the reactions of scientists opposed to the view that 'matter' had 'disappeared'.

Lenin's *Materialism and Empiro-Criticism* (1908) remains the best and most thorough analysis of this 'crisis'. Lenin clearly separates the philosophical category of matter from the objects of the various sciences and their theories. He shows that the rejection of *philosophical* materialism leads to an idealist position which ultimately disputes and denies the possibility of scientific knowledge and the reality of its object. Lenin's acumen in dissecting this event in the relation of philosophy and the sciences is generally and unfortunately obscured by the, often justified, criticism of his crude epistemological position.

9 See Comte (1896) and Mill (1963).

10 Kolakowski (1972) recognises this separation but does not see its nature and its consequences: 'His [Bernard's] importance in philosophical reflection consists in this, that he was perhaps the first to formulate so clearly the dividing line between philosophy and science. He made no attack on philosophy, but simply regarded it as a different kind of activity from scientific research' (p. 99).

11 Bachelard's concept of phenomenology has a quite different meaning from that associated with the work of Husserl and subsequent 'phenomenologists'. By a phenomenology Bachelard means a body of ideas and techniques which reproduce given appearances, an essentially pragmatic means of reproducing certain given effects. See note 29.

12 To take an example of this practice from the field of biology, materialistic Cartesian biology sought to prove, to materialise, the notion of the man-machine in the construction of automata which reproduced complex human actions by purely mechanical means. The 'toys' of Vaucanson had an ulterior motive:

> The quoted texts, taken from Quesnay, Vaucanson, and Le Cat, do not indeed leave any doubt that their common plan was to use the resources of automatism as a dodge, or as a trick with a theoretical intent, in order to elucidate the mechanism of physiological functions by the reduction of the unknown to the known, and by complete reproduction of analogous effects in an experimentally intelligible manner (Canguilhem, 1963, p. 510).

But they remained 'toys' and they could not become scientific instruments given the character of Vaucanson's 'research programme'. The automata were at best the mere *similation* of human functions by given technical means. In no sense were they constructs of Cartesian biology; that theory was not invested in them, rather it existed in a relation of parallelism and externality to these instrumentalities.

13 'As for Bacon and the other more modern philosophers who try a general systematisation of the precepts of scientific research . . . but works like theirs are of no use to experienced scientists; and by false simplification of things, they mislead men who wish to devote themselves to cultivating science' (Bernard, 1865, p. 225).

14 See the quote from Bernard in note 13 above.

15 'No philosopher, coming at a moment when science takes a fertile turn, should create a system, then, in harmony with the movement of science, and afterward cry out that all the scientific progress of his day is due to the influence of his system' (Bernard, 1865, pp. 224–5).

16 He therefore rejects the conventional nineteenth-century positivist view of philosophy as a realm of pure illusion which must be replaced by a study of the real. Durkheim, however, comes close to this positivist view.

17 See Charlton (1959) on the empiricist tendencies of positivism, its 'blind belief in fact'. It should be noted that Charlton regards Bernard as something of a positivist 'fellow traveller' with reservations. His discussion of Bernard is, however, a limited aspect of a wider theme and in this context Bernard's relation to the positivist movement is all that concerns him.

18 It 'leaves a space' in that while this non-philosophical philosophy is not conceptualised in the *Introduction*, the philosophy of the *Introduction* and its concepts do not negate or contradict it.

19 See note 34 of this chapter.

20 This is the object of Leibniz's 'monodology' – see 'Theodicy and monodology' in Leibniz (1951).

21 Scepticism is defined by its questioning of the possibility of the type of philosophical knowledge Leibniz sought; except in its relation to classical metaphysics scepticism becomes an absurd and impossible limitation on human, let alone scientific, knowledge. Kolakowski (1972) illustrates this point very well, see pp. 28–59.

22 See Bernard (1878–9), pp. 59–61.

23 Bernard uses the terms 'reason', 'ideas', 'intellect', etc., in the place of *theory*. This is an index of the absence of a concept in Bernard's problematic; an absence which will be considered in the next section. Bernard uses the terms of classical rationalism as a substitute for the absent concept of what theory is and what it works on. However, it is clear that the 'reason' or 'ideas' to which he makes reference are not, in fact, human rationality in general or just any ideas whatsoever but a specific form of reason and ideas with a specific character, scientific reason and scientific ideas. To avoid ambiguity in exposition and to signal this absence we have inserted 'theory' in brackets after terms such as 'reason' at certain points in the text.

24 'Givenness' is the mode in which *objects* must exist for a theory of knowledge based upon perception/recognition. Perception does not constitute its objects, it receives them. All theories of knowledge which conceive knowledge as a perception require a *subject*; this subject, even if he is a God, *sees* even if he does not have eyes. Knowledge is what the

subject *sees* of the object; knowledge is the surface of the object, or, if this be hidden behind appearances, the inner kernel of the object. In gestaltist/phenomenological variants of this conception the specific characteristics of the object are a function of the form of perception of the subject – in this case it is the *subject* which is given, in the character of its subjectivity is given what it can and will see.

25 The sensationalist problematic is the conception of knowledge in which knowledge is a function of the senses of the human subject perceiving or recognising objects external to and independent of him. Knowledge is displaced into the real – the recognition of an object is a knowledge of it. Idealist and scepticist theories of knowledge may exist as variants of this problematic. Idealism displaces the space of cognition from the exterior to the interior – the subject's internal cognition of mental objects is either more certain or ensures that the subject can recognise external objects on the basis of firm inner conceptions; it suffers from vertigo when confronted with the real. Thus the sphere of mind or consciousness is empiricised and the subject recedes; he now becomes the point of perception or recognition of the thoughts which confront him in the inner space of cognition. Descartes, therefore, is no more and no less of an empiricist than Locke. This sensationalist problematic generates an extreme form of the 'problem of knowledge' – the problem of whether what is perceived is truly a given real object or not, and the question of the guarantees of the perception. Thus we enter the terrain of the problems of appearance/reality, imagination and bias/true cognition; the cunning of the object and the bias and error of the subject open up endless traps for sensationalist knowledge. Scepticism preys on these difficulties to the full – it disputes, most effectively, the validity of any knowledge founded on experience, but it does so within the limits of a sensationalist epistemology. Scepticism is therefore an attack on the certainty of *all* knowledge, for it cannot conceive of a non-experiential knowledge – the rational materialism of the sciences. See Althusser, 'From *Capital* to Marx's philosophy' in Althusser and Balibar (1970).

26 See Bernard (1967), pp. 90–1.

27 Koyré (1968), chapter 3, discusses the role of imaginary experiments in Galileo's physics. These experiments are not 'frauds'; they are means by which Galileo defined the forms of materialisation and proof of his theories. As theoretical devices, strictly controlled, they were no less valid than more or less inaccurate attempts to do 'the real thing' with the techniques produceable at that time.

28 Bernard had from the very beginning of his scientific career recognised that blind empiricism was valueless in experimentation, no matter how careful and faithful an observer the experimenter was. Early on, he demonstrated the necessity of theoretically interpreting experimental results – he did so in respect of the question of the nervous system and the properties of recurrent sensitivity in the anterior spinal roots. His teacher, François Magendie, had in 1822 found them sensitive. Magendie was criticised by Longet for inconsistency in this

matter. Bernard was forced to come to the rescue of his empiricist mentor and show into the bargain the need for proper determination of the conditions of experimentation. For an account of this example see Bernard (1865), pp. 174–8. For another discussion of the same incident and an account of Magendie's empiricism, so complete that 'it would admit of contradictory facts', see Olmstead (1944).

29 Phenomeno-technique is a concept of Gaston Bachelard. Bachelard takes a strongly anti-realist position in respect of what it is on which science works:

> Between sensory knowledge and scientific knowledge there is a gap. Temperature is seen on a thermometer, one does not feel it. Without theory, one could never know whether what is seen and what one feels correspond to the same phenomenon (Bachelard, 1968, p. 9).

Science does not work on a given 'nature', the nature 'given' by sense data, but upon the materialities in *constructs* and which it knows only through its instruments, which are themselves constructs based upon its theory. The phenomeno-technique is 'incompatible dans son principe avec une phénoménologie' (Lecourt, 1969, p. 67). A phenomenology merely reproduces a given either by a technology which is constructed pragmatically with the repetition of that already-given 'nature' as its end, or by 'theories' which more or less plausibly account for or 'save' these given appearances. 'La phénoméno-technique étend la phénoménologie. Un concept est devenu scientifique dans la mesure où il est devenu technique, ou il est accompagné d'une technique de réalisation' (Bachelard, 1934, p. 61). Science produces phenomena which are not 'given' by the representations of the senses:

> It is an example of *experimental transcendence*, an expression which is not in our opinion an exaggerated one to define instrumentalised science as transcending the science of natural observation (Bachelard, 1968, p. 9).

Thus experimental science is never the reproduction of a given, 'it is not closed in upon itself' (ibid., p. 9). Scientific theory can never, therefore, have the order of a closed and completed system. Since theory is the condition of experimental production, the openness of the scientific problematic is a necessary condition of *experimental transcendence* engendered by the phenomeno-technique.

30 This doctrine of science as a pragmatic enterprise and experiment as an empiricist process of trial and error has been very pervasive in sociology. It has certainly underlain the work of sociologists of science like Hessen (1931) and Merton (1957) who see modern science as a product of a society in which pragmatism, craftsmen and artisans had a powerful social influence and contrast it with societies which placed a low value on practice matters and manual work. As Koyré (1968), chapter 4, argues, Galileo and the other scientists of the seventeenth

century were forced to construct scientific precision instruments to correspond to their theories' demands for precise measurement and to develop experimentally the theories of the new mechanics. They were forced to teach the artisans their business, for the technology of the seventeenth-century handicrafts and manufacture had no need of such precision and, indeed, was often, to the chagrin of the scientists, incapable of producing it. Modern physics' mathematisation of nature and its theoretical abstraction from given real phenomena proceeded in flagrant contradiction with common-sense social experience; as Koyré says: 'The empiricism of . . . modern science is not *experiential*; it is experimental' (Koyré, 1967, p. 90). See also Bernard's remarks on the mathematical pendulum (Bernard, 1967, p. 26).

31 As Bachelard argues, scientific instruments are 'materialised theories', the relation between theory and instrument is a necessary relation internal to science itself. When the instruments of production of phenomena and the theories which explain these phenomena are separated, then we are confronted with a mere technology of production and a more or less speculative theory which accounts for the given effects produced by this technology. See Lecourt (1969), pp. 66–9.

32 The philosopher most representative of this position in the philosophy of science is Pierre Duhem. Duhem maintained that accounts which 'saved' the appearances equally well had equivalent scientific validity. He argued that Galileo had introduced metaphysics into science in his belief that the order of nature could be known by science in other than phenomenalist manner. For Duhem, a Christian, all human knowledge was a knowledge of appearances, and the true knowledge of the essence of matter, of things, was present only to their creator. Duhem's conventionalism rejected the positions of metaphysical materialism and straightforward empiricism. It combined, however, speculative empiricism (hypotheses, unprovable in essence, which account for appearances) and a religious empiricism, i.e. God's knowledge of essences – God's essence as knowledge. Duhem (1969) outlines this position most clearly.

33 For Bernard's discussion of the role and limitations of statistics in the biological sciences see Bernard (1865), pp. 129–40. Durkheim regards correlation as one of the principal methods of his sociology; correlation *in itself* is evidence of a rational relation between phenomena. See chapter 3 of this text.

34 Canguilhem (1970) confirms this absence. His criticisms of Bernard's epistemology, in the light of Bachelardian epistemology, stress the extent to which Bernard takes the practice of the experimental sciences of his time as a fixed and necessary form, and therefore the extent to which his epistemological position is conditioned by a particular state of scientific development;

Claude Bernard pensait qu'on irait plus loin que Claude Bernard sur les chemins qu'il avait ouverts, il ne formait pas l'idée d'une biologie non-bernardienne' (Canguilhem, 1970, p. 170).

Confrontée à la théorie bachelardienne de la méthode, la théorie bernardienne se distingue par l'absence de dialectisation de ses concepts fondamentaux (ibid.).

35 This conceptual distinction is essential to any proper understanding of the role of theory in scientific practice. It necessarily problematises what all empiricist theories of knowledge assume to be obvious, that is, what it is on which scientific practice works. It transforms the role of theory in that it indicates that the object of a knowledge is not a given nature, but a domain of explanation constructed in thought. It renders impossible all realist and empiricist notions of verification and falsification; what a theory studies can never be the measure of that theory for it is a product of it. The retention of the notion of the real object in this distinction is essential; it differentiates this rational materialist theory of knowledge from idealism. It insists that the world is prior to and independent of thought – that the operations of knowledge attempt to *appropriate* this real concrete in thought. However, while matter is prior to and independent of thought it can only be known through the operations of definite theories and knowledges. For an extended discussion of this concept see Althusser (1969), pp. 164–73 and pp. 182–93.

36 The classical sensationalist problematic of matter/mind, subject/object, necessarily displaces the object of a dicourse into the real and the concepts of that discourse into the 'ideas' of a subject. Objects which are not given and yet are not the idealist's 'ideas', concepts which cannot be reduced to the conditions of existence of a subject's thoughts or perceptions are unthinkable in the terms of this problematic.

37 '. . . Bernard's fallibilism with respect to scientific theory – a doctrine held by many but never, to my knowledge, stated better' (Black, 1949, pp. 83–4); see also Kolakowski (1972), pp. 90–6.

38 See chapter 2, in particular the discussion of Bernard's experiments to demonstrate the falsity of Pasteur's position on fermentation. Here Bernard attempted an experimental refutation of a particular 'theory' which rested on vitalist premisses.

39 See our discussion in the introduction to this work.

40 For Descartes this aphorism was part of a philosophical *proof*. Descartes applied systematic doubt to all exterior knowledge and cognition in order to reduce experience to its sole ground of certainty. Hence the empiricism of Descartes's *cogito* – the existence of clear and distinct thoughts clearly perceived is a sufficient proof of the existence of the subject. Hence the unbreakable circle of Descartes's *cogito* – the subject which is to perceive these thoughts in an interior space cleared of extraneous mental furniture is the same subject whose existence is to be proved. In Descartes's variant of sensationalism the subject is presupposed and the proof entails an infinite regress.

41 Mathematical proofs are self-sufficient and require neither to correspond with common-sense experience nor to be validated by experimental proofs in another science, e.g. physics. Thus the construction

of a non-Euclidian geometry, which contradicts common-sense experience as much as anything can, preceded the physics in which it was to serve as a necessary theoretical tool, and physics' materialisation of its spaces rested upon its validity and not vice versa. See Aleksandrov *et al.* (1969), vol. III, chapter 17.

42 This is a common empiricist position in respect of mathematics: that mathematics is a descriptive syntax of the real, our instrument of scientific cognition. This conception of mathematics as an abstraction from the real can be found in many texts. We will only cite two here, one by a distinguished group of Russian mathematicians, see Aleksandrov *et al.* (1969), vol. I, chapter 1, and the other by perhaps the most original of modern philosophers, Husserl (1970).

43 The monist position ultimately leads to the reduction of thought to its biological conditions of existence, and to a conception of science as nature's self-consciousness, its laws revealed through particular conditions of matter. Monist materialism is closer in fact to spiritualism and mysticism than any dualism of matter/mind. Dietzgen (1906) is another example of nineteenth-century German materialist philosophy.

44 For Bernard's falling into a conception of the 'creative intelligence' which orders life, see chapter 2, in particular the section on reductionism.

Chapter 2   Bernard's Physiology

1 On Bernard and the history of the biological sciences in the nineteenth century, see the following (full references are given in the bibliography):

(i) *History of biological sciences in the nineteenth century, general works on physiology, and Bernard's life and work*

Canguilhem (1963), '*The role of analogies and models in biological discovery*', in A. C. Crombie (ed.), *Scientific Change*.

Canguilhem (1970), *Études d'histoire et de philosophie des sciences*; chapters on Comte, Darwin and Bernard.

Comte (1896), *The Positive Philosophy of Auguste Comte*, vol. II; Comte's discussion remains the best general account of the biological sciences in the first half of the nineteenth century.

Fulton (1931), *Physiology*; a general and simple textbook in the history of physiology originally intended for medical students.

Fulton (1966), *Selected Readings in the History of Physiology*; includes examples of the work of many physiologists.

Mendelsohn (1964), 'The biological sciences in the nineteenth century: some problems and sources', the most able and insightful short discussion of nineteenth-century biology; covers vitalist Naturphilosophie, the mechanist reaction, Bernard, and Darwin and evolutionism.

Mendolsohn (1965), 'Physical models and physiological concepts: explanation in nineteenth-century biology'.

Olmstead (1939), *Claude Bernard, Physiologist*; the best general account of Bernard's life and work.

Olmstead (1944), *François Magendie*; a biography of Magendie with much additional information on Bichat, experimental conditions in the nineteenth century, etc.

Olmstead and Olmstead (1961), *Claude Bernard and the Experimental Method in Medicine*; a version (with additions and being differently organised) of Olmstead (1939).

Virtanen (1967), 'Claude Bernard and the history of ideas', in Visscher and Grande (1967).

Visscher and Grande (1967), *Claude Bernard and Experimental Medicine*; a very uneven collection of essays on Bernard.

Wightman (1956), 'The emergence of general physiology'; an able general survey.

(ii) *Bernard and Cell Theory*

Holmes (1963), 'The milieu intérieur and cell theory'.

Mendelsohn (1963), 'Cell theory and the development of general physiology'.

(iii) *The Concept of Milieu Intérieur*

Holmes (1963), 'Claude Bernard and the milieu intérieur'.

Holmes (1967), 'Origins of the concept of Milieu Intérieur', in Visscher and Grande (1967).

Houssay (1967), 'The concept of internal secretion', in Visscher and Grande (1967).

(iv) *Vitalism and Materialism*

Goodfield (1960), *The Growth of Scientific Physiology*; an extended discussion of the vitalism/mechanism struggle in physiology.

Temkin (1946), 'The philosophical background of Magendie's physiology'; basic reading on French vitalism and German Naturphilosophie.

Temkin (1946), 'Materialism in French and German physiology of the early nineteenth century'.

(v) *The History of Medicine and the Theory of Disease*

Shryock (1947), *The Development of Modern Medicine*.

Shryock (1963), 'Medicine and public health'.

Temkin (1963), 'The scientific approach to disease: specific entity and individual sickness'.

(vi) Evolutionism

Burrow (1966), *Evolution and Society*.

Darwin (1968), *The Origin of Species*; introduction by J. W. Burrow.

Greene (1961), *The Death of Adam*; a history of the idea of evolution in Western thought.

Rádl (1930), *The History of Biological Theories*; primarily a history of Darwin's theory, Darwinism and evolutionism; it discusses, however, the reception of evolutionism in France, cf. p. 41.

2 See note 1, section iv of this chapter, for references to the literature on vitalism; see also Mendelsohn (1964).

3 Mendelsohn (1963), p. 419; for Bernard's views on Helmholtz, du Bois-Reymond, etc., see Bernard (1967), p. 74.

4 Mendelsohn (1963), p. 420.

5 Bernard often appears to adopt this agnostic position in the *Cahier Rouge*, cf. p. 30, p. 68, etc.

6 See chapter 1, pp. 36–9.

7 In this respect see pp. 76–7 of this chapter, where Bernard's position on the deduction of the causes of disease from symptoms is discussed. Reasoning from effects must always be speculative and empiricist, since it can never rest upon a rigorous determination of causes, but can only correlate its deductions with the frequency of their confirmation by events and hence determine their validity.

8 This translation is taken from Fulton (1966), pp. 325–7.

9 Bernard's concept of the *milieu intérieur* was an important part of this approach [basing physiology on the functions common to all living cells] because it related the higher organisation of animals to the cellular basis of general physiology. In addition it suggested a way to study all functions by altering the conditions of their surroundings (Holmes, 1963b, p. 335).

10 See Bernard (1865), pp. 163–8, for a discussion of glycogenesis; see also Larner (1967) in Visscher and Grande (1967), for a discussion of Bernard's discovery and subsequent developments in the field.

11 See Bernard (1865), pp. 168–70 for a discussion of the regulation of animal heat by the nervous system.

12 Holmes (1963b), p. 331.

13 This very pan-applicability of systems theory is taken by system theorists as a measure of its explanatory generality. One may well doubt, however, whether this 'theory' does not merely provide re-descriptions of given phenomena in terms of system concepts. See Emery (1969), particularly the essays of von Bertalanffy. Canguilhem (1963) presents a very penetrating critique of the use of systems models in biology.

14 See this chapter, p. 62, on the notion of the 'interdependence' of the parts of an organism.

15 See chapter 6, for Durkheim's position.

16 In this respect Bernard's conception of physiological analysis as the decomposition of higher level entities into units resembles Hjelmslev's method of analysis of the signifying chain; see Hjelmslev (1963) and Uldall (1957).

17   We must doubtless admire those great horizons dimly seen by the genius of a Goethe, an Oken, a Carus, a Geoffrey Saint-Hilaire, a Darwin, in which a general conception shows all living beings as the expression of types ceaselessly transformed in the evolution of organisms and species, types in which every living being individually disappears like a reflection of the whole to which it belongs. In medicine we can also rise to the most abstract generalisations, whether we take the naturalists' point of view and conceive diseases as morbid species to be classified nosologically, or whether we start from the physiological point of view and consider that disease does not exist, in the sense that it is only a special case of a general physiological state (Bernard, 1865, pp. 91–2).

In this, his most direct reference to Darwin in the *Introduction*, Bernard pays Darwin scant attention. He couples his work with that of writers who have seldom been recognised as scientists, such as Goethe, and he gives the Darwinian theory no more status than that of being part of general world-view, the theoretical basis of which is merely speculative: 'great horizons dimly seen'. This passage occurs in a section where Bernard is arguing against abstract generalisations in medicine which obscure and confuse the specificity of phenomenon.

18 This account is taken from Olmstead (1939).

19 Olmstead (1939) quotes the relevant passage from the lectures on pages 262–3 of his work.

20 Bernard is not consistent in this respect. On p. 166 of the *Introduction* he adopts the classic Comtian position that biology is a more complex science and he gives an extra-scientific specification of that complexity just as Comte does.

21 See Bergson's essay on Bernard in Bergson (1913); see also Bergson (1960), and Virtanen (1967), p. 21.

22 The *Cahier Rouge* is dominated by a simple major problem to which Bernard constantly returns; the 'creative' and 'intelligent' character of 'life'. In the *Cahier Rouge* Bernard discusses particularly the development of individual organisms, the egg, the control of the nervous system over the chemical phenomena of the organism, etc.

23 This exposition of Bernard's position owes much to the important paper of Canguilhem (1963). The discussion of models and analogies in this text as a whole has been strongly influenced by Canguilhem's insightful analysis. For a discussion of the notion of a causality based upon resemblance, see also Foucault (1970).

24 See Temkin (1963) on the theory of disease. Durkheim's position on pathology is the exact reverse of Bernard's, see chapter 4, pp. 115–22.

Chapter 3   Durkheim's Epistemology

1 Durkheim's use of the word 'ideological' (on p. 14 of the *Rules*) confirms rather than contradicts our representation of his theory, for he uses the word in its *original* sense. It was first used in the late eighteenth century by the ideologues, Cabanis, Destutt de Tracy, etc., as a term to denote the strictly bio-scientific analysis of thought and its laws. Durkheim uses the word ideological in the context of the analysis of ideas. Durkheim's theory of 'ideology' is far closer to this original non-societal theory than it is to modern Marxist or sociological theories of ideology. For an account of the ideologues see Temkin (1946a).

2 Durkheim's position is *realist* rather than 'materialist', in the nineteenth-century sense of the word. He believes that matter or reality exists apart from and independent of thought. He does not believe that thought is reducible to matter or that all reality (psychological and social reality) is reducible to a certain constitution of physical matter. The status of 'ideas' in Durkheim's text is that of representations or misrepresentations of the real; and the apparatus in which these representations take place (the *mind*) is not reducible to the real as such. In the strict sense of the term, 'materialism' is only applicable to monists like Haeckel.

3 Compare this with Bernard's position. While Bernard rejects Naturphilosophies and notions of first causes he does so because of their ideological effects on scientific work. Durkheim's rejection is largely due to his extreme realism and his opposition to any rationalist epistemology. For Durkheim's theory of knowledge only sense data are knowable, hence anything that cannot be known through the particular human faculties cannot be said to exist. This form of realism completely flounders when confronted with the triumphant rationalism of modern physics and the realities produced by its instruments which are inaccessible to human sense faculties. The last defence of realism in this case is its opposite but sister position, scepticism.

4 This position, the keystone of Durkheim's whole argument that the social is a reality independent of the individual, is philosophically very weak. The doctrine of the 'resistance' of the real to our will is a pragmatist appeal to common-sense experience. If we put the following question to Durkheim – how is it possible to know that things offer resistance to our will by reason of their inherent properties? – he can have no answer which is capable of proof. It is equally possible that the 'resistance' of things does not stem from their autonomous existence but from the inadequate vigour of our attempts to will them away, or, equally, that this apparent 'resistance', of which we can have knowledge only through the sensations, is merely a result of a defect in our sensory faculties. In standing on the ground of a sensationalist philosophy Durkheim exposed himself to the master of that terrain, George Berkeley. The defect of Durkheim's whole argument in the *Rules* is that to prove the existence of the *social* facts he relies upon the sensory experience of the human subject.

5 This conception of knowledge proceding by successive approximations to the real but never uncovering its essence is reminiscent of the position of Duhem; see Duhem (1969).

6 See note 4.

7 We are never told in what the difference of spontaneous and consolidated social life consists. How do social currents and actions 'crystallise'? The use of the notion of habituation (see p. 7 of the *Rules*) is a very weak explanatory device since Durkheim's notion of habit does not differ from the common-sense notion. Durkheim has no conception of social structure as anything but the consolidated resultant of social currents and acts. He has no conception of social structure as anything more than the manifest institutions of the family, law, state, etc.

8 We have seen that the notion of 'resistance' rests on a philosophically weak argument (see note 4). Similarly, Durkheim's use of the limitations of psychological and biological explanations of 'social' phenomena as one of his proofs of the existence of the field of sociology is a weak argument. Durkheim's critique of the inadequacy of existing explanations in these fields does not give us any proof of the inadequacy of all psychological and all biological explanations of social phenomena as such. It may be reasonably objected that Durkheim's sociology owes much to psychology, that it is a 'collective' psychology of 'representations' which are 'states of the collective consciousness':

> Social facts do not differ from psychological facts in quality only: *they have a different substratum.* . . . This does not mean that they are not also mental after a fashion, since they all consist of ways of thinking or behaving. But the states of the collective consciousness are different in nature from the states of the individual consciousness; they are 'representations' of another type. The mentality of groups is not the same as that of individuals, it has its own laws (Durkheim, 1966, p. xlix).

Society is mentalised; it becomes a society-subject: 'To understand the way in which a society thinks of itself and of its environment one must consider the nature of the society and not that of the individuals' (ibid.). If the difference is merely that individual psychology deals with individual subjects and sociology with a 'society' that has the characteristics of a collective subject, then the difference is not a difference in the type of theoretical explanation but merely in the 'things' to which it is applied. It is only the 'substratum' which is different in its form, collective versus individual, and not the type of theory.

In respect of the absence of a concept of social structure and in his insistence that social life consists of representations that exist in the collective consciousness, Durkheim does tend far more towards a collective psychology than a structural sociology. Indeed, theoreticians without a conventional sociological training tend to give this interpretation to Durkheim's work. Thus the Russian historian of social movements, B. F. Porshnev, in his book on social psychology, treats Durkheim as a collective psychologist who explained the phenomena of the 'social aspect of psychics' by 'coercion'; see Porshnev (1970), p. 182.

Similarly, the notion of 'social milieu' in Durkheim's *Rules* depends heavily on analogies with biology and tends toward a vitalist conception of physiological phenomena; see chapter 6.

9 Particularly noteworthy here are the penetrating criticisms of Lévi-Strauss (1945) which deal with this aspect of Durkheim's work.

10 See chapter 1, notes 11 and 29.

11 See chapter 1, note 32. It should be noted, however, that Duhem, as a conventionalist, accepted that alternative mechanisms of 'saving the phenomena' were epistemologically equivalent if they accounted for the appearances equally well and with equal economy. Thus Duhem (1969) attacks Galileo as a meta-physician for believing that the order of the universe could be uncovered in itself. Duhem would undoubtedly criticise Durkheim in exactly the same way. Durkheim is a *realist*; he uses phenomenalist positions only to oppose scientific rationalism.

12 The 'pre-critical' realism of Durkheim's position should dispel any conceptions of Durkheim's being a Kantian in respect of his theory of knowledge. Durkheim's realism contradicts Kant's position of the unknowability of the thing in itself:

> It is, therefore, not merely possible or probable but indubitably certain, that space and time, as the necessary conditions of all outer and inner experience, are merely subjective conditions of all intuition, and that in relation to these conditions all objects are therefore mere appearances, and not given us as things in themselves which exist in this manner. For this reason also, while much can be said *a priori* as regards the form of appearances, nothing whatsoever can be asserted of the thing in itself, which may underlie these appearances (Kant, 1968, pp. 86–7).

Durkheim does sometimes tend to suggest that we can only certainly know appearances and that things in themselves escape us (see p. 46 of the *Rules*) but this is by no means a consistent position; it is quite subordinate to his dominantly realist conception of knowledge.

13 On the question of the limits of 'sensationalist' knowledge and the erroneous character of modes of scientific knowledge based on human cognition, see Bachelard (1968), chapter 1.

It is possible for the individual subject to know the reality of the social realm, to receive and decode its 'message', because the sender of the message is a rational being, a society-subject which creates the social realm through the representations that exist in its (collective) consciousness. In this special sense, Durkheimian knowledge of society is 'understanding', but it is not the 'understanding' we are familiar with in the conception of Verstehensociologie, because the character of the meanings and the subject which transmits them are different in the two conceptions. The Durkheimian individual subject, *qua* scientist, must decode a rational message that is produced externally to and independent of him.

No individual subject can ever have direct and complete access to the essence of the collective consciousness since the sphere of action of that consciousness is the collective life, and its form of action in relation to the manifest facts of social experience is the partial and distorting form entailed in its causal mechanism of expression. The nature of social reality must therefore be *decoded* by the subject; it must be sought through 'clues' and 'symptoms'; social knowledge is neither spontaneous, nor simultaneous, it is asymptotic in practice because of the nature of the individual subject and its limitation. It is for this reason, and this reason only, that Durkheim's sociology avoids the mysticism of revelation. In the text of the *Rules*, Durkheim stresses the realist aspect of his epistemology and does not emphasise this asymptoticism; this is because of the dangers of phenomenalism and conventionalism that follow from such an emphasis and their consequences for this theory of knowledge based on perception of givens.

14 We should note here that the conception of induction which appears in this exposition is Durkheim's own construction and not Mill's. Mill's work is not at issue here, merely Durkheim's construction of it. For Mill's conception of induction see, in particular, Mill (1963), pp. 170–1, and pp. 181–6.

15 The strictures in the note above also apply here. For the conception of causality Durkheim is attacking see, in particular, Mill (1963), pp. 238–52. Mill is discussing cases of causes which 'compound their effects', that is, where causes intersect to produce a complex tissue of effects. Mill argues that the 'experimental method' is not valid in these cases.

16 Compare Durkheim's definition of experiment and observation with Bernard's. Note the difference between Durkheim's statement that experimentation exists when the phenomena 'can be artificially produced at the will of the observer', and Bernard's statements that the experimenter views natural phenomena 'to make them present themselves in conditions in which nature does not show them' and 'in conditions which nature often has not achieved'. Durkheim's definition reduces experiment into the artificial reproduction of given facts.

17 For a discussion of the role of measurement and scientific instruments see Koyré (1968), chapter 4.

18 For a discussion of the role of abstraction in political economy and, in particular, of the necessity of a concept of production in general, see, Marx (1857).

19 On this point, see, Rancière (1971–2), section 2.

20 On this point see Alpert (1939), part 1.

Chapter 4 Pathology and Morphology

1 See Bernard (1865), pp. 196–218.
2 See Durkheim (1966), pp. 50–8.
3 See Durkheim (1966), pp. 65–74.
4 For further discussion of the relation of the 'individual' and 'society' see chapter 5. See also the very interesting essay of Durkheim, 'The dualism of human nature and its social conditions', in Wolff (1964).
5 Zeitlin (1968) makes very telling criticisms of the ideological character of Durkheim's notion of the collective consciousness and its relation to 'given' social facts. But Zeitlin does not show by what mechanism these positions are produced in Durkheim's discourse, nor does he account for the theoretical structure of Durkheim's problematic.

The present text makes no claim to be a definitive analysis of the *Rules*; it merely attempts to point to the possibility and fruitfulness of its method of enquiry.
6 See pp. 55–8 of the *Rules*.
7 Compare Durkheim's position with that of Bernard on the relation of physiology and anatomy; see Bernard (1865), pp. 105–12. There is no question of the soundness of Durkheim's general conception of the relation of morphology and physiology in his social science; what is at question is his specific theoretical conception of that science.
8 It should be noted that Durkheim's conception of social elements as given and irreducible wholes is quite different from the concept of element in the science of chemistry. The principal difference consists in this, that the substances of chemistry are the products of its theoretical-experimental operations, while Durkheim's elementary units ('the horde') are merely speculative notions (Durkheim admits that the epistemological status of the notion of the 'horde' is that of a 'support' for the whole framework of his classificatory system, see p. 84 of the *Rules*). Substances in chemistry are not the products of an analysis of a given matter; chemistry analyses only 'pure' substances. The 'purity' of chemical phenomena is the result of this being products of the chemical operations of synthesis (Bachelard, 1968, p. 47):

> In the early days of organic chemistry people used to like to believe that synthesis merely served to verify the exactitude of a piece of analysis. Practically the reverse is true now.
> Chemical substances only get to be truly defined at the moment of their reconstruction. . . . As Marcel Mathieu says, 'although it is possible to apprehend molecular characteristics through organic molecules, it is, more especially, the development of methods of synthesis which has allowed us to construct with such certainty the edifice which constitutes organic chemistry'.

It is their character as intra-scientific products that enables their constituents to be uniformly and accurately reduced in analysis by

common procedures. This may give us some indication why Durkheim does not possess the equivalent of chemical compounds in his
morphology. Elements can only link one to another in 'mixtures' or
fuse into larger wholes, but *since they all have the same essential
substance* there can be no complex combinations of elements
in specific properties into compounds as in chemistry. There can
be no complex forms of substance since all substance is one and
elemental.

Durkheim's notion of element or atom is like the speculative
construction of the constituents of the universe in Naturphilosophie
(Democritus or eighteenth-century mechanical materialism). The
theoretical conditions of the existence of 'elements' in chemistry are
quite different. The order and the relation of the elements is determined by a theoretical construction, the Mendeleev table of the
elements. This theoretical construction is not the recording of the
results of 'discovery' in an orderly form, it is a means of producing
these phenomena of chemistry, of realising the objects which it unites.
The theory of atomic weights which constitutes the table, by means of
the atomic *series*, enables chemical science to produce phenomena
which had never existed in the world of sensations; elements that
could not be *discovered*, but had to be *thought*. Bachelard expresses the
significance of the Mendeleev revolution thus:

> Certainly, in studying the principle of the researches which came
> into existence in the Mendeleev organisation of elementary
> substances, it becomes apparent that ... *law surpasses fact*, that the
> *order* of substances imposes itself as a rationality. What finer proof
> can we adduce for the rational character of a science of substances
> than that it succeeds in predicting the properties of a yet
> unknown substance before its actual discovery (ibid., p. 49).

Similarly, Bernard's concept of histological unit (cell), does not
posit an entity without conditions, but the basic elementary form of
vital organisation, and this form has non-organic conditions of existence, the discovery of the character and role of which in its constitution, is the most important experimental task in physiology.

Durkheim's realist and sensationalist epistemology leaves him with
no opinion but to posit the elements of social life as givens.

9 This position stems from Durkheim's anti-individualist conception of
society, a conception which rightly rejects the reduction of social
relations to the needs or wills or individuals. Thus in Durkheim (1965)
and in Durkheim (1964), (particularly pp. 274–82) he rejects with
forceful arguments the 'fable' of individualist notions in which the
social is created by reason of the needs of pre-existing individuals:

> Collective life is not born from individual life, but it is, on the
> contrary, the second which is born from the first. It is on this
> condition alone that one can explain how the personal
> individuality of social units has been able to be formed and

enlarged without disintegrating society (Durkheim, 1964, pp. 279–80).

But these arguments are vitalist arguments since Durkheim posits social life as a given without conditions of existence which ever-always exists because it is in the nature of things. A vitalist conception of society is of equivalent epistemological status to the individualist conception; vitalism and reductionism form a couple, as Bernard has shown, the principle of their unity is their common conception of life as an essence, in the one case, accepted, and in the other, rejected.

10 It should be noted that this conception of the facticity of the social sciences as an infinite collection of individuals and events was a key element of the methodological position of Max Weber, a theory deriving from the idealist school of German historiography. For an excellent brief discussion of Weber's methodology and its epistemological foundation see Aron (1964). Weber's agnosticism in respect of the facticity of the social sciences is the exact opposite of Durkheim's realism.

This difference between Weber and Durkheim is another indication of the inaccuracy of attributing a Kantian or neo-Kantian epistemological position to Durkheim (at least in his writings before the *Forms*).

11 See p. 87 of the *Rules*. The example which Durkheim gives of a species which includes only one individual is the Roman Empire.

12 Durkheim's discussion of evolutionary theory is far more of the Lamarckian conception than of Darwin's. Durkheim places emphasis on environmental pressures and adaptation of characteristics to those pressures. He neglects the key element of Darwinian theory which differentiates it from previous conceptions, that is, the random variation of characteristics. It is this biological phenomenon of mutation, in no way directly determined by the environment, which determines the 'survival of the fittest', by determining the production of the 'fittest'. It is the relation between environmental change and random mutations which determines the character of the evolutionary process.

Darwin's theory of the evolution of species is not 'evolutionist', in the sense of social evolutionary theories. There is no teleology or necessary order in the succession of forms. The development of forms is governed by the contingent natural process of environmental change and random mutation.

It should also be noted that the Darwinian theory lacked any theory of the mechanism of the production of mutations; this theory of the laws of heredity was only developed later by Mendel.

13 In this respect, compare his criticisms of Spencer's failure to develop a clear *concept* of 'simplicity'; see pp. 81–3 of the *Rules*.

14 See note 12, particularly the reference to Mendel. It should also be noted that Durkheim treats the question of heredity in respect of the *fixity* of species characteristics, their transmission from one generation to the next, and not in respect of random mutations.

15 In the social realm this internal force is lacking. As a rule, a second generation is a different species from the parent-societies because the latter, in combining, give birth to an entirely new organisation (Durkheim, 1966, p. 87).

16 See note 10, p. 88 of the *Rules*.

17 See chapter 3, pp. 90–103.

18 See chapter 6.

19 Suppose, indeed, that these two collective consciences have no common meeting-ground, it is not possible for the two aggregates to have the continuous contact which is necessary, nor consequently, for one to abandon its functions to the other. For one people to be penetrated by another, it must cease to hold an exclusive patriotism, and learn another which is more comprehensive (Durkheim, 1964, p. 281).

Durkheim is here discussing the international division of labour, but this position holds equally well for the relation of segments within a single society. Thus the condition of the commerce of the segments is a higher moral unity.

20 See Durkheim (1965), pp. 67–75.

21 For Durkheim's exposition of the three main causes of this 'condensation', see Durkheim (1964), pp. 257–60.

22 Durkheim makes it clear that an increase in population volume is neither the only nor necessarily an independently effective pressure toward the division of labour; see Durkheim (1964), p. 261. Durkheim uses no form of law of population or explicit biological reductionism in his analysis of the division of labour.

23 See Durkheim (1964), pp. 266–9.

24 See Durkheim (1964), pp. 283–303, and Durkheim (1951), p. 336.

25 See Durkheim (1964), pp. 353–74.

26 See also in this connection, Durkheim (1964), Preface to the second edition, and Durkheim (1951), book 3, chapter 3, 'Practical consequences'.

Chapter 5 Individualism and Holism: Purpose, Function and Social Facts

1 The meaning of these terms will become clearer in the text; we will only give here some preliminary definitions. By 'humanism' we mean any conception of social science or social philosophy which is founded on an anthropology, that is, which takes as its point of departure an 'human essence' or a constitutive human subject, and, which conceives social relations and human actions as explicable in terms of the needs of that essence or the will of that subject.

Durkheim takes an anti-humanist position in the limited sense that he opposes any reduction of the social realm, a reality *sui generis*, to the needs or to the will of man. But Durkheim's position does not challenge humanism as such; humanism has its legitimate domain, the individual and the psychological.

2 Of course, we should not take Durkheim at his word. In our discussion of the *Division* in chapter 4 we saw that Durkheim is forced to introduce the individual, a given external to society, as an essential element of his explanation of the transformation from mechanical to organic solidarity. We have seen in chapter 3 that the 'givenness' of social facts is quite spurious, and, we shall see in the second part of this chapter the difficulties Durkheim gets into when he tries to explain the nature of social life and the source of social energy.

   Durkheim's position is sufficient in so far as he is opposing a certain reductionist conception of sociology, but insufficient in itself as an essential part of a system of social explanation.

3 See Durkheim (1965), p. 3, previously quoted in chapter 3.

4 Examples of such criticisms of Durkheim's sociology are: Berger (1963), Goldmann (1969), and Tiryakian (1962).

5 The notable exception in this respect is Montesquieu. Durkheim praises Montesquieu for his anticipation, albeit partial, of the method of explaining social facts by other social facts rather than reducing them to effects of the needs or will of individuals; see Durkheim (1965), pp. 36–60.

6 This is not, of course, to claim that Durkheim's own conception of sociology is an adequate or scientific one. Nevertheless, by adopting an anti-reductionist position, and by insisting that it is necessary to explain the existence of social facts by reference to concomitant conditions, Durkheim is able to produce a powerful critique of the individualism and evolutionism of Comte and Spencer.

7 Durkheim's hostility to any attempt to think the existence of the social in relation to the wills of individuals throws an interesting light on the discussion of the problem of 'order' in sociology. Parsons (1949) makes considerable use of this 'problem' to explain the necessity of social norms and social control. The 'problem' stems from the classical discussion of the nature of political authority in Hobbes (1960). Durkheim places this 'problem' squarely within the individualist problematic. For Durkheim 'order' is no 'problem' since he conceives the social realm as a given external to individuals, and in no way reducible to their needs or actions. The 'order' of society, the fact that societies exist as coherent wholes, is a fact of nature itself and that order is maintained by the articulation of the parts of society one with another and by the collective consciousness – unity as a *consciousness*. In insisting on the ever-already givenness of society to man or human individuals, Durkheim explicitly rejects any attempt to consider man without society or man's 'need' for society.

8 These arguments are merely repetitions of the arguments Durkheim uses to demonstrate the reality of the social which we have already discussed in chapter 3.

9 Methodological individualists such as Louch (1966) would definitely question this position.

10 See pp. 107–9 of the *Rules*.

11 Such theories *do* exist; an example is Gobineau's racist theory of

history. For a penetrating critique of Gobineau, and by implication of all such conceptions, see de Tocqueville (1959).

12 For the pertinent remarks of Durkheim on Comte, see pp. 19, 99, 119 and 125 of the *Rules*.

13 See p. 99 of the *Rules*:

> Thus, while the theories of psychology are insufficient as premises for sociological reasoning, they are the touchstone which alone can test the validity of propositions inductively established. 'A law of social succession,' says Comte, 'even when indicated with all possible authority by the historical method, ought to be finally admitted only after having been rationally related to the positive theory of human nature. . . .' Psychology, then will always have the last word (Durkheim, 1966, p. 99).

14 See p. 98 of the *Rules*.

15 See p. 121–4 of the *Rules* for Durkheim's discussion of the source of humanist theory.

16 See p. 124 of the *Rules*.

17 This, Durkheim claims, was what Rousseau sought to demonstrate in his conception of the 'state of nature'; see Durkheim (1965), pp. 66–75.

18 The section in question is chapter 5 of the *Rules*.

19 The individual is not *only* a domain of consciousness, the individual is also a domain of biology. This dualism of human nature is the way in which Durkheim recognises the physical desires and needs of men and the effect of their control and repression by social rules. Durkheim did not abolish man as a biological being; he did not reduce him to the order of consciousness, symbols and representation; he merely maintains that man's biological needs, while they are limited by and set limits to the social order, do not create the social order.

20 The psychology which Durkheim accepts as a necessary complement to sociology is a psychology which accepts the humanist conception of the subject as an integral consciousness developed in classical Western philosophy, but which attempts to study the 'laws' of that consciousness by the means of scientific method and proof. As we saw in note 1, Durkheim's anti-humanism is a partial one; he accepts the notion of the individual as a being of consciousness. Further, the 'duality' of human nature is the duality of man as a conscious being and as a biological animal. The subject is not de-centred by that duality, it exists in a relation to its own unconscious biological system and its desires and needs. This unconscious is *external* to the subject. Durkheim's notion of 'duality' in no way anticipates the Freudian de-centring of the totality of the psyche.

21 See chapter 2, and the discussion of anatomism for Bernard's position.

22 This contradicts Durkheim's other position in chapter 3 of the *Rules*, 'The normal and the pathological', that pathology cannot be defined by the chances of survival of the organism.

Chapter 6   Individualism and Holism: Vitalism and the Social Milieu

1 Both this chapter and chapter 5 are based on the chapter 'Rules for the exploration of social facts' in the *Rules*. Durkheim's exposition in this long chapter is continuous. We have broken it up into two distinct themes for purposes of greater clarity and economy of exposition. It will be noted how different in character and theoretical implication are the two arguments we have separated out in these two chapters. Durkheim's exposition in chapter 5 is not a continuous logical argument but a series of points and criticisms of various forms of reductionism.

2 For examples of this position, see Louch (1966), Mill (1963), Popper (1961), and Runciman (1970).

3 But note the important difference discussed below.

4 See p. 103 of the *Rules*.

5 Note Bernard's remark in this context cited in chapter 1, Bernard (1865), p. 113.

6 See in this context Durkheim (1966), p. xlviii.

7 Durkheim, in the Preface to the first edition of the *Rules*, strongly attacks any conception of social science which is nothing more than a theoretical elaboration of 'common sense' (p. xxxvii). He demands a science of 'discoveries' rather than a philosophy which consists in explaining phenomena by 'principles'. However, in the passages in which he develops his 'law' of association he is guilty of the very errors of the *a priori* philosophical method which he had previously exposed and criticised. We have noted before similar contradictions between his aims and his achievements.

8 Durkheim (1966), p. xlviii.

9 Durkheim (1966), p. xlix.

10 This last remark is our elaboration of Durkheim's position and is nowhere explicitly stated by him.

11 Durkheim (1966), p. xlviii.

12 Durkheim (1966), p. 103.

13 This conclusion which can be drawn from Durkheim's argument in these passages is directly contradictory with his attempt to establish sociology as an autonomous science.

14 The 'principle just enunciated' is as follows: 'The determining cause of a social fact should be sought among the social facts preceding it and not among the states of the individual consciousness' (Durkheim, 1966, p. 110).

15 This conception of the 'internal environment' of an organism as the 'aggregate of anatomic elements together with the way they are disposed in space' bears no relation to Bernard's conception of the *milieu intérieur*. Rather it resembles the anatomical reductionists' conception of living beings as assemblages of organs which Bernard attacked so strongly.

16 Durkheim in the *Division* insisted that the moral density of a society was a function of the extent to which individuals were forced into *social* relations one with another rather than the extent to which they engaged in purely instrumental economic contracts one with another. These economic relations are 'superficial' and a matter of 'civilisation'.

17 See pp. 114–15 of the *Rules*.

18 Bernard (1865), p. 108.

19 Durkheim (1966), pp. 102–3.

Bibliography

ALEKSANDROV, A. D. KOLMOGOROV, A. H. and LAVRENT'EV, M.A. (1969), *Mathematics: Its Content, Methods, and Meaning*, vols I–III, M.I.T. Press: Cambridge, Mass.

ALPERT, HARRY (1939), *Émile Durkheim and his Sociology* (republished 1961), Russell & Russell: New York.

ALTHUSSER, LOUIS (1969), *For Marx*, Allen Lane: London.

ALTHUSSER, LOUIS and BALIBAR, ETIENNE (1970), *Reading Capital*, New Left Books: London.

ARON, RAYMOND (1964), *German Sociology*, Free Press: New York.

BACHELARD, GASTON (1934), *Le Nouvel Esprit scientifique*, PUF: Paris.

BACHELARD, GASTON (1964), *The Psychoanalysis of Fire*, Routledge & Kegan Paul: London.

BACHELARD, GASTON (1968), *The Philosophy of No*, Orion Press: New York.

BERGER, PETER (1963), *Invitation to Sociology*, Doubleday: New York.

BERGSON, HENRI (1913), 'Centennial address', in E. Dhurout, *Claude Bernard: extraits de son œuvre* (1959), PUF: Paris.

BERGSON, HENRI (1960), *Creative Evolution*, Macmillan: London.

BERNARD, CLAUDE (1865), *Introduction à l'étude de la médicine expérimentale*, translated as *An Introduction to the Study of Experimental Medicine* (1957), Dover Books: New York.

BERNARD, CLAUDE (1867), *Rapport sur les progrès et la marche de la physiologie générale en France*. Translations of passages cited are from Fulton (1931) below.

BERNARD, CLAUDE (1878), *La Science expérimentale*. Translations of passages cited are from Fulton (1931) below.

BERNARD, CLAUDE (1878–9), *Leçons sur les phénomènes de la vie communs aux animaux et aux végétaux*, J. B. Ballière: Paris.

BERNARD, CLAUDE (1967), *The Cahier Rouge of Claude Bernard*, trans. by H. H. Hoff *et al.*, Schenkman: Cambridge, Mass.

BLACK, MAX (1949), 'The definition of scientific method', in R. C. Stauffer (ed.), *Science and Civilisation*, University of Wisconsin Press: Madison, Wis.

BRADLEY, J. (1971), *Mach's Philosophy of Science*, Athlone Press: London.

BURROW, J. W. (1966), *Evolution and Society*, Cambridge University Press: London.

CANGUILHEM, GEORGES (1963), 'The role of analogies and models in biological discovery' in A. C. Crombie (ed.), *Scientific Change*, Heinemann: London.

CANGUILHEM, GEORGES (1970), *Études d'histoire et de philosophie des sciences*, J. Vrin: Paris.

CHARLTON, D. G. (1959), *Positivist Thought in France during the Second Empire 1852–70*, Clarendon Press: Oxford.

COMTE, AUGUSTE (1896), *The Positive Philosophy of Auguste Comte*, 3 vols, ed. and trans. by H. Martineau, George Bell: London.

DARWIN, CHARLES (1968), *The Origin of Species*, introduction by J. W. Burrow, Penguin Books: Harmondsworth.

DIETZGEN, JOSEPH (1906), *The Positive Outcome of Philosophy*, Kerr: Chicago.

DUHEM, PIERRE (1954), *The Aim and Structure of Physical Theory*, Princeton University Press.

DUHEM, PIERRE (1969), *To Save the Phenomena*, University of Chicago Press.

DURKHEIM, ÉMILE (1915), *The Elementary Forms of Religious Life*, Allen & Unwin: London.

DURKHEIM, ÉMILE (1951), *Suicide*, Routledge & Kegan Paul: London.

DURKHEIM, ÉMILE (1957), *Professional Ethics and Civic Morals*, Routledge & Kegan Paul: London.

DURKHEIM, ÉMILE (1962), *Socialism and Saint Simon*, Collier: New York.

DURKHEIM, ÉMILE (1964), *The Division of Labour in Society*, Free Press: New York.

DURKHEIM, ÉMILE (1965), *Montesquieu and Rousseau*, Michigan University Press: Ann Arbor, Mich.

DURKHEIM, ÉMILE (1966), *The Rules of Sociological Method*, Free Press: New York.

EMERY, F. E. (ed.) (1969), *Systems Thinking*, Penguin Books: Harmondsworth.

ENGELS, FRIEDRICH (1954), *The Dialectics of Nature*, Progress Publishers: Moscow.

FOUCAULT, MICHEL (1970), *The Order of Things*, Tavistock: London.

FULTON, J. F. (1931), *Physiology*, P. B. Hoeber: New York.

FULTON, J. F. (1966), *Selected Readings in the History of Physiology*, Charles C. Thomas: Springfield, Ill.

GOLDMANN, LUCIEN (1969), *The Human Sciences and Philosophy*, Cape: London.

GOODFIELD, G. J. (1960), *The Growth of Scientific Physiology*, Hutchinson: London.

GREENE, JOHN C. (1961), *The Death of Adam*, Mentor Books: New York.

HAECKEL, ERNST (1908), *The Riddle of the Universe*, Watts: London.

HESSEN, B. (1931), 'The social and economic roots of Newton's *Principia*' in *Science at the Crossroads*, (Collected papers of the Delegation of Soviet Scientists, 2nd International Congress of the History of Science and Technology, London.

HJELMSLEV, LOUIS (1963), *Prolegomena to a Theory of Language*, Wisconsin University Press: Madison, Wis.

HOBBES, THOMAS (1960), *Leviathan*, Basil Blackwell: Oxford.

HOLMES, F. L. (1963a), 'Claude Bernard and the milieu interieur', *Archives Internationales d'Histoire des Sciences*, no. 65, Oct.–Dec.

HOLMES, F. L. (1963b), 'The milieur intérieur and cell theory', *Bulletin of the History of Medicine*, no. 37.

HOLMES, F. L. (1967), 'Origins of the concept of *Milieu Intérieur*' in Visscher and Grande (1967) below.

HOUSSAY, B. A. (1967), 'The concept of internal secretion' in Visscher and Grande (1967) below.

HUSSERL, EDMUND (1970), *The Crisis of European Sciences and Transcendental Phenomenology*, Northwestern University Press: Evanston.

KANT, IMMANUEL (1883), *Critique of Practical Reason and Other Works on the Theory of Ethics*, trans. by T. K. Abbott, Longmans: London.

KANT, IMMANUEL (1968), *Critique of Pure Reason*, trans. by N. Kemp Smith, Macmillan: London.

KOLAKOWSKI, LESZEK (1972), *Positivist Philosophy*, Penguin Books: Harmondsworth.

KOYRÉ, ALEXANDRE (1968), *Metaphysics and Measurement*, Chapman & Hall: London.

LARNER, J. (1967), 'The discovery of glycogen and glycogen today' in Visscher and Grande (1967) below.

LECOURT, DOMINIQUE (1969), *L'Épistemologie historique de Gaston Bachelard*, J. Vrin: Paris.

LECOURT, DOMINIQUE (1973), *Une Crise et son enjeu*, François Maspero: Paris.

LEIBNIZ, GOTTFRIED WILHELM (1951), *Selections*, ed. by P. P. Weiner, Scribners: New York.

LENIN, V. I. (1908), *Materialism and Empiro-Criticism, Collected Works*, vol. 14, Progress Publishers: Moscow.

LÉVI-STRAUSS, CLAUDE (1945), 'French Sociology' in G. Gurvitch and W. E. Moore (eds), *Twentieth Century Sociology*, Philosophical Library: New York.

LOUCH, A. R. (1966), *Explanation and Human Action*, Basil Blackwell: Oxford.

MACH, ERNST (1902), *The Science of Mechanics*, Open Court: Chicago.

MACH, ERNST (1959), *The Analysis of Sensations*, Dover Books: New York.

MARX, KARL (1857), 'Introduction' to *A Contribution to the Critique of Political Economy* (1971), Lawrence & Wishart: London.

MARX, KARL and ENGELS, FREDERICK (1962), *Selected Works*, vol. 2, Foreign Languages Publishing House: Moscow.

MENDELSOHN, EVERETT (1963), 'Cell theory and the development of general physiology', *Archives Internationales d'Histoire des Sciences*, no. 65, Oct.–Dec.

MENDELSOHN, EVERETT (1964), 'The biological sciences in the nineteenth century: some problems and sources', *History of Science*, vol. 3.

MENDELSOHN, EVERETT (1965), 'Physical models and physiological concepts: explanation in nineteenth-century biology', *British Journal for the History of Science*, vol. 2, no. 7.

MERTON, ROBERT K. (1957), *Social Theory and Social Structure*, Free Press: Chicago.

MILL, JOHN STUART (1963), *System of Logic* in *Philosophy of Scientific Method* (ed. E. Nagel), Hafner: New York.

OLMSTEAD, J. M. D. (1939), *Claude Bernard, Physiologist*, Cassell: London.

OLMSTEAD, J. M. D. (1944), *François Magendie*, Schumann: New York.

OLMSTEAD, J. M. D. and OLMSTEAD, E. H. (1961), *Claude Bernard and the Experimental Method in Medicine*, Collier–Macmillan: New York.

PARSONS, TALCOTT (1949), *The Structure of Social Action*, Free Press: Chicago,

POINCARÉ, HENRI (1913), *The Value of Science* (republished 1968), Dover: New York.

POPPER, KARL R. (1961), *The Poverty of Historicism*, Routledge & Kegan Paul: London.

POPPER, KARL R. (1968), *The Logic of Scientific Discovery*, Hutchinson: London.

PORSHNEV, BORIS F. (1970), *Social Psychology and History*, Progress Publishers: Moscow.

RÁDL, EMMANUEL (1930), *The History of Biological Theories*, Oxford University Press: London.

RANCIÈRE, JACQUES (1971–2), 'The concept of critique and the critique of political economy', *Theoretical Practice*, nos. 1, 2 & 6.

RUNCIMAN, W. G. (1970), *Sociology in its Place*, Cambridge: University Press.

SAUSSURE, FERDINAND DE (1966), *Course in General Linguistics*, McGraw-Hill: New York.

SHRYOCK, R. H. (1947), *The Development of Modern Medicine*, Knopf: New York.

SHRYOCK, R. H. (1963), 'Medicine and public health', in *The Nineteenth Century World*, G. S. Metraux and F. Crouzet (eds), New American Library: New York.

TEMKIN, OWSEI (1946a), 'The philosophical background of Magendie's physiology', *Bulletin of the History of Medicine*, vol. 20, pp. 10–27.

TEMKIN, OWSEI (1946b), 'Materialism in French and German physiology of the early nineteenth century', *Bulletin of the History of Medicine*, vol. 20, pp. 322–7.

TEMKIN, OWSEI (1963), 'The scientific approach to disease: specific entity and individual sickness', in A. C. Crombie (ed.), *Scientific Change* Heinemann: London.

TIRYAKIAN, E. A. (1962), *Sociologism and Existentialism*, Prentice Hall NJ.

TOCQUEVILLE, ALEXIS DE (1959), *The European Revolution and Correspondence with Gobineau*, Doubleday: New York.

ULDALL, H. J. (1957), *Outline of Glossematics*, part 1, *Travaux du cercle linguistique de Copenhague X*, Nordisk Sprog-og Kulturforlag: Copenhagen.

VIRTANEN, R. (1960), *Claude Bernard and his Place in the History of Ideas*, Nebraska University Press: Lincoln, Neb.

VIRTANEN, R. (1967), 'Claude Bernard and the history of ideas' in Visscher and Grande (1967) below.

VISSCHER, M. R. and GRANDE, F. (eds) (1967), *Claude Bernard and Experimental Medicine*, Harper & Row: New York.

WIGHTMAN, W. P. D. (1956), 'The emergence of general physiology', lecture delivered in the Queen's University of Belfast.

WILLER, D. and WILLER, J. (1973), *Systematic Empiricism: Critique of a Pseudo-Science*, Prentice Hall: New Jersey.

WOLFF, KURT H. (1964), *Émile Durkheim, Essays on Sociology and Philosophy*, Harper & Row: New York.

ZEITLIN, IRVING M. (1968), *Ideology and the Development of Sociological Theory*, Prentice Hall: New Jersey.

Index ─────────────────────────────